Southern Living.
1990
Garden Annual

Southern Living®
1990
Garden Annual

by the

Garden Department

of

Southern Living magazine

Oxmoor House®

© 1990 by Oxmoor House, Inc.
Book Division of Southern Progress Corporation
P.O. Box 832463, Birmingham, Alabama 35201

Southern Living® is a federally registered trademark of Southern Living, Inc.

All rights reserved. No part of this book may be reproduced in any form or by any means without the prior written permission of the publisher, excepting brief quotations in connection with reviews written specifically for inclusion in magazines or newspapers.

ISBN: 0-8487-1026-6
ISSN: 1048-2318

Manufactured in the United States of America
First Printing

Southern Living®
Senior Garden Editor: Todd A. Steadman
Garden Editor: Lois B. Trigg
Associate Garden Editors: Stephen P. Bender, Linda Askey Weathers
Assistant Garden Design Editor: Rita W. Strickland
Editorial Assistant: Kristen Sulser
Senior Garden Photographer: Van Chaplin
Garden Photographer: Mary-Gray Hunter
Production Manager: Clay Nordan
Assistant Production Manager: Wanda Butler

Oxmoor House, Inc.
Executive Editor: Nancy Janice Fitzpatrick
Production Manager: Jerry Higdon
Associate Production Manager: Rick Litton
Art Director: Bob Nance
Copy Chief: Mary Jean Haddin

Southern Living® 1990 Garden Annual
Editor: Vicki L. Ingham
Editorial Assistant: Karolyn Morgan
Production Assistant: Theresa L. Beste
Copy Assistant: Susan Smith Cheatham
Designer: Earl Freedle

To find out how you can order *Southern Living* magazine, write to *Southern Living*®, P.O. Box C-119, Birmingham, AL 35283.

Contents

Editor's Note

It is with great pleasure and pride that we offer our first *Southern Living Garden Annual*. It has been a long time in the making, and its publication is something many of us here at *Southern Living* have been looking forward to. I've heard so many times how cumbersome it can be to thumb through stacks of back issues for a particular story. In fact, many readers have specifically requested a book like this. So in our continuing effort to make your gardening endeavors more enjoyable and fruitful, we've responded to your wishes. What you hold in your hands is the result.

The *Southern Living 1990 Garden Annual* represents the garden and landscape articles published by *Southern Living* during 1989. Some of you may notice articles in this annual that did not appear in your issue of the magazine. That is because we publish different issues and stories for different states and growing regions. Likewise, it is possible that a story that ran in your copy of *Southern Living* may not appear in this book. This is because a story may have run only in your state, and printing it in this annual would preclude it from being published in future issues of *Southern Living*. There are only a few instances of this, however, and I feel certain you will find more "extra" stories than you will "missing" ones.

Reviewing the book, I am encouraged to see the range of subjects we've covered in the past year. Fruits, vegetables, trees, shrubs, and wildflowers are all included. Articles on a wide variety of annuals, perennials, and bulbs offer choices for filling your flower beds and containers with color and texture. Throughout we strive to provide the most up-to-date horticultural information about the most appropriate plant selections. This commitment to regional specifics is one of the many advantages *Southern Living* offers over national gardening magazines.

But knowing how to grow a plant is only part of creating a beautiful garden. Therefore, we offer ideas on landscape design to help you decide where to put the plants you add and where to build the structures that shape your garden. By sharing with you a private garden or a design feature such as parking, gates, or garden ornaments, we hope to spark your imagination. And we give tips on how to take care of your properly planted, well-designed garden.

As you can imagine, the credit for this book goes to many different people. First and foremost is the *Southern Living* Garden Department. Editors Lois Trigg, Linda Askey Weathers, Steve Bender, and Rita Strickland demonstrate their understanding of the gardening challenges and opportunities we face in the South. And it is primarily Van Chaplin and Mary-Gray Hunter who bring these plants and ideas to life with their award-winning photography. Together, this staff has almost sixty years of experience writing about and photographing Southern gardening. I think it shows.

Countless others were also involved: the art department that creates the look of each story, the copy desk that makes sure our facts are straight, and the production department that keeps track of all the information and makes sure that what we write is what is printed. But above all, it is you, the gardeners of the South, to whom we are most indebted. Without your desire to pursue the joy of nurturing a seed to full-fledged blossom, without your generosity in allowing us into your gardens to learn and share, and without your general support of gardening in the South, there would be no garden department and no *Garden Annual*. For that we thank you.

Please don't hesitate to write to tell us what you like or don't like about the book. Our goal is to serve you, and if you can think of a way for us to serve you better, then by all means, let us hear from you. We truly want you to feel that you have a stake in what we do here at *Southern Living*. We are a company built on the concept of sharing information, and what we give to you in the pages of this book and the magazine is a direct reflection of what the people of the South share with us.

I hope this *Garden Annual* provides you with the inspiration and motivation you need to get out there and garden. And I'll be disappointed if this book isn't ragged-eared and smudged come late fall. May the sun and rain be kind to you and may you come to respect nature even more through the time you spend in the garden. Happy gardening!

Todd Steadman

Todd Steadman
Senior Garden Editor

(**Top photo**) Back row: *Todd Steadman, Rita Strickland;* front row: *Linda Askey Weathers, Lois Trigg, Kristen Sulser, Steve Bender.* (**Bottom photo**) *Mary-Gray Hunter, Van Chaplin.*

Photographs: Cheryl Sales, Van Chaplin

January

A seed-starting lamp provides the necessary light for seedlings growing indoors.

Get the Garden Going

You don't have to wait until April to enjoy bedding plants.
Here's how to start them from seed right now.

If the frosty days of January have you itching to garden again, take heart. Not only can you plan your spring flowerbeds now, but you can also start seed indoors to get the neighborhood's first blooms.

Why sow seed yourself when you can just wait and buy finished plants from a garden center? There are several reasons. First, if you normally buy dozens of bedding plants, you'll save a lot of money by growing your own. Second, you'll have a much wider range of colors, sizes, and species from which to choose. Finally, as veteran gardeners will tell you, you never

really know a plant until you've grown it from start to finish.

Unfortunately, you can't simply cast seed in a pot of soil, think good thoughts, and pick a beautiful geranium three weeks later. Seed from different plants vary in their requirements for germination and growth. The seed of pansies and Madagascar periwinkle, for example, need total darkness to germinate; those of wax begonia and petunias need light. But don't be too concerned—with proper equipment, you can supply the correct conditions for most types of seed.

One way to begin is to sow seed

directly into a flat that's filled with seed-starting mix. This, however, will slow you down, for the seed of some flowers are so tiny that it's hard to sow them evenly in a flat. And when they sprout, you have to separate and transplant them to individual containers. It's much easier to buy one of the seed-starting kits available in most gardening supply catalogs. Such a kit usually consists of a plastic tray divided into small cells filled with seed-starting mix. All you need do is wet the mix according to directions and drop two or three seeds into each cell.

Unless you have a greenhouse, the

(Left) Common zinnias germinate five to seven days after sowing. (Center) Because impatiens seedlings grow slowly, sow seed 10 to 12 weeks before the last frost. (Right) Start pansies indoors for both fall and spring blooms. Photographs: Van Chaplin, Mary-Gray Hunter

next piece of equipment you'll need is a seed-starting lamp. A hood atop the bulb directs light onto the seedlings' leaves. Suspend the bulb about 12 inches above the leaves, and keep it on about 16 hours a day.

If you want a really early start with your flowers, you should also invest in a soil-heating cable. This device, placed beneath the seed tray, warms the soil and speeds germination for most plants (you probably don't need a heating cable to germinate pansies and other cool-weather annuals). All heating cables should be waterproof and run on house current. Some come with thermostats that turn off the current

when the soil reaches 74 degrees. Others don't have thermostats, so you'll have to unplug them when the soil reaches the right temperature (as indicated by a soil thermometer).

Given proper care, seedlings should emerge within 1 to 3 weeks after sowing. If you're using a seed-starting kit, pinch out all but the strongest seedling in each cell. Fertilize once a week with water-soluble 20-20-20 fertilizer. When a seedling gets to be about 1½ inches tall and has two to three sets of true leaves, poke your finger through the bottom of its cell, pop the plant out, and check the roots. If roots have filled the soil mass, it's time to transplant.

Transfer the seedling to a 4-inch pot, and let it grow.

If you've sown seed in a flat, use a pencil point to loosen and separate seedlings when they have at least two sets of true leaves. Gently lift a seedling out by a leaf, not the stem. Fill a 4-inch pot with soil, use a pencil to make a hole in the middle, and set the roots in. Firm the soil around the stem. Feed once a week with 20-20-20.

When the plants are ready to go outside, expose them to four or five nights of cool temperatures (45 to 50 degrees) to harden them off. Then plant directly into the garden when there's no danger of frost.

A GENERAL GUIDE FOR STARTING BEDDING PLANTS INDOORS

PLANT	SOIL TEMP.	HOW TO SOW	DAYS TO GERMINATION	WHEN TO SOW
Ageratum	70-75°	Barely cover with soil	5-10	6-8 weeks before last frost
Coleus	65-75°	Sow on surface	10-15	10-12 weeks before last frost
Geranium	70-75°	Barely cover with soil	5-15	12-16 weeks before last frost
Impatiens	70-75°	Sow on surface	15-20	10-12 weeks before last frost
Madagascar periwinkle	75°	¼ inch deep	15-20	12 weeks before last frost
Marigold	70-75°	¼ inch deep	5-7	4-6 weeks before last frost
Pansy	65-70°	¼ inch deep	10-20	August for fall and spring blooms, December for spring only
Petunia	70-80°	Sow on surface	10-15	10-15 weeks before last frost
Scarlet sage	70-75°	Sow on surface	10-15	6-8 weeks before last frost
Wax begonia	70-75°	Sow on surface	10-14	12-14 weeks before last frost
Zinnia	70-75°	¼ inch deep	5-7	4-6 weeks before last frost

"Structurally, I saw the pomegranates and hydrangeas as very compatible with the subject of the painting. In an odd way, they relate to the period feeling of the painting. There is something about the texture of what the people are wearing that evokes an earthiness, and I tried to pick that up. That's why I used cockscomb, liriope, and hosta. But it's the pomegranates that really make it work."
Arranger: Phillip Sides, Montgomery, Alabama. Artist: Barbara Gallagher.

Matching Flowers to Art

It can be as fun as it is challenging to match flowers to art. Here are a few guidelines, as well as some thoughts from the experts on how they approached these arrangements.

by TODD A. STEADMAN / photography MARY-GRAY HUNTER

In the world of nature, the flower is universally enjoyed as a thing of beauty. In fine art, it is painting that is perhaps most widely appreciated. So it stands to reason that man has tried for centuries to fuse the two—at times using flowers to herald the art, and at others letting art interpret flowers. But always, his attempt has been to make his world more beautiful.

Every year museums throughout the South have showings of arrangers matching flowers to art. The shows are well worth seeing, but you don't have to wait on the experts. Here are some ideas to help you get started with your own interpretations.

The photographs on these pages depict the work of several Alabama floral arrangers in combination with artwork from all over the world. The arrangers express their thoughts on what they wanted to accomplish and how they went about it for each composition. This is a perfect example of a picture being worth a thousand words.

Some Basic Considerations

More than anything else, matching flowers to art is a challenge of understanding. It's easy to look at a painting and know you enjoy it. And with a little practice, a person can learn the mechanics of basic flower arranging. But to understand the key elements of a painting and then use flowers to interpret those elements is no small task.

First, acknowledge and respect the intricacies that must be considered, but don't let them intimidate you. It's

"This particular painting contains such an obvious and mood-provoking subject that it almost creates its own environment. I took a literal approach and used the bird-of-paradise against a jungle-green wall to further the exotic, tropical feeling of the painting. It works, but it's not overstated. The painting and arrangement almost become one." *Arranger and artist: Monica Ard, Birmingham.*

"We started out by using a simple Oriental line and emphasized the sweep of the line with euphorbia. Then we filled in with freesia, garden roses, and cotoneaster. Of course, the arrangement is not pure Oriental or ikebana. It's more an American adaptation of Oriental flower arranging. I think it's a lot more fun the American way because you have more freedom." *Arrangers: Opal Yeates and Naomi Thomason, Birmingham. Artist: Unknown.*

"The colors, textures, and subject of this painting all have a harvest look, so we tried to play off of that—especially with the materials used: gourds, corn, miniature pumpkins, and the wicker basket. And then there is the goldenrod and ornamental grass. Using miniature pumpkins really helped keep everything at the proper scale. Because of the painting, this arrangement really lent itself to use of a lot of color." *Arrangers: Opal Yeates and Naomi Thomason. Artist: Barbara Evans.*

"Because this is a fairly small painting, I felt that it needed a fairly small arrangement and small flowers. I tried to use restraint on the arrangement so as not to overpower the picture—something easy to do. I also wanted colors that would blend with the setting of the painting. Using goldenrod, heather, and daisies gives a feeling that reflects the wild setting the woman is in, while the roses and snapdragons reflect the refined aspect of the painting." *Arranger: Lula Rose Blackwell, Birmingham. Artist: F. Sagasta.*

"We tried to keep the arrangement small so it would not compete with the painting—the amaryllis is so dramatic. As a result, the visual lightness of the vessel is important so as not to detract. And we had to search a long time to find foliage that relates to the amaryllis. We finally used some pineapple lily." Arrangers: Opal Yeates and Naomi Thomason. Artist: Betty Lassen.

largely a matter of developing your eye and practicing.

Consider whether you want to do a literal or an interpretive arrangement; both have merit and are equally valid. A lot will depend on the painting. If it's abstract, then you will have no choice but to interpret accordingly. The same is true for paintings of people. But if the painting has a floral subject, it can be fun to re-create the painting with real flowers. In almost every case, however, there will be interpretation.

Regardless of what style you choose, one of the most important elements will be color. Look for dominant colors in the painting, and decide if you want to match them or use complementary colors. Of course, to a certain degree you are limited by what flowers are available. But from your garden, the florist, and your imagination, you should be able to find what you need.

Another factor to keep in mind is line. Some paintings have very clear, strong lines that you can emulate. For example, a soft, soothing painting may be reflected by smooth, flowing lines in an arrangement. On the other hand, if the artwork is boldly graphic in its nature, it may be more appropriate to use jagged, abrupt lines. But remember, you don't have to be literal.

The same guidelines that apply to color and line apply to texture and form. Every painting will have a dominant texture and a form; it will be up to you to determine what they are and then react to them. For example, a large, bold painting with vivid colors will probably have a more coarse texture than will a pastel landscape.

The scale of the arrangement is also critical. Not only should it be appropriate for the painting, but it also should fit the setting. It is easy to go overboard and create an arrangement fit for a ballroom, but if it is to be used in your den, the arrangement will probably look out of place.

"For this arrangement, I used flowers and greenery in a textural way—much like the textural quality of the painting itself. At the same time, the lines of the arrangement reflect the lines of the painting, and the colors match the painting well. It's a simple arrangement. You just have to understand the painting first and not go overboard with the flowers." Arranger: Phillip Sides. Artist: Toni Tully.

*Freesias are pretty enough to be a favorite—
their delicate scent is a bonus.*
Photographs: Van Chaplin

Fragrant Delights

Although pleasant enough, the smells of a blazing fire, wool blankets, and hot cider can closet the mind in a fog of gray winter days. Sooner or later, thoughts turn to the sweet air of summer—which is good reason to add the garden-fresh scent of flowers to your home. As fragrance drifts about the room, you catch a hint of flowers before you ever see them.

Of course, not all flowers have such perfume. But there are a few that you'll treasure for your winter arrangements.

A big bouquet of **tuberoses** will not go unnoticed for long. They even appear to smell good. Their thick, waxy petals look like the daphne flowers that will soon be blooming outdoors. And they have the creamy color of gardenias. Borne from bulbs that normally bloom in summer, they are a luxury to be purchased from florists. Truly, tuberoses are a pleasing indulgence.

You'll love **freesias** not only for their distinctive scent but also for their bright colors and graceful form. The fragrance of freesias is lighter than that of tuberoses—but decidedly sweet. Growing the bulbs in your home will be difficult because they require bright light and cool temperatures. But whether you buy them or raise them in a greenhouse, they are delightfully versatile. Choose two or three stems for a

If a single stem of tuberose is delightfully sweet, imagine the fragrance of an entire bouquet.

delicate vase, or mingle them with other flowers for a fuller arrangement.

Houseplant enthusiasts will enjoy a cascading plant of **jasmine** (*Jasminum polyanthum*). While other fragrant flowers are a brief pleasure, the dark-green foliage of jasmine makes a handsome hanging basket all year long. And in winter, its trailing stems grow heavy with white flowers as the plant blooms in snowy profusion. Like Christmas cactus and poinsettia, jasmine needs long, uninterrupted nights; so keep it where it won't receive light in the evening. Ideally, it should be placed on a sunny windowsill and experience cool temperatures in the fall

while buds are forming. And remember, you can also cut branches for arrangements.

The fresh-scented **paperwhite narcissus** is familiar and rather easy to grow under average home conditions. Readily available as bulbs in the fall, they still may be available in garden centers that did not sell out. Just plant them and wait. You'll have flowers in about four to six weeks. However, with insufficient light, the stems can grow too tall to stand up on their own or look their best. So force enough bulbs so that you can cut the flowers and add their perfume to your winter arrangements.

Exotic Bromeliads Thrive Indoors

Let these intriguing dwellers of the rain forest bring an exotic look to your home. There are dozens of types to try; most are easy to grow.

by STEVE BENDER / photography VAN CHAPLIN

It would be nice to sum up bromeliads in a sentence or two, but these exotic plants just won't be pigeonholed. Depending on the species, they may adorn a tropical palm, embrace a desert cactus, or, in the case of the pineapple, provide a tasty snack. In addition to their remarkable variability, bromeliads possess another rare talent—a penchant for thriving indoors.

The native habitat of bromeliads explains somewhat why they do so well in the home. Most of the hundreds of species currently being sold hail from the steamy rain forests of Central, South, and North America. Shaded by a thick, jungle canopy, they survive with relatively little light, comparable to that in an average room.

Bromeliads fall into two broad categories: epiphytic and terrestrial. Epiphytic types cling to tree trunks and branches, gathering necessary nutrients and water from the air. Terrestrial types tie themselves to the ground, obtaining moisture and food through both roots and leaves.

Most houseplants flaunt either flowers or foliage, but bromeliads do both. Their flower spikes may be red, orange, yellow, pink, purple, or blue and range in size from ¼ inch to over 15 feet long. What's more, they often last for more than a month. Spikes vary in shape from the "flaming swords" of the *Vrieseas* to the water lily blooms of the *Guzmanias*.

As spectacular as the flowers sometimes are, they don't overshadow the foliage. The leaves may be striped, banded, spotted, or mottled with a number of contrasting colors. Gardeners especially prize the foliage of the *Neoregelias*.

There are so many shapes and colors of bromeliads from which to choose that you really can't blame people for overdoing them in the home. Yet too many different selections and species on display can overpower a setting. They may come from the jungle, but you don't want your living room looking like one. Remember: Variety is the soul of a collection, but well-ordered composition relies on restraint.

Gardeners just starting out with these plants need to know which ones to try. According to Bud Martin of Blossom World Bromeliads in Sanford, Florida, the five genera easiest to grow in the home (ranked in order from simplest to more difficult) are *Cryptanthus, Aechmea, Neoregelia, Guzmania,* and *Vriesea.* Here are capsule descriptions of each.

Cryptanthus: Known as "earth stars" because of the star-shaped arrangement of their leaves, these terrestrial

The mottled leaves of Vriesea fenestralis *accent this sideboard.*

plants seldom grow more than a few inches tall and 12 inches wide. Their flowers are insignificant, but they make up for this with gaudy foliage.

Aechmea: These most popular bromeliads blend colorful foliage and flowers. Most grow 2 to 3 feet tall, but some, such as *Aechmea chantii* Little Harv, can fill the corner of a room. Aechmeas can be either epiphytic or terrestrial.

Neoregelia: Generally growing 8 to 10 inches tall and 18 to 24 inches wide, these plants need bright, indirect light to produce their showiest foliage. Their flowers are attractive, though rather small. Both epiphytic and terrestrial plants belong to this group.

Guzmania: While some *Guzmanias* display flashy foliage, it's their riveting flower spikes of red, orange, and yellow that steal the show. Plants are mostly large, around 2 to 3 feet tall and wide, and epiphytic.

Vriesea: The upright spikes of these bromeliads often resemble red-hot pokers. But blooms also come in orange, pink, or yellow. The leaves may be solid green, banded, or mottled. Plants grow 12 to 30 inches tall and wide and are primarily epiphytic.

HOW TO GROW

There are hardly two environments more radically opposed than the tropical rain forest and the inside of your home. Yet bromeliads adapt well to either. Probably the biggest reason is their acceptance of low light. None of the species discussed requires direct sun. In fact, the hot, afternoon sun can burn them. As a rule, those with thin, flexible, spineless leaves tolerate dimmer light, such as might

The bloom of Vriesea splendens *shoots upward like a flame.*

The showy bracts of Aechmea fasciata *can last for more than a month.*

There's nothing little about Aechmea *Little Harv.*

It's hard to ignore Neoregelia *Aztec's burgundy-and-emerald leaves.*

Guzmania lingulata *Tricolor combines striped foliage and large, scarlet blooms.*

be found in the middle of a room lit by several windows. Those with colorful foliage or thick, fleshy leaves do best in bright, indirect light, or curtain-filtered sunlight. Low light does not affect flowering. "When a plant is mature and ready to flower, it will flower on its own," states Martin.

Most epiphytic bromeliads have a cup in the center of their foliage. In the wild, this cup collects rainwater and

Star-shaped Cryptanthus bivittatus *Pink Starlight*
is one of the easiest bromeliads to grow.

provides the plant with the moisture it needs. To simulate nature in the home, fill the cup with tap water, brought to room temperature, about every two weeks. Let the cup become nearly empty before refilling. Do not use water that has been run through a water softener.

A terrestrial bromeliad may or may not have a cup. If it has, fill the cup, and water the soil about every two weeks. If it hasn't, keep the soil moist, but not soggy. When you water, water thoroughly—excess water should run from the pot's drainage hole.

All of these bromeliads benefit from daily misting to increase humidity. They also require good air circulation and temperatures of at least 50 degrees. Foliar feed every two months with water-soluble houseplant fertilizer diluted to half strength.

Epiphytic bromeliads don't need soil—you'll often see people growing them on a piece of driftwood or a plaque of osmunda fiber. The trick here is to wire the plants in place until their roots get a firm grip. But you can also grow most epiphytes in pots. Just use a quickly draining soil medium, such as coarse sphagnum moss, perlite, or shredded bark, to anchor them in an upright position. For terrestrial types, any well-draining, general-purpose potting soil suffices. But if you prefer to make your own, mix together equal portions of compost, vermiculite, and coarse sand.

If you're not sure whether a particular bromeliad is epiphytic or terrestrial, just check the care card that comes with most plants or ask the nurseryman. For more information about these fascinating plants, write to the Bromeliad Society, 1508 Lake Shore Drive, Orlando, Florida 32803.

Choosing the right apple selection will give you a bountiful harvest.
Photograph: Van Chaplin

Picking the Best Apples

Choosing an apple tree is a lasting decision. You'll invest not only the money the tree will cost but also several years of care and training before you are rewarded with a harvest.

You can divide apples into two groups—those you want to grow and those you can grow. Ideally, you would like to find a selection that falls into both categories. While such criteria as flavor, size, and appearance are important, they are meaningless if the apple tree is not suited to the growing conditions in your area.

Gardeners must be mindful of the severity of winter. Hardiness is important, but with apples, you need to consider dormancy as well. You see, each apple selection needs a certain number of hours with temperatures below 32 degrees before their buds can break dormancy. This is called a chilling requirement. Gardeners in areas with mild winters, particularly in the Lower South, should select an apple with a low chilling requirement. These include Dorsett Golden, Anna, Brogden, and Ein Shemer. You can grow most other selections in the Middle and Upper South.

Another factor to consider is pollination. Apples must cross-pollinate with a second selection before they will set fruit. Some selections are better pollinators than others. Naturally, you need to choose two selections that flower at the same time. Good pollinators include Red Delicious with Golden Delicious, Granny Smith with Red Rome, and McIntosh with Lodi. Ein Shemer, Dorsett Golden, Yates, and Granny Smith are self-pollinating, but you will get a better yield if they are cross-pollinated. Stayman Winesap is pollen sterile, so don't count on it to pollinate other varieties. However, it can be grown in the company of Golden Delicious, Yates, Red Rome, or Granny Smith.

To extend the fruiting season, plant early-, mid-, and late-season selections. Early-fruiting selections include Lodi, Red June, Dorsett Golden, Anna, and Ein Shemer. Examples of mid-season apples are McIntosh, Molly's Delicious, Red Delicious, and Golden Delicious. For late-ripening fruit, plant Stayman Winesap, Yates, Red Rome, or Granny Smith.

If you only have room for a single tree, you can buy one that has several selections grafted onto it. This allows for cross-pollination and extended harvest, all on the same tree.

For maximum yield in minimum space, plant spur-type trees. These are usually grafted on dwarfing or semi-dwarfing rootstocks so that you have a tree that stays a manageable size but bears enough fruit to compensate for its smaller canopy.

The term "spur-type" is a little misleading. All apple trees bear their fruit on short twigs called spurs. But a spur-type tree has many more of them. Usually, a nursery or grower will find a branch on an old selection, propagate it, and sell a spur-type version of the old favorite. For example, Starkspur Winesap is a spur-type of Stayman Winesap.

Rootstocks can make a difference, not only in the size of your trees but also in how early they bear fruit. For freestanding trees, choose a semi-dwarf. If you plan to espalier the tree, choose a dwarf.

Dwarfing rootstocks and genetic dwarfs are entirely different. A genetic dwarf is not smaller because of its roots, but because the leaves and fruit on the stem are very compact. Genetic dwarfs are usually grown just for interest rather than to produce a quantity of fruit. However, they will bear full-size fruit on a small plant, even if grown in containers.

Once you've determined which trees you can grow, you need to decide which apples you want to eat. You can choose between apples for cooking or fresh eating. Of course you can cook any apple, but some will taste better than others. Good cooking apples include Stayman Winesap, Red Rome, and Granny Smith.

The apple you choose for fresh eating is strictly a matter of taste. You may like the sweetness of a Golden Delicious or prefer the full flavor of a McIntosh or the tart firmness of a Granny Smith. You need to sample different selections before deciding; you'll be amazed at the diversity in flavor.

Buying a Wheelbarrow? Here Are Some Tips

Sooner or later, anyone who works in the yard discovers he needs a cart or wheelbarrow to haul plants, fertilizer, tools, and other gardening materials. But do you need one that is big or small? Steel or plastic? Lightweight or heavy duty? The following information will help you choose.

Don't Skimp on a Wheelbarrow

If you're going to haul dirt, plants, pine straw, compost, bricks, firewood, or any other bulky or heavy items, you need a heavy-duty contractor's wheelbarrow. A small wheelbarrow is cheaper, but it has a shallow tray and its one-piece handle and undercarriage is harder to balance. A typical contractor's wheelbarrow has a deep tray and a sturdier undercarriage with a wide stance for better balance. Long wood

Select a good wheelbarrow to help you muscle a heavy load through the garden.

handles extend all the way to the wheel for good leverage. The wood also has a natural flex that helps with control. Various models of contractor's wheelbarrows usually hold 5 to 6 cubic feet (about the size of a large bale of sphagnum peat moss). Small wheelbarrows hold only 3 or 4 cubic feet.

A contractor's wheelbarrow weighs 20 to 30 pounds more than a smaller type. But most gardeners like the extra weight because the wheelbarrow feels sturdier. It also bounces less when rolling over bumpy surfaces. Look for one with a strong undercarriage. A flimsy one is apt to get bent, and then the wheelbarrow won't sit level.

If you don't like the heavy models (those weighing about 50 pounds), you can lower the weight by 10 or 15 pounds by choosing one that has a plastic tray. "Wheelbarrows with polyethylene trays are our biggest sellers," says John Flannery, product manager for Ames Lawn and Garden Tools in Parkersburg, West Virginia. "They don't weigh as much as steel trays, and they clean up nicely. Concrete and dirt don't stick to them the way they do to the steel trays. They cost less, too." The new polyethylene trays withstand sunlight and extreme weather, so you don't have to worry about cracking. Another bonus: They're quiet—no metallic clank when you drop something in the tray.

Besides the tray, handle, and undercarriage, you need to inspect the tire on a wheelbarrow. The tire supports the load and thus influences the feel and handling of the carrier. The best

tire is pneumatic; it's filled with air just like an auto tire. It makes for an easy, smooth ride. A semi-pneumatic tire is next best. It is a solid tire with an air cushion built into it. Solid tires are the least desirable. Because they do not have the give that air-filled tires have, they jostle the load more.

Garden Carts—When A Wheelbarrow Won't Do

Because of its one-wheel design, a wheelbarrow is easy to maneuver between garden rows, around shrubs, and in and out of other tight places. But when the load gets too big or too heavy, you can lose control and spill the contents. That won't happen with a garden cart; it's stable because it sits on two wheels. It's also easier to push across rough ground.

Garden carts come in two basic styles. The lawn (or leaf) cart is like a deep bucket, usually with the front side tilted at a 45-degree angle. That's so the front lies flat on the ground when you tip it forward, allowing you to rake leaves into the cart. However, you cannot shovel material out of this model. The second garden cart style resembles a wagon and has a flat bed. Usually made of exterior plywood with a metal frame, it's perfect for hauling bales of pine straw and other big loads. The flat bed is also easy to shovel from. This type cart generally holds 300 to 400 pounds—more than even the largest wheelbarrow—and is for the serious gardener. Look for a sturdy, noncorrosive frame and spoked wheels large enough to carry the load.

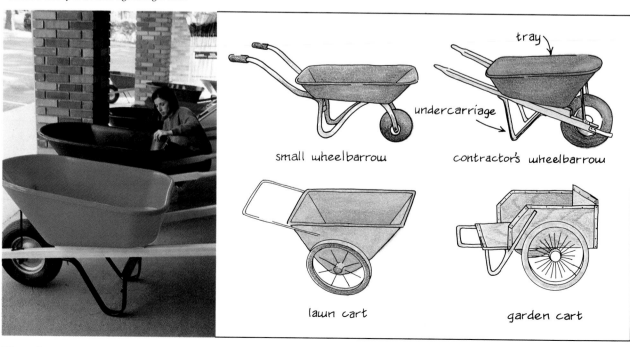

small wheelbarrow

contractor's wheelbarrow

lawn cart

garden cart

LETTERS
TO OUR GARDEN EDITORS

Cacti: What kind of plant food should I feed my cactus plants? *B. B., Norman, Oklahoma.* Cacti naturally grow in rather infertile soils, so they don't require much fertilizer. In fact, you shouldn't feed them at all during the winter. In spring and summer, feed them every two weeks with a low-nitrogen, water-soluble fertilizer diluted to half strength. Shultz Instant Liquid Plant Food 10-15-10 would be a good choice.

Planting under a maple: I have a large maple with a thick network of surface roots. I want to put a raised flowerbed underneath it. Can you suggest annuals, perennials, and bulbs that will do well in the dense shade? *J. E., Lynchburg, Virginia.* It's very difficult to grow anything beneath a big maple because shallow roots rob the soil of moisture and nutrients while thick branches hide the sun. You may be able to grow plants in a raised bed temporarily, but before long, the maple's roots will fill it and make gardening nearly impossible. For the time being, you can plant shade-tolerant annuals, such as impatiens, browallia, coleus, or caladiums. In the long run, however, you'd be better off mulching the bed or planting a ground cover such as liriope.

Weeping fig: My weeping fig was beautiful when I bought it, but it keeps dropping leaves. Can you advise me on the care of this plant? *M. S., Covington, Louisiana.* Your problem with weeping fig (*Ficus benjamina*) is quite common. This popular foliage plant is very temperamental and will drop foliage for no apparent reason. Dropping leaves usually follows a change in the plant's location. After it adjusts to the new light, temperature, and humidity, the problem lessens.

Weeping fig likes bright, indirect light and temperatures between 65 and 75 degrees. Let the top inch of soil go dry between thorough waterings. Fertilize monthly with water-soluble 20-20-20 fertilizer.

Snow damage: During a recent snowstorm, a heavy limb fell from a tree and nearly hit our power lines. What can we do to make our trees less susceptible to storm breakage? *D. C., Martin, Tennessee.* When planting shade trees, choose those that will have the strongest branches and hardest wood. As a rule, the faster a tree grows, the weaker its wood is. Silver maple (*Acer saccharinum*), Siberian elm (*Ulmus pumila*), Bradford pear (*Pyrus calleryana* Bradford), poplars (*Populus* sp.), and other rapid growers are notoriously weak wooded. Also, softwoods, such as pines, are weaker than hardwoods. For existing large trees, proper pruning is the best answer. In most cases, this involves removing growth from the ends of large branches to prevent a heavy buildup of snow or ice during a storm. Professional tree pruners are

A buildup of snow or ice on hardwoods, such as on this oak, rarely causes major breakage. Softwoods aren't as sturdy.
Photograph: Van Chaplin

best equipped to handle this job. If your trees are endangering power lines, the local power company will usually send a crew to do the pruning free of charge. However, because the crews prune only to remove the hazard and not to maintain aesthetics, the results can be less than satisfying to a discerning homeowner. A professional arborist can accomplish both goals. Look under the heading "Arborist" or "Tree Service" in the

yellow pages. Make sure that the arborist you choose is fully insured. Most belong to the National Arborist Association, the International Society of Arboriculture, or the American Society of Consulting Arborists. An arborist will listen to your ideas concerning the tree's appearance and can do the work in your presence. He may even diagnose structural weaknesses that can be corrected now.

Crimson King maple: We've recently planted an assortment of shade trees around our home, including red maple, sugar maple, and pecan. But one of them, a Crimson King maple, has made very little growth. Can you offer any suggestions? *A. G., Dekalb, Mississippi.* Crimson King, a purple-leaved selection of Norway maple (*Acer platanoides*), is naturally a pretty slow grower, especially right after transplanting. In addition, it's better adapted to the Upper and Middle South than in your area of east-central Mississippi. One thing you might do to encourage speedier growth is to fertilize the tree in early spring. You can do this by measuring about 2 pounds of 10-10-10 or 10-6-4 fertilizer for every inch of trunk diameter and broadcasting it in a circle around the tree. Start the circle about 2 feet from the trunk, and extend it about 3 feet beyond the dripline. Be sure to distribute the fertilizer evenly. Then water it in.

TIP OF THE MONTH
To give your houseplants an extra boost of sunlight during the dim winter months, cover the soil with aluminum foil. Just cut a circle of foil, slit it from the outer edge to the center, ease it around the stem, and fold down tightly around the rim of each container. The foil will reflect light up under the leaves. *Myrtice Phillips, Quitman, Georgia.*

Editor's note: We'd like to have your ideas—the ones that have worked for you. We're especially interested in vegetables, houseplants, shrubs, trees, and garden care. For each tip that is published, we will pay $10 and send you one of our garden books.

Submit as many ideas as you wish, but each must be on a separate sheet or card, along with your name, address, and telephone number. We may need to edit the tips, and none will be acknowledged or returned. Send to Gardening Tips, *Southern Living,* Box 523, Birmingham, Alabama 35201.

CHECKLIST
For January

☐ **Boston ferns**—This is a difficult time of year for Boston ferns growing indoors. They can be a nuisance, shedding leaflets all over the floor. Keep this problem to a minimum by placing the plants in bright, indirect light or direct morning sun. Also, keep the soil moist, and fertilize monthly. If you do lose your fern or it begins looking so bad you decide to discard it, consider buying a Dallas fern. A compact selection known for indoor hardiness, it resists shedding even when allowed to dry out.

☐ **Compost**—Even though it's cool outside, compost piles stay warm and active as bacteria work to decompose leaves and other materials. However, decomposition will practically stop if the pile gets dry. It's a good idea to let a soaker hose run on it for several hours once every two or three weeks.

☐ **Energy conservation**—If prevailing winter winds in your area are from a northerly direction, planting a windbreak could result in considerable savings on your fuel bill. For maximum benefit, select an evergreen species that will grow at least 1 or 1½ times as tall as your home. Plant the screen perpendicular to the wind direction at a distance not greater than three tree-lengths away from the house. If you choose trees with high canopies, such as pines or live oaks, underplant with tall shrubs. Gaps in the screen could actually increase wind velocity instead of decreasing it. A landscape architect can advise you on the most effective placement of the windbreak and can suggest suitable species.

☐ **Grafts**—Plants such as roses and fruit trees are usually grafted. You can easily find the graft union; it is the swollen part of the stem. In later years, you'll be able to see a difference in the color or pattern of the bark. When planting, be sure to set the graft union 1 or 2 inches above the level of the soil. Prune off any shoots that develop below the graft union.

☐ **Herbs**—You can start thyme indoors now and transplant it into the garden this spring. Sow seeds in a light, well-drained potting mix, and keep the soil moist. If your indoor temperature remains around 70 degrees, the seeds should germinate in about two weeks. Once the weather warms, set the container outdoors for a few hours each day to harden off the seedlings. Plant after the danger of frost has passed. Harvest thyme before it flowers, cutting the plant to within 2 inches of the soil line.

☐ **Houseplants**—Watch for signs of spider mites on your indoor plants. Their growth is favored by the hot, dry air of heated homes. Yellow, stippled leaves are your clue to turn the leaf over. If you find tiny white webs on the back, your plants are infested with spider mites. The first step is to give them a shower, paying particular attention to the backs of the leaves. Let the leaves dry, and spray with insecticidal soap. (You may want to do this outdoors.) Repeat this treatment weekly for three to four weeks to kill newly hatched mites.

☐ **Rose handbook**—The American Rose Society once again offers its yearly update on roses. The pocket-size "Handbook for Selecting Roses" rates the garden performance of over 1,000 selections based on evaluations by ARS members. For a copy, send $1 and a stamped, self-addressed envelope to The American Rose Society, Box 30,000, Shreveport, Louisiana 71130-0030.

☐ **Salt-tolerant bedding plants**—Tests conducted by researchers from the University of Florida and the Florida Extension service have pinpointed several bedding plants that will grow well on the coast despite salty ground water and ocean spray. They are dusty miller, gaillardia, geranium, gerbera daisy, lisianthus, and Madagascar periwinkle.

☐ **Tools**—This is a good time to get your garden equipment ready for the busy season ahead. Give your lawnmower its annual maintenance, such as sharpening the blade. Remove rust from tools by rubbing them with steel wool dipped in machine or motor oil. Linseed oil will protect wooden handles from rot. Sharpen your spade and edging knife to make garden tasks easier. Check your sprayer, and replace any old or worn parts.

☐ **Trees and shrubs**—The winter months are best for transplanting shrubs and small trees. First, have your new planting hole ready so you can replant immediately. Then dig up the plants carefully to minimize damage to the root systems. If many roots are lost, prune away a corresponding amount of top growth. Only the lateral branches should be pruned from trees with a single leader (main vertical branch). Water thoroughly immediately after replanting. Plants should receive at least 1 inch of water per week until they are re-established.

SPECIAL TIPS FOR THE SOUTHEAST

☐ **Transplants**—You may find that you need to grow your own transplants for unusual species or less common selections. That means you have to start early to have plants ready when the weather warms. Tomatoes, peppers, and eggplants all require seven to nine weeks from the time you sow seeds until you set them in the garden, as do wax begonias, impatiens, browallia, and verbena. Celosia, marigolds, and ageratum will be ready in five to six weeks. Usually the seed packet will tell you how long to allow between the time that you sow and the time that you plant. To avoid damping-off, a fungal disease that attacks seedlings, use the sterile soil mix sold for starting seeds. Growing plants should be kept in a greenhouse or on a sunny windowsill.

☐ **Vegetables**—Till your garden soil now to work in composted leaves and any other amendments recommended by your soil test. Tilling will also help destroy weed seeds as well as bring insects to the surface, where they will be victims of hungry birds or winter temperatures. The garden season begins later this month in the Lower South, where you can plant collards, turnips, Chinese cabbage, leeks, radishes, carrots, kale, kohlrabi, and spinach. Begin spraying cabbage and its relatives with *Bacillus thuringiensis* (Dipel or Thuricide) soon after you plant to prevent damage from cabbage loopers and imported worms.

☐ **Weed trees**—Not all weeds are annuals; some are trees. Cherry laurels, mimosas, mulberries, boxelders, willow oaks, sweet gums, and redbuds frequently pop up in beds where they don't belong. Remove these trees while they're only a few inches tall and when their roots are only a few inches deep.

SPECIAL TIPS FOR FLORIDA

☐ **Apples**—Before planting in the Sunshine State, be sure to choose apple selections adapted to the mild climate. Popular types that need only a small amount of cool weather to bloom include Anna, Ein Shemer, and Dorsett Golden. Plant at least two different selections so that cross-pollination will occur and trees will bear fruit. Mulch the area around the base of the trees, and keep it free of grass and weeds to help prevent disease. If you live in an area where there are rabbits, consider wrapping the trunks with hardware cloth or plastic tree guards. Rabbits love to nibble the bark of the trees and can kill a young tree by eating through to the live layer of wood.

☐ **Citrus**—Avoid spraying for insects while citrus trees are in bloom. Insecticides that kill mites, aphids, and other pests can also kill bees that are pollinating the citrus blossoms. If you must spray, do so in late afternoon after the bees are gone. Don't use insecticidal dusts, for they are more likely to be picked up by the bees' fuzzy bodies.

☐ **Flowers**—Now is the time to order flower seeds for spring and summer. To find out which selections do best in Florida, you can ask other gardeners. Or investigate the trial garden at Walt Disney World, where more than 400 selections are tested each year. (Results are distributed to nurserymen and other landscape professionals.) Some recent top performers include Jewel Box and Scarlet Toreador celosia; Early Sunrise coreopsis; Super Elfin and Impact impatiens; Tango New Guinea impatiens; Disco marigold; and Rose Madagascar periwinkle (also known as vinca).

☐ **Vegetables**—Gardeners in South Florida may now plant tomatoes, beans, and other warm-weather vegetables—just be prepared to protect them from frost. If the temperature dips into the 30's, cover the plants with boxes, a blanket, hot caps, or row covers. Don't use clear plastic unless you'll be around the next day to remove it should the weather warm. Otherwise, plants could cook under the plastic as heat builds up. Wait another two to three weeks to plant in Central Florida and until March in North Florida.

☐ **Vegetable pests**—Gardeners in frost-free regions should be on the lookout for cabbageworms and cutworms. Cabbageworms chew on cabbage, collards, broccoli, and other cole crops. To control the pests, dust foliage with carbaryl or rotenone. Cutworms often strike at night; they chew through the stems of young transplants at ground level, causing plants to topple like felled trees. Cutworms live underground and are difficult to kill, but you can thwart their efforts by shielding transplants with collars. You can make a collar from a plastic or paper cup. Simply cut off the bottom so the cup forms a tube; then slip it over the plant. Twist about an inch of the cup into the ground so it will stay in place. Now the pests can't reach the stems.

SPECIAL TIPS FOR TEXAS

☐ **Annuals**—Turn the soil in annual beds in preparation for spring planting. Along with destroying weed seeds, this also brings insects to the surface, where birds can eat them or winter temperatures kill them. When daytime temperatures consistently reach about 40 degrees, plant cold-hardy annuals, such as larkspur, calendulas, and poppies, for early spring flowers.

☐ **Blackberries**—Plant these fruiting brambles in January. Make sure the selection you choose is suited to your part of the state. In the northern half of Texas, consider Womack; to the south, Brison. Brazos does well in all but the extreme west, while Rosborough was developed for use in most of Texas. Consult your local office of the Texas Agricultural Extension Service for more information.

☐ **Native Plant Society of Texas**—Using native plants in your landscape can mean less watering and fewer insect and disease problems. To learn more about plants indigenous to the Lone Star State, write to the NPST at P.O. Box 891, Georgetown, Texas 78626.

☐ **Planting roses**—If you prepared your beds last fall, you'll be ready to plant as soon as bare-root roses are available. Dig wide planting holes about 4 feet apart, and build a cone of soil in the bottom of each one. The cone should be tall enough to raise the bud union slightly above the soil line when a plant is placed atop the cone. Spread the roots out fully, cover them with soil, and water thoroughly. If planting is delayed because of weather, the roses should be heeled in (the roots covered with loose soil and mulch) until you can plant.

LOVE THOSE CATALOGS

The new garden catalogs have arrived, but most of us set them aside during the busy holidays. Now is the time to plan this year's garden.

Once you get on a few mailing lists, it seems to be no problem to get the catalogs. But prior to that, where do you begin and how do you get those specialty catalogs? The answer is usually to request them. The advertisements in gardening magazines often include order cards that you can tear out and send back. Also examine source books, such as *Gardening By Mail 2*, by Barbara J. Barton. This regularly updated compendium lists companies for plants, seeds, and equipment, as well as plant societies, gardening magazines, libraries, and books. The third edition, published by Houghton Mifflin, will be available in bookstores in March 1990.

When you finally have the catalog in hand, follow a few guidelines to ensure that your orders are filled and returned without delay.

☐ If the company is new to you, place a small order to test their quality and service. Carefully read the ordering information included in each catalog to be sure that you meet the required minimum order. And be sure to specify on the form that substitutions are unacceptable.

☐ Some companies do not ship year-round, usually because they are shipping live plants that would suffer from extremes in temperature. Others cannot ship to certain states due to pest control regulations.

☐ Finally, keep a copy of your order form for reference.

Take time to shop the new catalogs to order the latest for your garden.
Photograph: Mary-Gray Hunter

February

A Sweet Harvest of Grapes

Pick a bunch of sweet grapes, rinse them under the hose, and enjoy a snack from your own backyard.

by LINDA ASKEY WEATHERS, STEVE BENDER, AND LOIS TRIGG

Photographs: Van Chaplin, Mary-Gray Hunter

Most of us are familiar with our native muscadine grapes that drop from the treetops in autumn, but we assume that bunch grapes have to be shipped to our grocer from other regions. However, many Southerners are finding that bunch grapes are a rewarding and delicious addition to their garden.

Bunch grapes get their name from the fact that the fruit is clustered rather than spread along stems, as muscadines are. Basically, bunch grapes are divided into two groups—wine grapes and table (or dessert) grapes. Both grow well in the South. The key is to choose the right selection for your area and give them proper care.

MAKE THE RIGHT CHOICE

Basically, there are three types of grapes that will grow in the South. *Vitis labrusca* is a native bunch grape. Concord is probably the best known selection of this group, but Fredonia, an improved selection, ripens earlier and more evenly.

The European grapes, *V. vinifera*, are a troubled but much sought after group. These are the famous wine grapes as well as the better known seedless table grapes. Because they are best suited to the moderate winters and dry summers of the Mediterranean and of California, they can have a hard time in the South. If you decide to try these grapes, buy plants grafted onto rootstocks that are resistant to phylloxera and nematodes, which are soilborne pests.

Where you live will determine which grapes you can grow. Steve Sorensen, vineyard manager at Biltmore Estate in Asheville, North Carolina, explains, "For each region in the Southeast, there are grapes that will and won't grow." To find out which ones are best for your garden, contact your local agricultural Extension agent. In addition, each state has a publication that includes preferred selections as well as management techniques.

Hybrids are the answer in most regions of the South. These are the result of crosses between native American grapes and European grapes. Dr. Jim Moore at the University of Arkansas is breeding seedless table grapes for the South. "We feel that seedless is the preference of everyone, whether they are buying grapes in the supermarket or growing them," he says.

*(**Opposite page**) Grapes seem even sweeter when you pick them from your own garden. Design: Harvilee Harbarger, ASLA, Huntsville, Alabama.*

Hybrids for Florida

For decades, Floridians have tried hard to grow bunch grapes from Northern states and Europe. But it seemed that the state sidestepped its reputation as a gracious host when it came to these grapes. Over and over again, the vines eventually died because of a culprit called Pierce's disease. A bacterium that loves hot, humid weather, this disease causes leaves to dry and vines to wither as it invades the plant.

Fortunately, back in the 1940's, the University of Florida began a visionary research program to overcome the disease. In the years since, breeders have combined the disease-resistant genes of bunch grapes native to the state's woodlands with the more refined European and American varieties. These crosses have yielded unique grapes with a likeness to Concord and Sauvignon Blanc, yet they grow in Florida's near-tropical climate in spite of Pierce's disease. The results are hybrid bunch grapes—Blanc du Bois, Blue Lake, Conquistador, Daytona, Lake Emerald, Orlando Seedless, Stover, and Suwannee—the only bunch grapes suited for Florida.

When buying Stover or Orlando Seedless, purchase plants grafted onto Tampa rootstock. They will be more productive. Conquistador is best on Dog Ridge rootstock. The rest of the recommended varieties do well on their own roots.

Hybrids for the Southeast

In general, hybrids recommended for the home garden in the Southeast include Mars (seedless, deep blue table), Saturn (seedless red table), Canadice (seedless green table), Seyval and Vidal Blanc (white wine), and Foch and Millot (red wine). Gardeners in the Lower South must choose selections resistant to Pierce's disease. Recommended selections for this region include Blanc du Bois, Blue Lake, Conquistador, Daytona, Lake Emerald, Orlando Seedless, Stover, and Suwannee.

Hybrids for Texas

For a long time, Thompson Seedless reigned as the top table grape in both the grocery and garden. People liked the pale-green, seedless fruit for its sweet, if somewhat thin, taste. Then seven or eight years ago, a serious challenger appeared on the scene: Flame Seedless. At first, some shoppers balked at the new red grape, preferring to stick with the tried and true. But now Flame is challenging Thompson as the number one grape.

What makes Flame Seedless so good? As the name tells you, it doesn't have seeds. Add to that an attractive color and a taste that's richer and more complex than Thompson's.

Unfortunately, Flame Seedless won't grow all over Texas. Due to the state's immense size, growing conditions vary tremendously. Flame Seedless grows best in North and West Texas. But if you live elsewhere, don't despair. Delicious alternatives exist for gardeners in every part of the state. For example, those in Regions 2 and 5 (North-Central and Central Texas) can grow Reliance, a tasty, seedless pink grape. And gardeners in Regions 3 and 6 (East and South Texas) should try Orlando Seedless, the only seedless grape resistant to Pierce's disease.

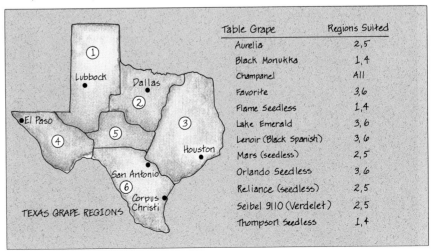

Table Grape	Regions Suited
Aurelia	2, 5
Black Monukka	1, 4
Champanel	All
Favorite	3, 6
Flame Seedless	1, 4
Lake Emerald	3, 6
Lenoir (Black Spanish)	3, 6
Mars (seedless)	2, 5
Orlando Seedless	3, 6
Reliance (seedless)	2, 5
Seibel 9110 (Verdelet)	2, 5
Thompson Seedless	1, 4

TEXAS GRAPE REGIONS

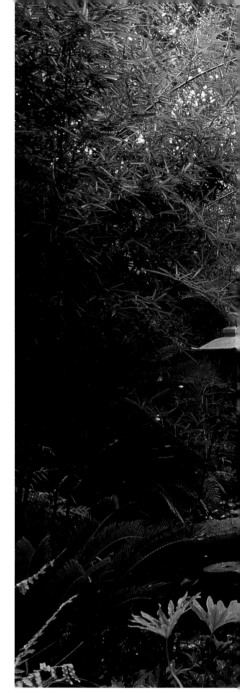

A Jewel in the
JAPANESE STYLE

You might pass by the plain gray wall of this New Orleans garden without a second thought. Yet behind its bright-red doorway lies an Oriental treasure.

by RITA W. STRICKLAND / photography VAN CHAPLIN

To the Japanese, gardens are more than pretty pictures. They are symbols of natural order and harmony. Because of his long-standing admiration for Japanese culture and art, this New Orleans homeowner requested that his architect, Pio Lyons, AIA, reserve a special place for just such a garden when plans for his new house were developed.

In keeping with ancient Japanese tradition, the space Lyons provided is rectangular and totally enclosed. The house wraps around two sides of the garden, and a high wall completes the enclosure. Visible from almost any point on the ground floor, the garden also can be seen from an upstairs bedroom balcony. "It's the focal point for the whole house," says Landscape Architect Luis A. Guevara, ASLA, of Design Consortium Plantscapes, who designed the garden.

Using many time-honored principles developed by Oriental masters, Guevara created a garden that he describes as "Japanesque." "I don't call this a Japanese garden because I believe that true Japanese gardens can be designed only by the Japanese," he says.

One of the techniques Guevara borrowed is miniaturization: If objects in the distance are disproportionately smaller than those nearer the viewer, the distant objects will seem much farther away, and the garden will appear larger. The water feature, an integral part of most Japanese gardens, is one example. "The pond is wide nearest the viewer; then it tapers back toward the waterfall, which by Western standards seems too small," Guevara says. But it's purposely small to make the viewer feel as if he were seeing the cascade across a larger landscape.

Likewise, if coarse-textured plants are used in the foreground and finer textured selections are used to the rear, a sense of greater space is achieved. This effect is enhanced if vibrant colors are kept near the viewer and duller shades placed farther away. "We used yaupons in the background. They're fine textured and gray green in color, so they seem to fade into the distance compared to the coarser leaves and brighter greens of the plants toward the front."

The Japanese also make use of scenery beyond the garden—the borrowed view—to give the impression of increased space. In this case, live oaks visible above the wall give the garden additional depth and serve as a faint reminder that this is, after all, New Orleans, not Kyoto.

There is a traditional Japanese belief that unusually shaped rocks are inhabited by *kami,* or spirits, and that their presence in the garden ensures its fertility. "So we looked for boulders with sculptural shapes that could also represent a mountain or cliff in the miniaturized landscape," Guevara says.

Placed beside the still pool, these rocks form a striking vertical accent.

On the garden floor, scattered around the boulders, dark-gray river stones, smoothed by centuries of running water, provide a contrast in both color and texture. "They create a naturalistic edge for the pool and form a beautiful pattern," says Guevara.

Across the pond, peeking out amid the foliage, a Japanese lantern resembles a temple in the distance overlooking a peaceful lake. "The lantern was originally much taller," Guevara says, "so we sank the bottom into the earth. We didn't want its height to interfere with the false perspective we'd created." This stone ornament is most beautiful in the evening when a candle flickering in its firebox is re-

flected on the water's surface.

Many evergreens, such as cleyera, azalea, sasanqua, and ardisia, are native to Japan but thrive in the Louisiana climate, so Guevara used them liberally in his design. A small Japanese maple graces one side of the waterfall, while aquatic lilies float lightly on the surface of the pool. And bamboo, which forms a lacy canopy overhead, makes the garden seem like a clearing carved out of the forest—just like the ancient sacred spots that were the first gardens of Japan.

(**Above**) *Visible from almost every room, this well-planned garden is the focal point of a New Orleans home.* (**Right**) *To the Japanese, large boulders, a tapering pool, and a small waterfall represent the landscape in miniature.*

By virtue of their size, miniature roses can turn an ordinary cream pitcher into a porcelain vase. Photograph: Beth Maynor

Roses in Miniature

Whether you garden or not, chances are you love roses. And miniature roses carry no less appeal for their diminutive size. In fact, they may be even more in demand.

"They're the most popular thing in the rose world as of now," observes Dr. Charles Jeremias, president of the American Rose Society. "We have anywhere from 60 to 75 new ones come out every year. They're popular because they're easy to grow. You can grow them in raised beds, flowerpots, hanging baskets, flue liners, whiskey barrels; you can grow them almost anywhere you want."

In the garden, miniature roses fit into a flower border beautifully, bringing color all season long. Jeremias explains, "They repeat blooming every five to six weeks just like regular roses if you deadhead them, that is, cut off the spent blooms as soon as they are finished." You can also plant them as an edging for your rose garden.

And they offer unique opportunities for arrangements. Containers too small for other flowers are perfect for a bouquet of miniature roses, which can add a special touch on the bedside table, at a place setting, or beside the powder room sink. They also work well in large bouquets. Insert stems into water picks. Then tape water picks to long floral picks, and insert them into the arrangement as you would do with any long-stemmed flower.

The Specifics

The original miniature rose that sparked all of this interest was Roulettii, a rose known in the early 1800's. It was lost for almost 100 years, only to be rediscovered in a Swiss window box around 1918. Roulettii is still available today—among hundreds of other selections.

Many of the early miniature roses, even when fully open, had blooms no bigger than the size of a nickel. These are now known in the trade as micro-minis and will grow only 8 to 14 inches tall.

In the last 20 years, hybridizers have concentrated on producing flowers that, when one-half to three-fourths open, have high-pointed centers similar to those of modern hybrid teas. Plant heights will vary from 24 to 36 inches, depending on selection, climate, and culture. But even on taller plants, canes and foliage are small.

Most roses require frequent pesticide sprayings, and miniatures aren't any different. However, their small size means spraying takes less time and requires smaller quantities of chemicals.

"The biggest problem with miniatures is spider mites," explains Jeremias. "When they get on those tiny leaves close to the ground, it's hard to get down and spray them. That's why people grow them in raised beds and containers."

For good nutrition, Jeremias recommends one application of slow-release fertilizer in the spring. However, he says you may also apply 10-10-10 in the spring at the rate of 1 tablespoon per plant to get the roses started. Continue with monthly applications of 10-10-10, or switch to a slow-release type.

If you have grown full-size roses, then you will find that the pruning technique is the same for miniatures. The time to prune is when you see the rosebuds swelling. Begin by cutting out the tangle of wood that grows toward the center and removing any dead branches. Then you can simply reduce the height of the plant as desired by cutting back canes to an outward-facing bud. However, if the rose is a spreading type, cut to an inward bud to make it grow more upright. While some miniatures scarcely need pruning, other selections will need to be cut back to maintain their compact habit.

Miniature roses offer all the color choices you find in other roses. Some of the better known selections include Red Beauty, Snow Bride, Rainbow's End (red and yellow), Rise 'n' Shine (yellow), Minnie Pearl (pink), and Jean Kenneally (apricot). Climbing miniatures are also available, such as Jeanne Lajoie (up to 10 feet) or Magic Dragon (up to 15 feet). For hanging baskets or a ground cover, try Red Cascade or Ralph's Creeper. And if you don't already have plenty of choices, each year brings new ones.

LETTERS

TO OUR GARDEN EDITORS

Baby's-breath: Is it possible to grow baby's-breath in our area? Both times that I tried, the plants died. *H. P., Fort Myers, Florida.*
Baby's-breath (*Gypsophila paniculata*), a perennial whose delicate sprays of white or pink flowers are favorites for flower arrangements, isn't well suited to the Lower or Coastal South, as summers there are too hot and humid. So you'll have to be content with getting flowers from a florist. Gardeners elsewhere in the South who want to try it should provide full sun and well-drained, slightly alkaline soil. Do not fertilize. Established plants resent transplanting, so choose a permanent location.

Maples: Would you please advise me about which maples are best adapted to southwest Louisiana? *J. L. G., New Iberia, Louisiana.*
Probably the best choice for your area is red maple (*Acer rubrum*). This fast-growing shade tree reaches 60 feet tall and features handsome, silvery bark and attractive foliage. In the Upper, Middle, and Lower South, the leaves may turn red or yellow in fall. Red maple prefers moist, fertile soil but is quite adaptable to other soils. If you'd like a smaller tree, consider Southern sugar maple (*A. floridanum*) or chalk maple (*A. leucoderme*). Both are essentially smaller versions of the more familiar sugar maple (*A. saccharum*) and grow 25 to 30 feet tall.

Kaffir lily: My Kaffir lily bloomed the first year, but now all the leaves that come out of the stalk turn yellow, then brown, then die. What's wrong? *O. B. W., Kosciusko, Mississippi.*
It sounds as if you have been overwatering. Kaffir lily (*Clivia miniata*) likes plenty of moisture when it's blooming and actively growing, but then enjoys drier soil during its dormant period in the fall. It's also possible that your plant needs repotting. If so, spring is a good time to do this. Move the plant to a container at least 2 inches larger in diameter than the previous one. Be careful not to damage the roots. Use a porous, well-drained potting mix consisting of equal parts sphagnum peat moss, perlite, and coarse sand. Water sparingly until the plant begins actively growing; then increase watering to keep the soil evenly moist. Feed every two weeks from spring to fall with water soluble 20-20-20 fertilizer diluted to half strength.

Aloe: After my *Aloe vera* plants reach a certain size, the bottom leaves start to dry up and die. What are the conditions needed to stop this? *T. D., Southern Pines, North Carolina.*
Medicinal aloe (*Aloe barbadensis*), often sold as *Aloe vera,* is a succulent plant well suited to growing in pots. However, older plants may become so crowded that outer leaves shrivel. One way to surmount this is to start a new plant from a leaf cutting. Simply cut a leaf, and let it dry on a table overnight; then insert it in moist potting soil. It should root within several weeks.

Brown leaves can also result from overwatering. Aloes need well-drained soil that is allowed to go dry between thorough waterings. Water very sparingly in winter, perhaps once every two weeks. Feed once a month with water-soluble 20-20-20 fertilizer diluted to half strength.

Daffodils: My daffodils have been growing in the same spot for a number of years but never bloom. What could be the cause? *E. T., Lexington, Kentucky.*

Periodically, daffodils need to be divided to keep them blooming prolifically.

Photograph: Mary Carolyn Pindar

Over the years, your daffodils have probably become too crowded. This spring would be a good time to divide and replant them. Use a garden fork to lift the clump; then shake off all the soil from the roots. Divide the bulbs into separate plants; then plant 4 to 6 inches deep and 6 to 8 inches apart in loose, fertile, well-drained soil. Water thoroughly. Full sun or light shade is fine. Next spring, sprinkle some Holland Bulb Booster (9-9-6) or 5-10-5 fertilizer over the soil surface just as the daffodil foliage emerges.

Tree stump: An enormous poplar tree at the end of our driveway died last year. We are now faced with the problem of how to utilize the stump. Can we make it an interesting focal point for our backyard? *B. W., Raleigh, North Carolina.*
The stump will eventually rot, so you shouldn't try to make it a permanent garden feature. Instead, we suggest you contact a local tree service and ask them to remove it. They have equipment that can take out the stump from below the soil line so you can plant grass, shrubs, or flowers in its place. However, if you prefer to leave the stump alone for the time being, you might use it as a pedestal for a birdbath or potted plant.

TIP OF THE MONTH

Here's an easy way to grow lots of sweet potato plants for a small garden. Place a sweet potato, root end down, in a glass of rain water, so that the opposite end sticks out of the water about 1 inch. Move the glass to a sunny spot. In a week or so, roots and sprouts will appear. When the sprouts get to be 5 or 6 inches long, pull them off and put in another glass of rain or snow water (water with chemicals causes them to rot). These sprouts will root, and you can set them in the garden after the danger of frost has passed.
Rosie Stephens, McKenzie, Tennessee.
Editor's note: We'd like to have your ideas—the ones that have worked for you. We're especially interested in vegetables, houseplants, shrubs, trees, and garden care. For each tip that is published, we will pay $10 and send you one of our garden books.

Submit as many ideas as you wish, but each must be on a separate sheet or card, along with your name, address, and telephone number. Send to Gardening Tips, *Southern Living*, Box 523, Birmingham, Alabama 35201.

CHECKLIST
For February

☐ **African violets**—If your African violet isn't blooming properly, make sure it's getting the correct amount of light. Levels that are either too high or too low can interfere with flower production. A plant receiving insufficient light will have dark-green leaves supported on long, weak stems. Too much bright sunlight will give the leaves a yellow appearance. Generally, your violet should be placed in a south- or west-facing window during the winter, in an east- or north-facing window during the summer.

☐ **Aphids**—Be on the lookout for these tiny, sucking insects—especially on the new growth of such plants as photinias, tulips, and daylilies. Infestations cause distorted growth and leave behind a sticky residue that is an invitation to disease and ants. Control with insecticidal soap, malathion, Diazinon, or Orthene applied according to label directions.

☐ **Apples**—Prune apples every year for the best quality fruit. Now that the branches are bare, this is the best time to do it because you can easily see the form of the tree. Ideally, there should be one central leader and several main branches radiating from it. Consider removing a major limb to achieve better form and to help prevent limb breakage when the tree is loaded with fruit. Also remove water sprouts—those long, upright shoots that grew last summer. They have no flowerbuds and, if left on the tree, will crowd more productive limbs. Next, take out the lesser of two limbs that cross or any limb that grows inward, judging each for its size, fruitfulness, and contribution to the overall form of the tree. Prune any broken, dead, or diseased wood, and spray the tree with dormant oil to eliminate overwintering insects.

☐ **Bare-root plants**—This is the time of year when nurseries, garden centers, and discount stores are stocking bare-root trees and roses. The plants are dormant; however, if left too long in warm temperatures, they will begin to sprout. Only buy plants that are still dormant or those that the nursery has planted in pots. Before planting bare-root nursery stock, soak the roots in water overnight. If you're not ready to plant, cover the root system with moist soil or compost, and store in a shady location. When ready to plant, set trees in a well-prepared bed at the same depth they were growing (look for soil stains on the trunk). Roses should be set so that the graft union is about an inch above the soil line.

☐ **Dahlias**—You can plant tubers after the last frost. Dahlias like a loose soil, so prepare the bed by forking or tilling at least 8 inches deep. Work in plenty of compost or organic matter. Plant tubers of the large-flowered varieties 3 to 4 feet apart. Space small bedding dahlias 12 to 18 inches apart. Be sure to set stakes for large varieties when you plant so you won't disturb their roots after the plants are growing.

☐ **Dogwoods**—If you are thinking of planting this Southern favorite, remember that a dogwood needs a well-drained site. In areas with a high water table, you'll need to plant a dogwood as you would an azalea, by setting the root ball in a shallow depression and mounding soil around it. Also, select a site that receives partial shade. That way your tree will develop the graceful, tiered branches that are characteristic of dogwoods in the forest. If grown in full sun, dogwoods flower well, but they may die during hot, dry summers.

☐ **Forcing spring blooms**—Azalea, flowering quince, vernal witch hazel, redbud, forsythia, star magnolia, and many other spring-flowering shrubs can be forced to bloom early indoors. Cut branches that have plenty of fat flowerbuds, and place them in a container of warm water; store where temperatures are between 60 and 65 degrees. Change the water every three or four days, and every week, cut an inch from the base of each stem. Most selections will begin to bloom within three weeks.

☐ **Liriope**—If your liriope has unsightly, damaged foliage, mow it now before spring growth begins. Set your mower blade about 3 inches above the ground, and slowly run over the tops of the plants. Repeat, going in the opposite direction. Make sure the blade is high enough to avoid cutting any new leaves emerging at the center of the clumps.

☐ **Perennials**—An economical way to plant large masses of perennials is to grow your own plants from seeds. You can even start now if you have a cold frame or greenhouse, and then set the seedlings in the garden after all danger of frost has passed. Use a sterile potting soil to prevent damping off, a fungal disease that attacks emerging seedlings. Perennials that are easily grown from seeds include blue salvia, columbine, Shasta daisies, blackberry lilies, coreopsis, purple coneflower, cardinal flower, bee balm, and yarrow.

☐ **Pruning**—This is a good time to prune most shrubs. Before you cut, identify specific problems, and work with a goal in mind. For example, if the plant has overgrown its location, you can reduce its size while still maintaining its character. Take out each tall limb at its point of origin. If the plant needs to be restored to a more natural habit, take out any limbs that are dead, crossing, or growing toward the center. After that, thin the branches as needed. Spring-flowering shrubs have already formed flowerbuds, so wait until after they bloom to prune.

Always try to maintain the natural form of a plant unless it is used in a formal situation. If a plant constantly needs pruning to control its size, consider replacing it with one that won't outgrow its location.

☐ **Soil**—Before trying to work your soil judge its condition with this simple test. Squeeze a small amount of soil in your hand; then drop it from about the height of your waist. If the soil doesn't crumble easily, wait until it is drier before you till; otherwise it will form rock-hard clods.

SPECIAL TIPS FOR THE SOUTHEAST

☐ **Flowers**—Gardeners in the Lower South can set out seeds of hardy annuals; gardeners in the Middle and Upper South should wait another month or two. Choices include sweet alyssum, calendula, cornflower, poppy, sweet pea, larkspur, forget-me-nots (*Myosotis*), and phlox.

☐ **Vegetables**—When those first mild days lure you outdoors to work in your garden, begin by renewing the soil. Add a 4-inch layer of organic matter, and turn it in 8 to 12 inches deep. Because organic matter continually breaks down, thereby improving drainage and fertility, it should be an annual addition to the soil.

In the Lower South, you can begin planting root crops, such as carrots, beets, radishes, turnips, and Irish potatoes. By the end of the month, you can set out transplants of cole crops, such as broccoli and cabbage.

If you live in the Middle or Upper

South, begin raising transplants of cole crops to plant in the garden six to nine weeks from now.

☐ **Weeds**—Apply pre-emergence herbicides now in the Middle and Lower South. You can apply them to an established lawn as well as newly planted ground cover and shrub beds. Dacthal or DCPA granules can be applied to the soil in early spring to kill weed seeds as they germinate. Later, when plants grow together, weeds will be less of a problem.

SPECIAL TIPS FOR FLORIDA

☐ **Annuals**—Feed calendulas, pansies, petunias, snapdragons, and other cool-season annuals so they will continue to grow and bloom. Use a balanced, slow-release fertilizer that contains organic nitrogen, such as 6-6-6. Apply about 1 cup per 10 square feet of bed. In South Florida, you can also plant warm-season annuals. Some that are tried-and-true include begonias, gomphrena, impatiens, marigolds, and portulaca. Gardeners in North Florida should wait until March to plant.

☐ **Citrus**—Plant bare-root citrus trees this month. Keep a 3-foot circle around each tree free of grass and weeds, which rob the tree of water and nutrients. To help keep new weeds from sprouting, mulch with a light layer of bark or pine straw. Don't mulch right up to the bark of the tree; leave some space so the trunk doesn't stay moist and invite disease. After the tree begins to sprout new leaves, apply a fertilizer especially blended for citrus, such as 14-7-10. Citrus fertilizer contains iron and other elements the trees need.

☐ **Grape pruning**—Your county Extension office now has a videotape on grape pruning available to check out and take home. It's a thorough lesson in all aspects of pruning—from the tools you'll need to selecting and cutting the canes. To reserve the tape, "Pruning Bunch Grapes in Florida," call your county Extension office.

☐ **Leaf drop**—Gardeners in South Florida shouldn't worry about leaves dropping from avocado, citrus, ficus, mahogany, live oak, mango, and wild tamarind trees. They're just shedding old leaves as new ones appear. Add them to the compost pile, or shred with your mower and work them directly into the soil.

SPECIAL TIPS FOR TEXAS

☐ **Lettuce**—There are many selections of lettuce recommended for Texas gardens. For leaf types, try Black-Seeded Simpson, Prizehead, Saladbowl, and Red Sails. Loosehead types include Bibb, Buttercrunch, and Boston. Romaine and Paris Island Cos should also do well. Crisphead lettuces, or icebergs, are harder to grow in Texas. But if you are anxious to experiment, try the Great Lakes, Mission, or Vanguard selections.

☐ **Potatoes**—Plant potatoes about four weeks before the last killing frost predicted in your area. For much of the state, that means late this month; in the Panhandle, wait until March. Varieties recommended for Texas are LaSoda (red skinned), Pontiac (red skinned), and Kennebec (white skinned). Cut seed potatoes into sections about the size of an egg, each with two to four eyes. Allow the sections to dry until a thin, callous layer forms over the cut edges (about two or three days). Dig a trench about 4 inches deep in prepared garden soil. Place the pieces 12 inches apart in the trench; then cover. As the plants grow, mound the soil around the stems to a height of about 8 inches. You can harvest new potatoes when the plants begin to flower, but wait until after the vines have died to harvest the mature crop.

LAST CALL FOR BROCCOLI

In Texas, Florida, and the Lower South, there is still time to grow a spring crop of broccoli. Texas gardeners can set out transplants two weeks before the last killing frost predicted for your part of the state. In South Florida, plant early in February. In North Florida, set out transplants through February into early March. Gardeners in the Lower South can set out transplants of broccoli during the last two weeks this month and continue planting during the first weeks of March. For Middle South gardens, March and April are the best months to plant; in the Upper South, wait until April.

But no matter where you garden, beat the hot weather by planting varieties that mature early (eight weeks or less). These include Bonanza, Green Comet, Green Goliath, and Early Emerald. Broccoli that matures in hot weather has a mealy texture; sometimes a head doesn't even form—just a tall stalk of yellow flowers.

Premium Crop, Waltham 29, and other varieties that take longer to mature should be planted in fall.

Before you set out transplants, fork or till the soil, and work in a 3-inch layer of rotted compost, manure, or sphagnum peat moss. Also incorporate about 1 cup of 6-6-6 per 10 square feet of planted area. Use a formula that contains slow-release nitrogen.

Space plants 18 to 24 inches apart because crowded plants won't form big heads. Be sure to water regularly as broccoli does best if the soil is continuously moist; alternating moisture and dryness will stunt growth. About a month after planting, feed again with 2 tablespoons 6-6-6 per plant.

Be prepared to protect broccoli from cabbageworms and cabbage loopers—its two worst pests. Cabbageworms are green and velvety. Cabbage loopers are green with a faint white stripe. Dust the plants with Dipel, Thuricide, or Caterpillar Attack. These products contain *Bacillus thuringiensis*, a bacterium that kills the caterpillars without harming beneficial insects. Be sure to cover all the leaves thoroughly, and reapply after rain.

Harvest broccoli when the hundreds of tiny flowerbuds that form the head are still green and tightly closed. As they enlarge and begin to open, the head loses quality and has a mealy texture. After harvesting, pull the plants to make space for crops that are heat tolerant.

Harvest broccoli when the head is full size but while the buds are still tightly closed.
Photograph: Van Chaplin

March

GARDENER
THE SOUTHERN

DESIGN
The First Step

A green lawn makes the garden. It is the place for warm-weather picnics, pup tents, touch football, and garden parties. With good design and proper care, it will survive all this and still look great. And it doesn't take every weekend to keep it that way. It only requires an understanding of what your lawn needs and then a willingness to do the right things at the right time.

However, each factor influences another. Fertilizer affects how often you mow. Mowing height affects how often you need to water and how many weeds you have. But these are only guidelines—you have to strike the right balance. On the pages that follow, you will find recommendations for each aspect of lawn care.

Gardens without grass are hard to imagine. "I think the lawn is the fabric that the rest of the design is built on," says landscape architect Jay Starbuck, ASLA, of Birmingham. And it doesn't have to be a huge expanse to be effective. In many cases, all that's needed is a small area of turf.

Most often our lawns satisfy both functional and aesthetic needs. While they provide a comfortable surface for outdoor activities, they must also be pleasing to the eye. Successfully combining the two can be difficult.

First you have to consider the physical characteristics of your lot, including its strengths and shortcomings. Then you must decide exactly what you require of a lawn, both as outdoor living space and as part of a visual composition. Using this information, a final design can be developed that takes advantage of your site's special qualities, meets your family's needs, and looks great, too.

Your lot may be open to the sunlight or possess a shady canopy of trees. It could be flat with a drainage problem, or sloping and subject to erosion. Soil conditions, which may vary within the space of a few feet, will also affect what you can grow and where you can grow it.

"Existing trees frequently determine which areas are, or are not, suitable for lawns," says Gregg Coyle, ASLA, of Athens, Georgia. Shade presents difficulties for many Southern grasses. In addition, competition for nutrients and water can cause stress in turf growing beneath trees. "We usually design the landscape so that those problem areas are planted with some type of shade-tolerant ground cover or shrub," says Dallas landscape architect Steve Dodd.

Turf is also useful in stabilizing sloping areas, but only if they aren't too steep. Coyle says, "I would never plant a lawn grass in an area that rises more than 1 foot vertically for

every 4 feet of horizontal length. It just isn't safe to mow." Again, ground covers or shrubs that grow well on steep slopes are more suitable for these areas.

Most grasses need good drainage. That can be a problem if you have a heavy clay soil, your lot is flat or concave, or there's a great deal of rainwater runoff from nearby rooftops or paved areas. These cases may require underground drainage systems or the construction of swales to channel the water away. If drainage is a problem, a landscape architect can suggest the best solution.

After you've taken into account all the site factors, it's time to study the way you and your family will use the lawn. "I always interview my clients to find out just what their interests are and what kind of lifestyle they have," Coyle says. Grass makes an excellent playing surface, so you'll probably need larger lawn areas if you have children. Of course, you must be prepared for the added maintenance of wear and tear on the turf. If you entertain regularly, locate lawn areas adjacent to your terrace or deck to provide overflow space for guests. And remember, permanent pathways should be built in areas that are subject to heavy foot traffic.

This is also the time to think seriously about maintenance. "You have to consider how much time you're willing to commit to working on your lawn," says Charleston landscape architect Sheila Wertimer. "If I'm designing for someone who sees the garden mainly as a picture or backdrop,

Maintaining your lawn can be a big job, but a lush carpet of green is well worth the effort. Landscape Architect: Harvilee Harbarger, Huntsville, Alabama.
Photography in the Special Section by Van Chaplin, Mary-Gray Hunter

Most grasses don't grow well in deep shade, so the shape of a lawn is often guided by existing trees.

then I use turf sparingly because it takes a lot of maintenance. On the other hand, if the client is enthusiastic about lawn care, I feel free to increase the size somewhat." It's important to remember the practical side as well: Make sure you can reach lawn areas with a mower, and that all areas are large enough to maneuver in easily.

Last, but by no means least important, is the fact that the lawn should visually enhance the rest of the garden. Starbuck explains, "It's very difficult to appreciate the natural elements in the landscape unless you have something to compare them to. And one of the easiest ways to accomplish this is to play the manicured look of turf against the informal character of other plants."

Wertimer adds, "Even the coarsest grass is a fine texture in comparison to woody plants. And I think the greens of Southern grasses play nicely against the palette of colors found elsewhere in the garden."

Another visual function of lawns is to lend emphasis to other features. "Because the lawn is on the ground plane, it accentuates the vertical elements. It becomes a peaceful

Small plots of turf are easy to maintain yet make a bold statement in the landscape. Landscape Architect: Steve Dodd, Dallas.

Lawn areas located near a terrace or deck provide overflow space for entertaining. Landscape Architect: William Ray, Louisville.

A garden that has geometrically shaped lawn panels, such as this one, usually presents a more formal character than one with looser, curving lines. Landscape Architect: Naud Burnett, Dallas.

surface that leads the viewer's eye where you want it to go," Wertimer says.

All too often, one suburban lawn simply blends into the next. You can avoid this pitfall by planting shrubs and trees to enclose smaller areas within the garden. This will give a feeling of containment, making each a separate outdoor room. "These lawn areas define space in a wonderfully simple way and help to organize the garden," Wertimer explains. It's also much more satisfying visually, because your eye finds a place to rest, rather than wandering.

The shape a lawn assumes depends on topography, existing plants, architectural styles, and personal preference. In Charleston, the landscape is flat, most gardens are small, and the houses have an air of formality. There Wertimer often employs geometric panels of lawn. The hills around Birmingham, however, present different opportunities. "Considering the topography we have to work with, I prefer a curvilinear shape," says Starbuck. "I don't find a lot of need for strict formality. Balance, yes, but not symmetry." And in Dallas, Dodd sometimes combines the two. "Even if we locate formal areas near the house,

Broad, sweeping curves are more pleasing to the eye than short, wiggly ones. Landscape Architect: Richard Dawson, Houston.

the design usually becomes more curvilinear as we move out into the landscape."

Whatever the final shape of the lawn, it's often the line formed by its edge that has the greatest visual impact. If this line doesn't please the eye, neither will the lawn. Establishing a pleasant curvilinear line can be especially difficult. Often, the result is too many wiggles worming their way across the landscape. Instead, the edge should flow smoothly, with broad sweeping curves. "Each curve should be a measured arc, a small segment of a perfect circle," Coyle says. Once established, this line can be a challenge to maintain unless some hard edging is employed. "I usually use a brick border that repeats paving used somewhere else in the garden. That way, the edging becomes a design element in itself," says Wertimer. "Often it consists of a course of brick level with the ground to run a mower wheel along, and upright bricks behind that to slightly raise the beds." There are other styles and materials suitable for mowing strips and edging. But whichever you choose, most designers agree it's well worth the investment. "It eases maintenance, and keeps lines crisp," says Dodd.

St. Augustine is superbly adapted to the Lower and Coastal South, and it tolerates shade better than other warm-season grasses. Landscape design: René Fransen, ASLA, New Orleans.

Choose the Right Grass

Whether you're planting a new lawn, renovating an old one, or just patching a few bare spots, the type of grass you choose can make or break the project. Turf specialists divide lawn grasses into two groups: warm-season (Bermuda, bahia, centipede, St. Augustine, and Zoysia) and cool-season (Kentucky bluegrass, perennial ryegrass, tall fescue). Warm-season grasses grow fast in hot weather and go dormant when it's cool. Cool-season grasses behave just the opposite. The farther south you live, the more likely you are to grow a warm-season grass.

Once you determine the correct group of grasses for your area, the next choice involves the grasses in that group. Factors to consider at this point include desired texture, ease of establishment, shade tolerance, the amount of maintenance you are willing to do, and which hardiness zone you live in (see chart on page 43).

Warm-Season Grasses

The most widely used grass in the South has to be **common Bermuda.** Exceptionally drought tolerant and quick to establish, it can form a solid lawn from seed in just one year. It also tolerates salt spray, so it's good for growing near the coast. On the down side, it isn't very cold hardy and won't grow even in light shade. Moreover, it spreads aggressively by rhizomes, readily invading flower and shrub beds.

Improved Bermuda selections, such as Tifway, Tifgreen, Texturf, and Tufcote, feature a finer texture and better color. However, they require more frequent watering, fertilization, and mowing to maintain their appearance. These are the grasses of golf greens in the Coastal and Lower South.

Though hardly a glamorous grass, **centipede** has a lot going for it. It grows in highly acidic and poor soils where other grasses won't, it requires less

mowing than other grasses, and it needs little or no fertilizer. On the other hand, it is shallow rooted and less drought tolerant than Bermuda or Zoysia. And it may need iron occasionally to keep it from yellowing.

A rapidly spreading grass, **St. Augustine** is most widely grown in Florida and along the Gulf and South Atlantic Coasts. In fact, it is sometimes called Charleston grass because it is so frequently planted there. Hardy selections will grow in areas as cold as Atlanta, Birmingham, and Dallas. St. Augustine is quite coarse, possessing wide, stout blades. It grows better in light shade or salt spray than most other warm-season grasses.

Older types of St. Augustine, such as Bitter Blue, often fall victim to insects, disease, and cold temperatures. But newer selections, such as Raleigh and Seville, resist pests and withstand colder weather. They also hold their

In winter, Zoysia turns a beige color, resembling a carpet. Landscape design: Jay Starbuck, ASLA, Birmingham.

green color long after Bermuda, centipede, and Zoysia have turned brown.

Floratam, and the newer selection called Floralawn, are resistant to chinch bugs. Although they are excellent choices for Florida and Texas, they can be damaged by cold weather in cooler regions. They're more drought resistant, however, than Raleigh and Seville.

St. Augustine selections can be divided into two groups: those with a typical growth habit and semidwarf selections. Seville and the soon-to-be-released Jade and Delmar are good examples of semidwarf selections. They offer finer texture and low growth habit; therefore, they need to be cut a little shorter.

Zoysia is the South's most refined grass. Soft, lush, and thick as a carpet, it chokes out weeds and fills in bare spots. It tolerates drought, grows in sun or light shade, has few insect or disease problems, and needs little maintenance. It also turns an attractive beige color in winter. But it's available only as sod or plugs and can be expensive and slow to establish.

The most widely available Zoysia selections are Emerald and Meyer (Z-52). Emerald is noted for its fine texture—truly a pleasure to walk on. Meyer is a bit coarser but hardier.

Bahia is rarely used for lawns outside the Coastal South, where it will tolerate nutrient-poor, sandy soil. It is coarse textured and easy to grow from seeds. With the exception of mole crickets, it has few pests. This low-maintenance grass requires fertilizer only once or twice each year. The selection recommended for lawns is Argentine; one named Pensacola is best left to roadsides.

Cool-Season Grasses

Probably the world's most beautiful lawn grass, **Kentucky bluegrass** does best where summer temperatures drop to 70 degrees or lower at night. So it's restricted to the Upper South and cooler areas of the Middle South. Bluegrass exacts a price for its beauty—lots of water, fertilizer, and maintenance. But it's quick to establish and spreads rapidly. Recommended selections include Adelphi, America, Eclipse, Vantage, and Windsor.

Like bluegrass, **perennial ryegrass** thrives in cool temperatures. It doesn't spread by rhizomes, however, so it takes longer to form a thick lawn. Perennial rye is often mixed into a bluegrass lawn as a "cover crop" because it germinates quickly and holds the soil until the bluegrass gets going. Homeowners in the Lower and Coastal South also use this or annual ryegrass to overseed their Bermuda, centipede, St. Augustine, or Zoysia lawns in fall. The ryegrass keeps its green color all winter then dies when the others turn green in spring. Some of the better selections of perennial ryegrass are Citation, Premier, and Regal.

Tall fescue blends good qualities from both warm- and cool-season grasses. It holds its green color all winter and resists drought, insects, diseases, and wear better than bluegrass or ryegrass. It is not as tough or drought resistant as Bermuda and Zoysia, however. And in the hottest parts of the Lower and Coastal South, it may gradually die out.

Most people think of tall fescue as a coarse grass, thanks to the still popular, but outdated, selection, Kentucky-31. But new selections, which include Falcon, Finelawn, Houndog, Jaguar, and Rebel, sport as fine a texture as bluegrass. Tall fescue doesn't spread by rhizomes, so you'll need to sow seed several times. In some areas, tall fescue is now available as sod.

You can improve the insect and disease resistance of all cool-season lawns by using a seed mix that contains several selections of the type of grass you want. For example, an excellent tall fescue mix might include equal portions of Falcon, Rebel, and Finelawn. And a good bluegrass mix might blend Adelphi, America, and Windsor. Some garden centers will custom-blend grass seed for you. You can also purchase ready-made mixes in bags.

RECOMMENDED GRASSES FOR THE SOUTH

Grass	Hardiness+	Texture	Drought Resistance	Shade Tolerance	Fertilizer Needs	Method of Establishment
Bahia	LS,CS	Coarse	Excellent	Poor	Low	Seed
Common Bermuda	MS,LS,CS	Medium	Excellent	Poor	Moderate	Sod, seed, sprigs, plugs
Improved Bermuda	MS,LS,CS	Medium to fine*	Moderate	Poor	High	Sod, sprigs, plugs
Centipede	LS,CS	Medium	Moderate	Poor	Low	Seed, plugs, sprigs, sod
Kentucky bluegrass	US,MS	Medium	Poor	Poor	High	Seed, sod
Perennial ryegrass	US,MS	Medium	Poor	Poor	High	Seed
Tall fescue	US,MS,LS	Medium to coarse*	Moderate	Moderate	Moderate	Seed, sod
St. Augustine	LS,CS	Coarse	Moderate	Good	Moderate	Sod, sprigs, plugs
Zoysia	MS,LS,CS	Medium to fine*	Excellent	Good	Moderate	Sod, plugs

+ *US = Upper South, MS = Middle South, LS = Lower South, CS = Coastal South*
For map see "Letters to Garden Editors," page 59.
* *Texture depends on selection*

The Way To Water

Regular watering is essential to a healthy lawn. And after several summers of drought, watering has become a major concern for gardeners. After all, if your city adopts water rationing policies, you'll have to shut off your sprinklers.

A lawn that has been properly managed will be deeper rooted and more resistant to water stress. One way to encourage deep rooting is to water only once a week, but water well.

Applying an inch of water each week should moisten the soil to a depth of 4 to 6 inches, depending on your soil type. If your soil is sandy, you'll find that it requires less water to moisten it, but it loses water more quickly. In that case, apply ½ inch of water every three to four days.

Dr. Art Bruneau, Turf Extension Specialist at North Carolina State University, cautions that on heavy clay soils water may begin to run off long before an inch has been applied. This is a common occurrence on lawns with heavy traffic. He recommends timing how long it takes until water runs off, moving the sprinkler to another area, and then coming back after the first watering has had time to soak in. In the future, you'll know just how long you can run the sprinkler in one spot.

You can gauge the amount you apply by setting tuna or cat food cans at intervals beneath the area covered by the sprinkler. When they are almost full, you've applied an inch.

Another virtue of thorough but infrequent watering is that you toughen the lawn. Bruneau observes, "Most people water until they get their first water bill. Then they shut if off. That's like taking a plant out of a moist greenhouse and planting it in the hot sun." You have to let cool-season grasses "harden off" for the summer. Don't water until grass blades begin to curl (the first sign of wilt), the lawn has a blue-gray cast, and footprints remain in the turf.

Although the best time to water is in the early morning (less evaporation and more water pressure), you have to take advantage of every opportunity. In some communities, watering is only permitted at night during rationing. You may need to set your alarm to

Water is essential to healthy turf, but you can reduce the amount of water you use and improve the condition of your lawn by irrigating properly.

move or shut off the sprinkler, but you can save yourself some trouble with an inexpensive water timer. Some sprinklers have them built in and will turn your water off automatically. There are more costly models that can be programmed to turn on and off on a weekly schedule.

"If you're going to all the trouble and expense of maintaining a sodded, manicured lawn, you owe it to yourself to consider installing an irrigation system," says Landscape Architect Gregg Coyle. "One that's well designed will apply just the right amount of water to your lawn and turn itself on and off. This type of irrigation is very efficient because so little water or time is wasted."

Types of Sprinklers

Sprinklers come in a variety of types, and some may be better for your garden than others. Ideally, you want a sprinkler with even coverage. And look for one that suits the size of your garden, as well as your pocketbook.

Oscillating sprinklers are the most popular, with deluxe models covering up to 4,000 square feet. However, the coverage area can be adjusted from one side to the other. Some models are more easily adjusted than others, so compare mechanisms before you buy.

Water may drift on windy days, and you will have some evaporation, but the application is gentle enough for even newly seeded lawns. However, the openings can become clogged, resulting in uneven application. You'll find a wide range of prices and quality.

Impulse sprinklers are growing in popularity in the South, according to Linda Neill, Advertising and Merchandising Manager for Gilmour Group in Louisville. There is less drift, they water at a greater rate, and they can cover more area. Because of the greater water pressure, the sprinkler is less likely to clog than an oscillating sprinkler. However, they may not function properly under poor water pressure. Features to look for on different models include adjustments for the height and diffusion of the spray, as well as the full-circle and partial-circle coverage.

Rotary sprinklers apply water through whirling arms with either two or three nozzles. The spray and the coverage area are adjustable, and models with wheels are easily moved without your getting wet.

Stationary sprinklers are ideal for small gardens and condominium courtyards. They have a fixed pattern. The coverage area is adjusted by varying the water pressure.

Ground covers used in problem areas, such as under this tree, can replace a lawn that has grown thin due to shade and root competition.

Give an Old Lawn New Life

The way to tell if your lawn is worth renovating, or if it should be dug up and started anew, is to look at the health of the existing grass. Is the lawn weedy just in patches? Or, if weeds are everywhere, is there healthy grass underneath? Is the grass the type you want? If you can answer yes to any of these questions, then the lawn is probably worth renovating. And in most cases, it's easier and less expensive to redo the lawn than to replace it.

The first step in renovating a lawn is to identify and alleviate the problems that caused it to decline. The most obvious way to start is to get rid of the weeds (see page 52). But there are other problems you may not see at first glance.

Thatch

If the lawn feels spongy under your feet, it is probably resting atop a thick layer of dead stems and plant debris called thatch. This material keeps water from passing through, harbors insects and diseases, and keeps the roots from growing deep into the soil. A thin layer of thatch (½ inch or less) is not harmful. It protects the roots from extreme heat and cold and can help hold in moisture. But heavy thatch makes a lawn more susceptible to damage from drought and disease.

You can remove thatch with a thatch rake—a handtool with knifelike blades that cut into the soil and pull out the dead material. Such a rake is fine for lawns less than 1,000 square feet, but for larger areas, you'll probably need power equipment.

You can rent a power rake or dethatcher from equipment rental companies. Run these over your lawn to loosen thatch, and then use a bag attachment on your mower or a rake to remove this material from the lawn. A power rake is not usually needed for common Bermuda, and it is not recommended for St. Augustine because of the damage it would cause. Plan on using the handtools for these grasses.

Soil Compaction

All soils have tiny pores that hold air, water, and nutrients essential for healthy grass. When the soil is compacted, these pores are squeezed, and the grass roots are deprived of necessary elements. In cases where the soil has been compacted by a lot of foot traffic or repeatedly driven over, you'll need to take an extra step in renovation—aeration.

Aeration, also called coring, involves using a special machine that punches the soil with a row of closely spaced, hollow tubes that cut out cores of soil. This perforates the soil to let in water and air. As the machine travels across the lawn, it drops the tiny cores of soil on top of the grass. Rake them for the compost pile, or drag a piece of chain link fence over the lawn to break up the cores. This type aerator is preferable to one that has solid spikes that punch holes in the soil. Most large equipment-rental businesses will have this equipment available.

Bare Spots

Sometimes lawn problems are more localized, and you can just patch bare areas of a lawn. But here again, you would be wise to correct the problem before replanting. If the grass died because it was in a low spot, raise the grade by filling in with topsoil and raking it level with the surrounding turf. If the soil is compacted by traffic, either divert the traffic or make a mulched or paved path. If tree roots are the problem, redesign the shape of the lawn so that you can use a ground cover or mulch beneath the tree.

You can use sod to custom-fit the worst spots. Just be sure that the sod you use is the same type as the existing grass. The many selections of St. Augustine, Bermuda, centipede, and Zoysia sod vary in color and texture. The same is true for cool-season grasses, such as tall fescue and bluegrass, which are started from seed.

Replace any thin turf by using a knife or sharpened spade to cut a distinct line in the healthy grass. Then use a turning fork to loosen the soil. If the soil is heavy clay or sand, add organic matter to improve soil structure. Then rake to the finished grade. Cut sod to fit the bare area or sow seed, depending on the type of grass you are growing. Care for the newly planted areas as you would a new lawn, keeping them moist during the first critical weeks.

Routine Renovation

To look its best, a lawn needs renovating about every third year. For warm-season grasses, use a power rake in early spring, followed by the recommended pre-emergence herbicide and fertilizer. This will keep weeds out while encouraging growth and thickening of the turf.

Cool-season lawns should be renovated in early fall, following summer treatment for broadleaf weeds. A power rake will not only remove thatch, but it will also open the turf to light. Remove all debris from the lawn. Bluegrass will spread and thicken, but fescue will need additional seeds. Use half the normal seeding rate (see page 48) as you already have a partial stand of grass.

Keys to a successful renovation include diverting traffic, improving drainage, and then patching bare areas with new sod.

If you want to change to another type of grass or you feel that your lawn is past renovating, spray the entire lawn with Roundup according to label directions. Allow two weeks for the lawn to turn brown; then proceed with soil preparation for a new lawn.

Thatch is the dead material that builds up in the turf. You can remove it by hand from small lawns with a thatch rake. Larger areas require special equipment.

(**Left**) *Soil preparation is the key to establishing a new lawn, whether patching an area or starting from scratch. Till the soil deeply, working in any soil amendments recommended by the soil test.* (**Right**) *Rake the soil to smooth it over while removing debris.*

Use a water-filled roller to firm the soil and reveal any depressions that may hold water and kill the new turf.

Starting From Scratch: Sod vs. Seed

Although there are many types of grasses, there are but two major ways to start a lawn: seeding and sodding. Both have their merits.

Sowing seeds is the least expensive way to establish a new lawn. Compared to using sod, seeding is a bargain. Eight pounds of fescue seed can cover 1,000 square feet of lawn for less than $20, and a bale of wheat straw to mulch the seeded ground costs about $3.50. At $2 to $5 per square yard, sod can take a chunk of your budget. On the other hand, sod gives an instant lawn and can be installed almost any time of year.

Besides cost and time of year, another consideration is the type of grass you choose. Some types must be seeded, others sodded, so the choice is made for you.

Soil Preparation

Whichever method of establishment you choose, you have to prepare the soil properly before planting. Till the area to break up dead grass and compacted soil. When you till, work in any lime recommended by a soil test as well as a 1- to 2-inch layer of organic

matter. If you are sowing seeds of a cool-season grass, apply a high-phosphorus starter fertilizer at this time. To keep weeds from sprouting, apply a product that also contains pre-emergence weed killer, such as Tupersan (siduron). Then use a steel garden rake to level the ground and collect chunks of dead grass and stones. If all the old grass didn't come up with the tiller's first pass, till and rake the soil again. Remember, you are establishing a finished grade, so include any contours needed for drainage. If your soil is poor, you may want to top the prepared soil with 2 to 3 inches of topsoil and rake it smooth.

A good watering or gentle rain will help settle the loose soil, but this can take time. The best idea is to go over the area with a roller. This specialized tool—like a barrel with long handles—can be rented at most rental equipment centers. It can be filled with water to make it heavy, but a half-filled barrel is weighty enough to firm the soil without compacting it. Rolling the soil helps reveal sunken areas so you can fill and level prior to planting. Shave off high places with a spade. Be ready to plant

shortly after preparing the soil, as a heavy rain can undo a lot of hard work.

Sodding

When you are ready to plant, water the area the night before to be sure the ground is moist. It's easiest to lay sod if you start at a straight edge, such as the street or driveway. If there aren't any straight edges, then simply divide the area into quadrants with stakes and string, and place the sod on either side of the strings. As you reach irregular areas, fit the pieces by cutting the sod with a knife or spade.

Lay each rectangular strip of sod as tightly against the adjacent strip as possible without overlapping. Stagger the

Seeding is very economical and the only way to establish some types of grasses.

Lay the sod in a staggered pattern as you would lay brick. Use a knife to cut pieces to fit odd-size areas.

joints between strips as you do with bricks when building a wall. This creates a smooth turf and protects the edges from drying. If sodding a slope, lay the long side of each strip across the face of the slope. After all the sod is in place, press it down with the roller to ensure the roots contact with the soil.

Water the sod daily for the first two weeks and then every other day, weaning gradually until you're watering just once a week. When the grass begins to grow, mow and fertilize as you would an established lawn.

Seeding

Always begin with quality, certified seed. And if you can't decide between named selections, ask the dealer. One may be better adapted to your site than another. Be sure to check the label for the following items: name(s) of selection(s), weed-seed content, germination percentage, and date tested.

Sow cool-season grass in late summer or fall; sow warm-season grass in spring. For best results, follow the rates recommended at right.

Sow seeds using a drop spreader or a hand-cranked seeder—if you do it by hand, you'll end up with a spotty lawn. To ensure even coverage, sow half the seed in one direction, and the other half at a right angle to the first.

To be sure the seeds are in good contact with the soil, roll it with a half-filled roller, or rake it lightly to partially cover the seeds. Then lightly cover the bed with a sprinkling of weed-free wheat straw to help protect the seeds from drying or washing. Don't remove the straw when the seed germinates. Just let it rot in place.

Water daily with a gentle, but soaking, sprinkle. Once the grass is 1 to 2 inches tall, water every two or three days. Fertilize after the second or third mowing, and allow one full growing season before applying a weedkiller.

Options

Although by far the most common methods of establishing a lawn, seeding and sodding are not your only alternatives. Gardeners who are long on patience and short on money may want to plug or sprig the grasses that spread. Both are relatively easy to do.

Purchase St. Augustine, centipede, Zoysia, or hybrid Bermuda grown specifically for plugging, or use a sharp knife to cut a 3-inch square plug from a piece of sod. In a prepared bed make a hole large enough to accommodate the plug, and place a teaspoon of slow-release fertilizer into the hole. Set the plug so the grass is at ground level. Space plugs 12 inches apart. At that rate, you will need 7 square yards of sod or about 56 flats of plugs to cover 1,000 square feet. Keep the plugs moist the first couple of weeks. Thereafter, water as you would an established lawn. They should form a nice lawn in one to two seasons.

Sprigs are 4- to 8-inch-long runners of grass. You can either shred sod or cut your own sprigs from an established lawn. Shoots that are cut off when you or a neighbor edges the sidewalk, driveway, or shrub bed will serve nicely as sprigs. Prepare 3-inch-deep trenches, fill halfway with loose soil, set the sprigs 1 to 1½ inches deep, and finish covering with soil. You can also use a tool, such as a screwdriver, to make holes in the soil. Insert the end of the sprig, and step on it to firm the soil.

Although plugs have a better chance of surviving, sprigs may actually cover more quickly. Regular mowing encourages them to spread laterally.

SEEDING RATES
POUNDS PER 1,000 SQ. FT.
Bahia: 5-10
Common Bermuda (hulled): 1-2
Centipede: ½
Bluegrass: 2-3
Perennial rye: 5-10
Tall fescue: 5-10

Fertilize for a Healthy Lawn

To put it bluntly, your lawn needs fertilizer. Not too much, not too little, but just the right amount. A well-fertilized lawn competes with weeds and better withstands attack by insects or diseases. It's also better able to withstand extreme cold or heat and doesn't delay turning green at the beginning of the growing season. Learning how to fertilize properly takes a little research, but it's certainly worthwhile.

What Is a Good Fertilizer?

Of the many brands of fertilizer on the market, obviously some are better than others. A good lawn fertilizer contains more nitrogen than other types of plant foods, and contains at least 25% or 30% of the nitrogen in a slow-release form. Look on the label for the words "slow-release" or "controlled-release" nitrogen. It will be more expensive, but it's money well spent because a good quality lawn fertilizer feeds the lawn gradually over several weeks. A good slow-release fertilizer contains nitrogen, phosphorus, and potassium in approximately a 3-1-2 ratio, such as 21-7-14 or 18-6-12. However, you will find many variants for specific grass types. For example, centipede grass, which doesn't like too much nitrogen or phosphorus, is best fertilized once a year with a formula that reflects its needs—such as 15-0-15.

Don't buy lawn fertilizer in which all the nitrogen is ammonium nitrate, ammonium sulfate, or urea. The nitrogen in these types of fertilizers breaks down too quickly. What isn't taken up by the grass soon after applying is washed away and may end up in ground water. It can also seriously burn the lawn. This is not only a waste of money but also poses a threat to the environment.

How Much Do You Apply?

The amount of fertilizer you apply will vary depending upon its nitrogen content and the type of grass you have. The best advice is to select a name-brand fertilizer formulated for your type of grass and apply at the rate recommended on the label. Don't be tempted to overapply—you may burn the grass and encourage problems with

insects and diseases. Too much fertilizer will make the lawn grow faster, too. That means more mowing.

When Do You Apply?

No matter which type of grass you have, it needs fertilizer most during its growing season. That means for most warm-season grasses (bahia, Bermuda, St. Augustine, and Zoysia) the rule of thumb is to fertilize in spring, summer, and fall. Centipede is the exception. It actually declines if overfed. Fertilize it just once a year in spring. With all warm-season grasses, make the spring application about two or three weeks after the grass turns green.

A word about fall fertilization of warm-season grasses. It may seem questionable to apply fertilizer to a warm-season lawn at the end of its

Using a rotary spreader will make quick work of fertilizing a large lawn.

growing season, but fall fertilization helps the lawn store food for next spring and makes it more tolerant of extreme cold in winter—especially if you haven't fertilized since spring. For this feeding, the key is using a fertilizer that is *low* in nitrogen and high in potassium, such as 8-8-25. In most of the South, the best time to apply is in late August or early September.

Cool-season grasses will be hungry in fall, winter, and spring. Usually one application at the beginning of each season is enough. For example, you can apply regular lawn fertilizer in September, low-nitrogen, high-potassium fertilizer in November, and regular fertilizer again in February. In the Upper South, you can delay the spring feeding until March.

It is important to remember that the suggestions given here represent the general rule. Factors such as your specific type of lawn, soil, amount of rainfall, and type of fertilizer all affect the frequency of application. If you are uncertain about what you need, check with a garden center or your agricultural Extension agent.

You Need a Spreader

Use a spreader to distribute fertilizer evenly over the lawn. This will prevent the green spots and streaks that appear if you just throw the material out by hand. There are two basic types of spreaders: drop and broadcast. A drop-type spreader is more accurate, but it's also slower because it drops a swath only as wide as the hopper of the spreader. Drop-type spreaders are better if your lawn is small. For lawns 5,000 square feet or more, you'll probably want a broadcast spreader. It scatters the material with a whirling action, throwing it in a swath at least 6 feet wide. The width of the swath is adjustable to 10 feet or more on most types, so for large lawns this saves many footsteps. However, if you are spreading a fertilizer/weed killer combination, it's best to use a drop-type spreader along the edge of shrub and flowerbeds to be sure that none of the material is accidentally scattered among the ornamentals. Many weed killers are safe for lawns but not for flowers and shrubs. As a rule, trees aren't bothered.

Mowing Wrong Just Won't Cut It

Mowing regularly and at the proper height keeps the lawn healthy and weed free.

Each summer weekend, we dutifully march behind our lawnmowers, confident that we have put the yard in order. But there's more to mowing than simple cosmetics. Proper mowing can mean the difference between a lush, green carpet and a sickly looking weed patch.

The cardinal rule of mowing is this: *Mow frequently enough to maintain the desired height, but never remove more than one-third of the grass blades in one cutting nor more than 1 inch of top growth.* Doing so can cripple a lawn.

There are two types of lawnmowers: rotary and reel. The rotary mower is far more common. It uses a twin-edged rapidly spinning blade on a single shaft to cut by force of impact. A reel mower, on the other hand, uses whirling blades attached to the wheels to cut with a scissorslike action. Reel mowers make a much cleaner cut. But they're harder to use and maintain.

What's the correct mowing height? That depends on the type of grass. As a general rule, warm-season grasses can take closer clipping than cool-season kinds. For mowing heights of specific grasses, refer to the chart on the next page.

Mowing the lawn at the highest recommended heights offers several distinct advantages. Among them are:
- Fewer weeds. A lawn cut at 2 inches or higher, for example, will contain significantly less crabgrass.
- Less disease. Taller grass is less stressed and more resistant to fungal attack.
- Better root system. Mowing too low reduces root growth, making the grass more susceptible to drought.
- Reduced mowing frequency. This is because the rate of blade growth slows as the grass grows taller. So a lawn cut at 2½ inches will need less frequent mowing than one cut at 1½ inches.

- Reduced watering frequency. Grass that's closely cropped requires much more water to stay green.

People growing new lawns from seed may wonder how tall the grass should be before its first cutting. The rule is: Make the first cut when the blades are about 1 inch taller than the recommended, minimum cutting height. Thus, for Kentucky bluegrass, make the first cutting at about 3 inches. Thereafter, cut the grass lower—at 2 to 2½ inches.

- Mow when the grass is dry. You'll get a cleaner cut, the mower will use less gasoline, and clippings won't mat.
- Keep the mower blade sharp. A dull blade will tear the grass, making the lawn more susceptible to disease and drought.
- Cut grass in shade a little higher than grass in sun. Shaded grass needs the extra leaf surface for photosynthesis to compensate for reduced sunlight.

You can adjust the cutting height on most mowers at half-inch increments from ½ inch to 3 inches.

RECOMMENDED MOWING HEIGHT*

Bahia	2½" to 3"
Bermuda	
Common	1" to 1½"
Improved	½" to 1"
Centipede	1½" to 2"
Kentucky bluegrass	2" to 2½"
Perennial ryegrass	1½" to 2½"
St. Augustine	
Common	2½" to 3"
Semi-Dwarf	1½" to 2½"
Tall fescue	2" to 3"
Zoysia	1" to 2"

*Mow ½" to 1" higher during hot, dry weather.

Removing clippings is usually a matter of taste and not a necessity.

To Bag or Not To Bag

Most of us remove grass clippings as a matter of course. We either rake them up or use a bagging lawnmower. But should we remove them? In most areas, it appears that a concern for aesthetics is the only reason to do so.

For one thing, grass clippings usually decompose rapidly and don't contribute to thatch. More importantly, they contain significant amounts of nutrients, which they return to the lawn when they decompose.

According to Felder Rushing, Extension horticulturist for the Mississippi Cooperative Extension Service in Jackson, "People who catch their clippings are just throwing away fertilizer." In fact, 100 pounds of dry clippings taken from the average lawn can yield approximately 3 to 4 pounds of nitrogen, ½ pound of phosphorus, and 1 to 2 pounds of potassium. By leaving these clippings on the lawn, you can cut its fertilizer requirements by 25%, saving lots of money. Using less fertilizer also means that less nutrients will leach into ground water or run off to pollute lakes and streams.

Leaving clippings in place isn't always practical for St. Augustine lawns in Florida and along the Gulf Coast, unless the grass is mowed quite often. High rainfall there makes the grass grow lush and fast. And if you've been on vacation and the grass has grown exceptionally high, you'll probably want to bag. In either case, clippings can be collected and composted and their nutrients returned to the garden.

Clippings on the lawn need not be unsightly or messy, if you mow properly. One key is not letting the grass get too tall before cutting it, thereby reducing the volume of clippings. You should never cut more than an inch at a time.

When you mow, do so when the grass is dry. Wet, mown grass forms clumps and mats, which take a long time to break down. Dry clippings, on the other hand, can be easily dispersed by a mower as it runs across the lawn. On a sunny day, they'll disintegrate within hours; should any persist, just use a soft rake to scatter them. Another alternative is to use a special "mulching" mower or mower attachment to grind clippings into very small pieces and distribute them evenly over the lawn.

In the end, the question of whether or not to remove clippings comes down to personal choice. Bagging clippings certainly won't *hurt* the lawn, but leaving them requires less work and fertilizer and is better for the environment.

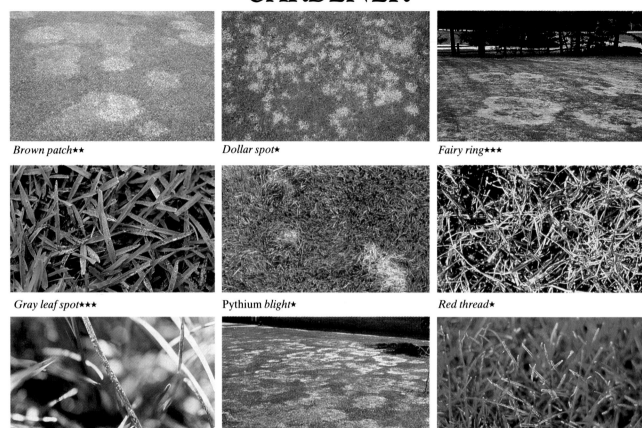

Brown patch★★

Dollar spot★

Fairy ring★★★

Gray leaf spot★★★

Pythium *blight*★

Red thread★

Rust★★

Spring dead spot★★

Slime mold★★

★Photographs reprinted from the *Compendium of Turfgrass Diseases*, The American Phytopathological Society, St. Paul, Minnesota
★★Photographs courtesy of The O.M. Scott & Sons Company   ★★★Photographs courtesy of Edward A. Brown, University of Georgia

About Those Ugly Diseases

Brown patch appears as circular, blighted spots when the weather is warm and humid. The disease attacks all grasses and is worse on lawns that are overfertilized. Spray with Terraclor, Daconil 2787, or captan.

Dollar spot first shows up as bleached spots 1 to 6 inches in diameter; the spots may overlap to form large areas of dead grass. It attacks all grasses except centipede, St. Augustine, and tall fescue. Lawns that are starved for nutrients are the most susceptible. Effective fungicides include benomyl, Daconil 2787, and Fore.

Fairy ring is easy to identify by the dark-green rings it forms. Eventually the grass along the edge of the rings will die. All grasses are susceptible during moist, warm spells in spring and fall. There are no fungicides to kill fairy ring. If the fungus attacks, care for the grass properly so it will fill in.

Gray leaf spot is a pest of St. Augustine. It first appears on the leaves as tiny spots with a gray center. As the disease progresses, the grass looks scorched. Gray leaf spot appears during warm, humid weather and is most likely to attack a lawn that is overfertilized. Spray with Daconil 2787.

***Pythium* blight** is a serious pest of bluegrass and annual and perennial ryegrass. It especially likes an overseeded or new lawn that's been sowed too thickly. First signs are circular spots of dark-green, water-soaked blades. They are about 6 inches in diameter. Sometimes you'll see white fungal threads on the blades. As the grass dies, the threads disappear and the blades turn reddish brown then straw colored. To prevent the disease, don't sow a new lawn too thickly. You can also spray with captan.

Red thread is a problem in the Upper South on Kentucky bluegrass, red fescue, tall fescue, perennial rye, and occasionally on Bermuda and Zoysia in Tennessee and other northern fringes of its range. The blades of infected grass turn yellow and shrivel from the tips. Later a red, threadlike fungal growth may appear. It is worse in cool, humid weather. Treat red thread with Daconil 2787 and Fore.

Rusts first make the lawn look yellow and thin in spots. Then red, rust-like spores appear on the grass blades. All grasses except centipede and Bahia are susceptible, but rusts are worse on Zoysia and Kentucky bluegrass, especially if underfed.

Spring dead spot is exactly what the name says. Patches of grass don't turn green in spring as does the rest of the lawn. The disease primarily affects Bermuda lawns in the Middle and Upper South. The only cure is to replant or encourage the dead areas to fill in.

Slime mold is an ugly, but harmless, mold that may appear when the weather is humid. It likes all types of grasses, so don't be alarmed if it shows up in your lawn.

Blue phlox and bearded iris are a winning combination for a spring flower border.   Photographs: Van Chaplin, Mary-Gray Hunter, Beth Maynor

Blue Phlox: One of Nature's Best

*Color your spring with blue phlox, a Southern wildflower
that makes an excellent garden perennial.*

by LINDA ASKEY WEATHERS

Spring dawns quietly in the wild-flower garden. But blue phlox is boisterous by comparison to more subtle blossoms.

It is most at home in a green wood-land setting, and that is where you'll find blue phlox growing wild in many regions of the South. The blue flowers meld with the green, white, and pale yellows of early spring. Yet they are strong enough to hold their own among bolder colors.

"It's one of the nicest perennials a garden can have," says Dan Franklin, landscape architect in Atlanta. "In my garden, it blooms with the late tulips."

It is also striking when combined with hyacinths, bearded iris, candytuft, yellow pansies, or forget-me-nots.

Blue phlox (*Phlox divaricata*), some-times known as wild sweet William, begins to flower as early as March in the Lower South and as late as May in the Upper South. Although the display usually lasts about two weeks, Nash-ville gardener Becky Talbot notes, "This past spring was so cool that the blue phlox bloomed for a month." In her garden, it blooms with the Lenten roses, celandine poppies, and prim-roses. "If you've got a lot of celandine, the effect of the blue and yellow is

always very strong." You can get the same color combination by pairing blue phlox with daffodils.

You would think any plant that grows with tulips and Lenten roses could tolerate both sun and shade. However, full sun is not ideal. Bill Funkhouser of Funkhouser's Gardens, Inc., in Dahlonega, Georgia, says that the foliage gets very compact and red-dish in full sun. But move the same plant into the shade and it will loosen up and recover its normal form.

In spite of its name, blue phlox isn't always blue. Most of the wild forms have the slightest hint of pink,

although there are actually no true pink-flowered selections. The selection called Dirgo Ice is a pale, lavender-flowered form, Fuller's White is obviously white, and Louisiana Blue is a strong blue. For larger flowers, try Laphammi, a subspecies with blue-violet flowers that lack the characteristic notch on each petal. Chattahoochee, named for the town in North Florida where it was found, is a popular hybrid. It has a maroon eye in the center of each blue flower and seems to stay in bloom longer than the others. Unlike its parent, Chattahoochee likes full sun and sandy soil.

With the exception of Chattahoochee, blue phlox enjoys the moist, organic soil of a rich woodland. However, Funkhouser has observed, "It's amazingly drought tolerant. Think about it growing wild in the woods. It has to take some drought." Blue phlox is much less susceptible to powdery mildew than other species, but Funkhouser has seen powdery mildew on blue phlox when it has been stressed by dry conditions. While it may live through a dry summer, it's best to give it rich, moist soil.

And the soil can be either acid or alkaline. Becky Talbot believes that, as is the case with French hydrangeas, a slightly acid soil may make the flowers a deeper blue than a more alkaline soil.

Although blue phlox can be propagated, if simply left alone it will multiply all by itself. "It seeds all over the place, and it's marvelous," says Franklin. "I let it go to seed, particularly through the wildflower garden." Each plant will spread gradually into a clump, so you can also increase blue phlox by dividing clumps every third year in the spring. Otherwise, root stem cuttings after flowers fade.

Blue phlox will remain green through winter. While it may not be an asset at this season, it will be there among the hardy perennials. And you can be reasonably sure that, except in the southernmost tips of Florida and Texas, this wildflower will thrive in all regions of the South no matter what the seasons may bring.

For sources of blue phlox, send a stamped, self-addressed, business-size envelope to Blue Phlox Editor, *Southern Living,* Box C-119, Birmingham, Alabama 35282.

(**Top**) *Blue phlox is bold enough to hold its own with a patch of bright-red tulips.*
(**Left**) *Fuller's White offers color variation plus all the fortitude of the original plant.*

Careful Planning Casts a Spell

Because it contains a series of smaller areas, this courtyard gives the illusion of much greater space. Yet there's no sleight of hand involved—just a knack for organization and a flair for design.

by RITA W. STRICKLAND / photography BETH MAYNOR

Envision a secluded spot where the morning sun sparkles through a canopy of gnarly oaks. The air is filled with the sweet scent of Carolina jessamine. A warm breeze rustles the leaves of Southern magnolias. Water splashes into a fountain. Does the term "enchanting" come to mind?

That's just the word these Houston homeowners use to describe their garden, and rightly so. Here, each small area has a charm of its own; in combination, they cast a spell.

But such a composition doesn't happen by magic. It's the product of careful planning and attention to detail—Landscape Architects Richard Dawson and Lawrence Estes, ASLA, are experts at both. In this case, their work started as soon as the homesite

had been selected, long before construction began.

Dawson and Estes worked closely with the architects to develop a design that treats home and garden as inseparable. "Because the property isn't very wide, the house is tall and narrow from front to back," Estes says. "We located the courtyard on the east side of the lot so the house would shade the garden from the hot afternoon sun." Service areas, driveway, and parking take up the west side of the site.

The unity of the indoors and outdoors becomes obvious the moment you enter the house. The courtyard is constantly in view through the long, low windows and double doors of the downstairs living area. A high brick wall stretches from the house and en-

closes the courtyard, binding the two visually as well as physically. And the pavers that floor the family room extend into the garden as well.

The doors of the living and family rooms open onto a central terrace, the focal point of which is an elegant raised fountain resting against the garden wall. Recessed brick panels in a herringbone pattern call attention to its three low jets, and ferns cascade from terra-cotta pots atop the wall.

A zigzag path of stepping pads leads from the fountain terrace to a small, rustic arbor at the north end of the garden. Each pad is made of a single stone paver banded with brick. Used throughout the courtyard, this brick banding repeats the material of the house and garden wall. In addition, it

(**Left**) *An arbor made of rough cedar beams and smooth stone columns becomes a separate space within the larger courtyard.*
(**Right**) *Herringbone panels in the brick wall call attention to three jets of water in this raised fountain.*

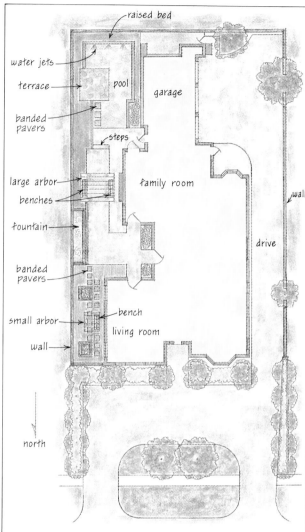

Seen from a second-floor balcony, the dark pool looks deep and inviting.

raised bed

water jets

terrace

pool

garage

banded pavers

steps

large arbor

family room

benches

fountain

wall

drive

banded pavers

bench

small arbor

living room

wall

north

provides an interesting contrast to the stone and lends a detailed, finished look to the design.

On the other side of the fountain terrace, there's a similar but larger arbor supported by smooth stone columns. "Although we didn't need the arbor for shade, we used the overhead structure to give the feeling of being in a separate space," Estes explains. "And it helps break up the long, slender garden." Benches placed between the columns make it just the right place for a quiet conversation.

Two steps lead down from the arbor to a dark-blue swimming pool at the south end of the courtyard. "The land around Houston is so flat, even a minor change in elevation can be dramatic, especially in a small garden," Dawson says. "To make the grade change seem even greater, we built a

low wall along the back of the pool to raise the planting beds there," adds Estes. This wall also houses spray jets, which transform the pool from recreational to decorative with the flip of a switch.

In one corner of the pool, a small dining terrace seems to float like a lily on a pond. "When you're on that terrace, you have the feeling that water is all around you," says Dawson. "The sound of the spray blocks most of the outside noise, so you really feel cut off from the rest of the world." To add a dash of adventure, stepping pads totally surrounded by water are the only access to this terrace. Identical in design to those at the far end of the courtyard, these pads add yet another thread of continuity to the garden.

Ease of maintenance was a primary concern in the choice of plants. Be-

cause the pool and fountain play such an important role in the design, mostly evergreens were used to minimize cleanup. And to reduce the amount of shearing necessary, slow-growing varieties, such as Wheeler's Dwarf pittosporum and dwarf yaupon were used to form the low, clipped borders.

Even among the evergreens, however, seasonal interest is an important consideration. In this garden, each time of year has its show-offs, from the blossoms of azalea and jessamine that decorate spring, to the berries of holly and nandina that brighten the winter.

"We also reserved space for bedding plants in some of the planters and in the low terra-cotta bowls we placed throughout the garden," Estes says. In Houston's moderate climate, that means a spectacular display of color is possible almost every day of the year.

LETTERS

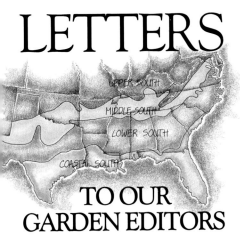

TO OUR GARDEN EDITORS

Mimosa: About 12 years ago, I planted a mimosa tree to shade my front lawn. It bloomed nicely for a number of years and is over 30 feet tall. However, last summer it suddenly dropped most of its leaves and now appears to have died back. I can't find any insects on it. Is this a one-year occurrence, or should I cut down the tree?
E. E. A.,
Myrtle Beach, South Carolina.
Mimosa (*Albizia julibrissin*) is naturally a short-lived tree, primarily because of its susceptibility to a wilt disease called *Fusarium*. This disease, which can quickly kill a mimosa at any age, causes the foliage to wilt and drop. Unfortunately, there is no cure for *Fusarium*; it's almost always fatal. So consider replacing your tree with a longer lived species that's immune to the disease. A good choice for you would be Shademaster thornless honey locust (*Gleditsia triacanthos inermis* Shademaster). Although this tree doesn't have showy blooms, its foliage and growth habit are somewhat similar to mimosa's. It grows fast, provides good shade, isn't fussy about soil, and tolerates heat and drought. And unlike some other honey locusts, it doesn't drop seed pods.

Cosmos: Every year my cosmos blooms well, but the plants tower above eye level. I give them plenty of sun and extra phosphate. What is wrong?
F. D.,
Nashville, Tennessee.
Most likely, you're growing the old-fashioned types of cosmos that naturally become tall and leggy. For more moderately sized plants, try either Diablo (orange-red flowers) or the Bright Lights series (several colors). These selections grow 3 to 4 feet tall. For even shorter plants, try Sunny Red or Sunny Gold.

Roly-polies: We didn't get to harvest many strawberries last year due to all the roly-polies (bugs that roll up into a ball when you touch them). What can we do to control them?
V. G.,
Frisco City, Alabama.
Pill bugs or sow bugs (popularly known as roly-polies) are actually small crustaceans that feed on roots and plant debris near the soil line. But, as you discovered, they won't pass up a juicy strawberry lying on the ground. Your first course of action should be to eliminate their hiding places, such as rocks, bricks, and timbers. Then apply a thick mulch of pine straw around your strawberry plants, so that the fruit won't rest on the soil. If this doesn't work, you may have to mix up a gallon or two of Diazinon solution and drench the soil in early spring, or sprinkle Diazinon granules on the soil surface and water them in. Be sure to follow label directions carefully.

Japanese kerria: I've seen a bush in the spring that has bright-green stems and yellow flowers that look like pom-poms. What is it?
W. F.,
Pinola, Mississippi.
Our best guess is double Japanese kerria (*Kerria japonica* Pleniflora). This lanky, arching shrub grows 6 to 8 feet

The golden-yellow blossoms of Japanese kerria are a springtime delight.
Photograph: Mary-Gray Hunter

tall and thrives in both sun and shade. Its golden-yellow blossoms are fully double, and the species sports single blooms. Bright-green stems make it easy to spot in winter. This shrub likes well-drained soil and grows throughout the South, except South Florida. Pruning immediately after it finishes flowering will encourage new, vigorous growth and plenty of flowers for the following spring.

Amaryllis: Please tell me the right way to plant amaryllis bulbs outside and how to care for them.
R. S. B.,
Savannah, Georgia.
Many gardeners wonder what to do with amaryllis bulbs (*Hippeastrum* sp.) after they've finished flowering indoors for the holidays. In Savannah, as well as the rest of the Lower and Coastal South, they can be planted outdoors in the spring. Select a sunny spot, and plant the bulbs 2 to 3 inches deep in fertile, well-drained soil. While the leaves are still growing in spring and summer, give the bulbs plenty of water. Feed every two weeks with water-soluble garden fertilizer diluted to half-strength. Toward the end of summer, cease feeding and reduce watering, eventually letting the soil go dry. This will induce dormancy. Cut the leaves off when they turn yellow. Resume watering and feeding when new green growth appears in spring.

Amaryllis bulbs aren't winter hardy in the Upper and Middle South. Gardeners there should grow them in pots outdoors in summer and bring them in for the winter. Follow the same schedule as above for watering and feeding.

Dogwood: I have about 2 pounds of dogwood berries that I stored over winter in my refrigerator. How do I plant them to get seedlings in spring?
M. C.,
Buchanan, Tennessee.
By keeping the berries in the refrigerator over the winter, you've satisfied the chilling requirement for germination. Your next step should be to peel the pulp away from the seed. Then sow the seed about 1 inch deep into either an empty garden bed or a container filled with potting soil. Keep the soil moist. The seed should germinate this spring.

TIP OF THE MONTH

I always mix my carrot and radish seed together, then sow very thinly in garden rows. The radishes mature first, so I harvest them before the carrots are ready. By the time I've harvested all the radishes, the carrots are properly thinned. This saves lots of work, and no plants are wasted.
Ginny Terry,
Jackson, Ohio.

Editor's note: We'd like to have your ideas—the ones that have worked for you. We're especially interested in vegetables, houseplants, shrubs, trees, and garden care. For each tip that is published, we will pay $10 and send you one of our garden books.

Submit as many ideas as you wish, but each must be on a separate sheet or card, along with your name, address, and telephone number. We may need to edit the tips, and none will be acknowledged or returned. Send to Gardening Tips, *Southern Living,* Box 523, Birmingham, Alabama 35201.

CHECKLIST
For March

☐ **Bedding plants**—When you buy transplants of flowers and vegetables, remember that bigger is not always better. Plants that have outgrown their container and have become leggy will not perform as well as those that have just filled out their pot. If you have a choice, select the ones that have not yet started flowering. Also choose transplants grown in individual cell packs over those that have several plants growing in one larger pot. Individual transplants will suffer less transplanting shock.

☐ **Cold damage**—If your trees or shrubs were damaged by cold this winter, wait until later in the spring to prune. That way, new growth will be more abundant, making damaged portions clearly evident. If the entire plant appears dead, wait awhile before you replace it, as some plants will sprout new growth from the roots. Even if grafted selections resprout, however, they may still need to be replaced; the new growth will not be the desired selection.

☐ **Mealybugs**—Watch out for these white, cottony masses on the stems and leaves of houseplants. Mealybugs feed on sap, causing leaves to be deformed. Severe infestations can even kill plants. You can often control minor cases by wiping the insects with a cotton swab soaked in alcohol. If spraying becomes necessary, be sure to use a pesticide specifically labeled for use on the affected plant, and apply it in strict accordance with label directions.

☐ **Mulch**—Renew mulch in flowerbeds and under trees and shrubs. A layer of mulch 2 to 4 inches thick will reduce weed problems and protect against moisture loss. Pine straw is an excellent all-purpose mulch; it lasts for months and won't wash away except in extremely heavy rains. Various kinds of bark mulches also work well. Avoid using bark mulches on slopes as they tend to float away during prolonged rainfall.

☐ **Perennials**—Divide overcrowded clumps of cannas, chrysanthemums, coreopsis, and perennial phlox as soon as they begin showing growth. Lift clumps with a spading fork; then cut the clumps into smaller divisions. Discard any weak or diseased portions, and reset divisions at the same depth as they were previously growing. Your plants will be healthier and more vigorous if rejuvenated every two to three years.

☐ **Pesticide information**—There is a toll-free number you can call if you have questions about pesticides, whether they concern general safety, toxicity, symptoms of poisoning, or disposal procedures. Reach the National Pesticide Telecommunications Network at 1-800-858-7378. The phone lines are staffed by specialists at the Texas Tech Health Sciences Center.

☐ **Raised beds**—If your garden site is too wet to plant in early spring, consider making raised beds. Border the beds with railroad ties, landscape timbers, or pressure-treated 2 x 12 boards. You can even make temporary beds by simply mounding the soil. Make the beds as long as you like, but for easy maintenance, build them no wider than 4 to 6 feet across (so you can comfortably work from either side of the bed). Don't worry about these beds drying out too quickly in summer. Just add plenty of organic matter at the start to help hold soil moisture.

☐ **Soil compaction**—Whenever you plant vegetables, trees, or flowers, you should always work the soil and add organic matter and amendments, such as lime and fertilizer. One of the most overlooked benefits of this process is simply loosening the soil. This allows the roots to grow deeper where they will find water and nutrients. Light, fluffy soil also has a lot of space between soil particles. This space supplies oxygen to the roots and lets water drain through the soil. Keep this in mind when you are working in your beds. Avoid stepping on freshly prepared soil, as that will compact it. Repeated foot traffic will make the soil quite hard and inhibit root growth. Put boards across vegetable beds to distribute your weight more evenly across a wider area. Place stepping stones at intervals in shrub and perennial borders to provide a place to stop to work.

SPECIAL TIPS FOR THE SOUTHEAST

☐ **Columbine**—Although traditionally considered a perennial for partial shade, columbine actually grows into a stronger, more vigorous plant in full sun, producing a thicker mound of foliage and a better show of flowers. And the foliage tends to be more resistant to leaf miner. This larval insect feeds between the upper and lower surface of a leaf, leaving the pattern of its winding trail. While leaf miners seldom kill a plant, heavy infestations will weaken and mar the summer foliage. Apply an insecticide that contains acephate, such as Orthene, for control. If damage is slight, just remove affected leaves.

☐ **Fruit trees**—Newly planted fruit trees need to be trained so they will be able to support heavy loads of fruit. The key is to have limbs growing at right angles to the trunk, even though limbs of many trees have a natural tendency to grow upward. It is easy to train them while they are young. If the branches are only a year old, you can use round toothpicks. Pull the upright limb down to the point where you feel resistance. Then hold it in place with a toothpick by putting one pointed end into the trunk and the other into the limb. Older limbs will need limb spreaders, constructed of sections of 1 x 1 lumber, cut 1 to 2 feet long. Drive a finishing nail into each end, and then clip off the head at an angle. Position these just as you would toothpicks between the trunk and an upright limb. Let limb spreaders remain in place for at least one year.

☐ **Trees**—This is a good time to plant trees. The weather is warm enough for the gardener, yet the plants are still dormant. However, your work is not done when the roots are in the ground. Shade trees need to be trained while they are young to grow sturdy limbs that will withstand storms. The National Arbor Day Foundation has published a guide that will explain what you should do and when—and it's free. Send your name and address to: How To Prune, National Arbor Day Foundation, Nebraska City, Nebraska 68410.

☐ **Vegetables**—Although most vegetables in the cabbage family are transplanted into the garden, many cool-weather vegetables can be sown directly into the soil where you want the seeds to grow. These include beets, spinach, English peas, edible-podded peas, lettuce, turnips, Swiss chard, kohlrabi, and carrots. Follow the directions on the seed packet for proper depth and spacing.

SPECIAL TIPS FOR FLORIDA

☐ **Bananas**—Start your own banana plants using the suckers of large plants. Suckers should be about 4 feet tall and have plenty of healthy roots. Choose an area that drains well, and dig a planting hole about 3 feet wide and 2 feet deep. Space plants at least 8 feet apart. Bananas need rich soil, so amend the backfill with plenty of compost, manure, or other organic matter. Work into the soil 1 pound of 4-8-8 at planting time. Set the plants at the same depth they were growing, and mulch to keep down weeds. Banana plants need lots of moisture, so water regularly when there is no rain. And fertilize every two months for a year, increasing the amount of fertilizer by ½ pound each time. This may sound like a lot, but bananas' rapid rate of growth demands it.

☐ **Flowers for shade**—If you want color in the shady areas of your garden, a number of annuals and bulbs will do the job. Some of the most popular include caladiums, begonias, browallia, coleus, annual phlox, and torenia. Impatiens will also grow in shade, but they do best with a little filtered sunlight. You can also plant ferns as a companion for many of these plants. Southern shield fern and Boston fern will remain as a permanent cover year after year.

☐ **Ginger**—Fresh ginger roots from the grocery store can be used to start a planting. Buy nonrefrigerated roots, and plant in the vegetable garden or other clear area with loose, rich soil. Plant about 2 inches deep; water regularly. Leaves should sprout within four weeks.

☐ **Hydrangeas**—To grow blue hydrangeas in parts of Florida where the soil isn't acid, treat the soil with aluminum sulfate. This makes the soil acid and supplies aluminum ions—both help turn the flowers blue. You can purchase aluminum sulfate in small bags. Work the amount recommended on the label into the soil around the plants, and water it in well. Repeat in summer and fall.

☐ **Leaves**—In South Florida as new growth forces old leaves to fall, gather the leaves and add them to your compost pile, or grind them to make mulch. Use a leaf grinder or run over leaves with your mower, catching the clippings in the mower bag. You can also use the shredded leaves as a soil amendment.

☐ **Mangoes**—Watch for powdery mildew on mangoes. This disease appears as a white, powdery film on the leaves and blossoms. You can prevent the disease by spraying with sulfur every week from now until early summer. Spray on a calm day to avoid spray drift.

☐ **Vegetables**—In North Florida, this is the beginning of the planting season for summer vegetables. It's the last month to plant in South Florida. You can set out transplants of tomatoes, eggplant, and peppers. Squash, okra, cucumbers, and melons are best started from seed. Be sure to set up stakes or cages for tomatoes, cucumbers, and eggplant at the time of planting. If you wait until later, you may disturb the

plants. Also be sure to label so you won't confuse different varieties; use a permanent marker to write the name on wooden sticks.

SPECIAL TIPS FOR TEXAS

☐ **Figs**—You can grow this fruit tree in most of the state, except in the extreme west and the Panhandle. If you're in the northern part of their hardiness range, plant figs to the south of your home where they will receive some protection from winter cold. Two recommended selections are Celeste and Texas Everbearing. Figs are self-fertile, so you needn't plant two; however, Celeste will ripen before Texas Everbearing, so you can extend your harvest by planting one of each. Fig trees planted now should begin to bear within two to three years.

☐ **Onions**—For the largest bulbs, get your onions in the ground early. Sets no larger than ⅝ inch in diameter are best because they are the least likely to flower. Plant larger sets to harvest as early green onions.

☐ **Pansies**—In South and Central Texas, feed pansies planted last fall. Sprinkle 5-10-10 between the plants at the rate of ½ pound per 25 square feet of planting bed. Gardeners in North Texas should plant two to four weeks before the last expected frost. Keep plants watered well, especially during cold snaps. Remove faded blooms regularly to encourage continued production.

MOONFLOWER BRIGHTENS THE NIGHT

Like its cousin the morning glory, moonflower (*Ipomoea alba*) is only open about 12 hours. But unlike the morning glory, moonflower could be called a night glory, as its big white blossoms are in their prime at night. You can actually watch them open. Big twisted buds unfurl into flowers that are up to 6 inches wide. They seem to glow in the dark as they reflect moonlight or even outdoor lights. This is the perfect, fast-growing summer vine for a fence or trellis by a porch or patio where you can enjoy its sweetly scented blossoms.

Moonflowers open in late afternoon and close the next morning.
Photograph: Van Chaplin

Moonflower is easy to grow. Just plant the big seeds in spring about the same time you plant tomatoes, marigolds, and other warm-weather plants. The seeds are hard, so it's best to soak them for a day before planting. Presoaked seeds should sprout in a week. Choose a location that receives full sun. Moonflower will grow in partial shade but will bear fewer flowers.

The soil should be well drained and moderately fertile. If it is too rich, you will get a lot of vine but not many flowers. When seedlings are a few inches tall, feed with water-soluble 20-20-20 mixed at half its usual strength. If your soil is sandy, repeat this feeding monthly to maintain healthy growth.

Once established, moonflower will grow several inches per day until it gets 15 to 20 feet tall. It climbs by wrapping itself on a fence, trellis, or other support. The large leaves form a good screen all summer. In fall the vine is killed by frost. In South Florida it will live for several years, but you might want to replant every spring to keep the planting vigorous.

April

Clematis Is Always a Surprise

An otherwise quiet little vine, hybrid clematis blooms with a fury.
This is one flower that's hard to resist.

by LOIS B. TRIGG

Each spring when clematis begins to bloom, one has to wonder how such big, showy flowers could suddenly appear from almost nowhere. The thin, delicate vines stand forgotten throughout the year, then burst forth with saucer-size flowers that last for at least two weeks.

There are dozens of clematis, but these big ones are hybrids of several species and are simply known as hybrid clematis. You can find the plants in nurseries each spring packaged in neat little boxes with pictures showing the different flower colors—white, blue, red, purple, and shades in between. The boxed plants look weak and wiry, but given a chance, they'll grow into a vigorous vine 8 to 20 feet long, depending on the type you choose.

Many hybrid clematis bloom in spring, and some bloom again in the fall. There are also hybrids that bloom only in summer. If you choose carefully, you can enjoy clematis from April to September—just buy several selections with staggered bloom times. Although clematis vines live indefinitely, they are somewhat like an annual. After the flowers are gone, the green foliage seems to disappear until it drops in fall.

Clematis will grow throughout the South except in South Texas and Central and South Florida, where it is too hot. Cold weather is never a problem.

FLOWERS IN SUN, ROOTS IN SHADE

When you plant clematis, don't leave the roots exposed. Always choose a spot where the vine can grow out into the sun but the roots can hide under a terrace, walkway, or even a layer of mulch. And in the Lower South, you may need to limit the sunshine. For example, gardeners in Montgomery, Alabama, would be advised to find a spot with morning sun and afternoon shade, especially for the colorful selections. Henryi, a popular white, seems to do fine there in sun throughout the day.

Give clematis a good start and it will grow 3 or 4 inches a day in spring. A good start means adding plenty of organic matter so that the soil is light and drains well. Ideally, you want to prepare a spot about 2 feet deep and 2 feet wide, but if this seems like too much work, at least prepare the soil to the depth of a turning fork. Work ½ cup of slow-release tree-and-shrub fertilizer into the soil.

Set the plant so the crown is 2 to 3 inches deep. Burying a pair of buds on the stem below the ground provides insurance in case something happens to the brittle top. After planting, cut the vine back to the first pair of above-ground buds. That way, it will branch to encourage a fuller plant. Mulch with pine bark or pine straw; then water well and regularly. Don't ignore this plant during dry weather or it could easily die.

Clematis climbs with gentle tendrils—it doesn't tug like ivy or wisteria and so is perfect for lightweight structures, such as lattice. It does twist its tendrils around whatever it can reach, however, even itself. To prevent a tangle, support the vine and point it in the direction you want it to grow. Check the fast-growing vine weekly to be sure it stays on course. Plants growing on walls will need wire to cling to.

PROPER PRUNING MAKES THE VINE

The trickiest part of growing clematis is knowing when to prune—if you do it at the wrong time, you will cut off the year's blossoms. But prune properly, and you will encourage lots of blooms. Spring-flowering types don't need pruning at all unless you just want to control size. In that case, prune immediately after blooms fade. Clematis selections in this category include Duchess of Edinburgh, Belle of Woking, Henryi, Nelly Moser, Red Cardinal, and The President.

If your clematis blooms in summer and fall, then you should prune hard in late winter, cutting each stem back to the last pair of buds. This encourages lots of new growth on which the blossoms are borne. Selections in this group include Jackmanii, Comtesse de Bouchaud, and Ernest Markham.

(**Right**) *A spring bloomer, Henryi clematis drapes over a garden wall.* (**Below**) *This lattice-filled arch comes alive with the white blooms of Henryi. The handsome foliage remains through summer after the blossoms fade.* Photographs: Van Chaplin, Mary-Gray Hunter

(**Below**) *Although the pale blossoms appear delicate, they will stay fresh for two weeks or more, even in rain.* (**Center**) *Red Cardinal is a deep, rich red that blooms in spring.* (**Bottom**) *Nelly Moser blooms in spring and late summer. Its pale-pink petals are marked with deeper pink bars.*

Because of its dense, mounding shape, Indian hawthorn is ideal for mass plantings near walkways and entrances.   Photographs: Van Chaplin

Indian Hawthorn Likes Sand, Salt, and Sun

What looks like pittosporum, blooms like mountain laurel, and grows where many other plants won't? The answer is Indian hawthorn. Not only does it boast glossy, evergreen foliage, but it also takes to the shore like a teenage surfer.

Native to Japan and Korea, Indian hawthorn (*Raphiolepis indica*) is a dense, mounding shrub growing 4 to 6 feet wide and 3 to 4 feet high. It's usually compact and spreading, although some upright selections become small trees. Each oval or elliptical leaf is 2 to 3 inches long and about 1 inch wide, with a dark-green upper surface and light-green underside. A novice gardener could easily mistake the plant for Japanese pittosporum (*Pittosporum tobira*).

Fragrant flowers appear in March and April. Reminiscent of mountain laurel, they're borne in large clusters at the tips of the branches. Sporadic blooms may also appear in late summer or early fall. Pink and white are the dominant flower colors. Popular selections include Enchantress (a compact grower with rose-pink flowers),

Fascination (compact with pink-and-white flowers), Snow White (dwarf with white flowers), and Majestic Beauty (a tall-growing hybrid with light-pink flowers).

Ralph Graham, director of landscape operations at Sea Island, Georgia, suggests several ways to use Indian

hawthorn in the garden. "We use the dwarf kinds in mass plantings and foundation plantings," he says. "The taller kinds, such as Majestic Beauty, we grow as standards, either planted in the ground or in containers."

Graham's neighbor to the south, Landscape Architect Bob Hartwig, of Jacksonville, Florida, recommends planting the compact selections under low windows, around decks and patios, near entrances and walkways, and in oceanfront plantings.

Oceanfront plantings—that's where Indian hawthorn can really shine. "It seems to love our sandy soil, as well as the summer sun and heat," notes Graham. "It's also quite salt tolerant—we plant it even on the ocean side of our houses." In this location, it's a good substitute for such salt-sensitive evergreens as hollies, camellias, and azaleas.

Indian hawthorn does best in full sun, although it tolerates partial shade. It prefers moist soil but, once established, withstands drought. Excellent drainage is important. Pruning, though seldom necessary, should be done directly after flowering in spring. Leaf spot is an occasional problem, but you can control it by spraying with either benomyl or Daconil according to label directions.

If Indian hawthorn has a weakness, winter hardiness is it. Injury occurs when the temperature drops much below 10 degrees. So while the shrub is an excellent choice for Florida, the Lower, South, and the Gulf and South Atlantic Coasts, gardeners in the Middle and Upper South should either select another plant or plant Indian hawthorn in pots and bring it inside for the winter.

Indian hawthorn is also an excellent choice for foundation plantings, especially when set off by shrubs with brighter green foliage, such as Japanese boxwood.

Planting beds for shrubs and flowers soften large, exposed walls.

A zigzag retaining wall levels this lawn.

Now This Garden's On the Level

When John and Virginia Tomlinson bought their Louisville, Kentucky, home, there was, as they say, both good news and bad news. The good news was that the lot had excellent drainage. The bad news was that the backyard sloped so severely, it was hard to stand up.

"The view in back was nice, but there was no usable space," recalls Virginia. "The only place with any sun was on that very steep slope. I wanted a level spot so I could grow something."

The Tomlinsons hired Landscape Architect Edmund Ely, ASLA, to devise a solution. Ely began by designing a series of redwood decks that leads from the side of the house down to the lawn below. The upper deck, which sits 10 feet above the lawn, is level

with the house's sunroom. Family and guests can exit from the sunroom to the upper deck then descend to the lower deck and lawn. Built-in benches along the rim of the lower deck provide plenty of seating.

A large, bare wall beneath the sunroom was the next area to receive attention. Ely installed a number of planting terraces bordered by low retaining walls to soften this stark surface. The terraces also give the Tomlinsons level gardening space in which to grow low shrubs, flowers, and ground cover.

One of the landscape's more noteworthy features is a zigzag retaining wall at the rear of the lawn. Built of pressure-treated 6 x 6 timbers, the wall helped to transform the slope into a level lawn. Ely decided on

the zigzag arrangement because it's structurally stronger than a straight wall would be. "And since it's viewed mostly from above, it creates an interesting pattern that a straight wall lacks," he says.

A grass path leads from the lawn down to the exposed side of the retaining wall. Planting boxes at the foot of the wall mirror the wall's zigzag pattern. Virginia plants perennials in most of the boxes but reserves one box for a cutting garden and another for tomatoes. By summer's end, both the annuals used for cutting and the tomatoes get leggy, but the wall hides them.

The decks and lawn are tailormade for dining and entertaining. Lighting in the steps, under the benches, and in the trees brightens the garden at night. Electrical outlets on the upper deck allow Virginia to plug in coffeemakers and other appliances for meals and parties. "I serve people on the upper level and let them drift down and be seated on the lower level," she explains. With a backdrop of beautiful hardwood trees, each get-together is a pleasure.

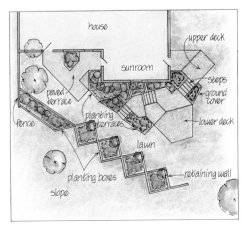

The small size of cherry tomatoes makes them perfect for salads and snacks.

Cherry Tomatoes Love Summer

When nights are above 70 degrees for several days in a row, standard-size tomatoes go into a lull—one that lasts as long as the warmer weather. But there are many cherry tomato types that don't mind the heat at all.

You can call a round tomato that measures less than 1½ inches in diameter a cherry tomato, but there are a few that grow to about 2 inches in diameter and look like miniature standard tomatoes.

Seed catalogs usually list all small-fruited tomatoes as either cherry,

patio, or basket types, and they all share one thing in common—their size. Most are very sweet and have thin skins, making them perfect for salads and snacks.

Even among the cherry types there are differences in heat tolerance. Dr. Jay Scott, associate professor of Vegetable Crops and tomato breeder at the University of Florida's Experiment Station in Bradenton, suggests that gardeners try several selections of cherry tomatoes to see which of their favorites will take the most heat. Among those he has seen do well in Florida's warm nights are Small Fry, Cherry Grande, and Sweet 100. One that does not is Red Cherry Large. In Fort Meyers, Linda Sapp of Tomato Growers Supply Company recommends Baxter's Early Bush Cherry for its summer vigor. But these are just four—test a few on your own. Look for selections that are resistant to verticillium and fusarium wilts and nematodes; in catalogs or on labels they are marked VFN.

Even though their fruit is small, some cherry tomato plants can be just as rambling as those that bear big, sandwich-size fruit. Sweet 100, a vining type, gets taller and taller throughout the season, eventually reaching 4 to 5 feet. Bush-type selections, such as Patio Prize and Small Fry, grow less than 4 feet tall.

It's not too late to plant cherry tomatoes, even if you must start from seed; just choose selections that mature early. Seedlings will be big enough to set in the garden within three to four weeks after planting; they'll start producing at about seven weeks. Before planting, work plenty of compost or other organic matter into the soil along with ½ cup 10-10-10 per 10 square feet. Or you can drop 1 tablespoon of slow-release fertilizer, such as Osmocote, into each planting hole.

Set young transplants deep enough so that the lowest leaves are 2 inches above the ground. When the transplants are 4 to 6 inches tall, mulch them with compost or a 3-inch layer of pine straw to help conserve moisture and keep down weeds. Be sure to provide a wire cage or stake to support the stems of tall types. This keeps them off the ground and helps prevent disease. Shorter ones appreciate staking, too, especially in a rainstorm.

Although their fruit is smaller, some cherry tomato plants will grow just as tall and rambling as plants that bear much larger fruit. Photographs: Mary-Gray Hunter

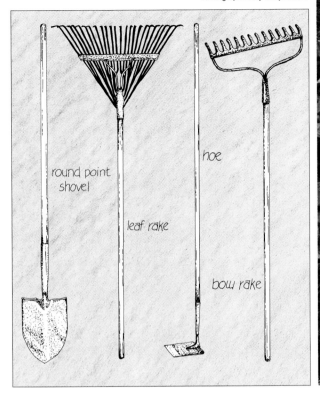

A Guide to Garden Tools

It's an understatement to say tools make gardening easier; they make it possible. From pruning to raking to planting, tools become the gardener's right hand. Here are seven basic garden tools that no serious gardener should be without.

■ With a **round point shovel** you can dig planting holes, shovel mulch or gravel, build raised beds, and even mix concrete. This tool is a must. Look for one with a long, smooth wooden handle that won't splinter. Also look for a shovel with a closed back—that's the place where the handle comes down into the blade. An open groove in the back provides a place for mud to collect, causing the handle to rot and the blade to rust. The top edge of the blade should be rolled over slightly; that way the shovel won't hurt your foot when you bear down on it.

■ A good **leaf rake** isn't just for fall—it helps a gardener year-round. You can use it to gather grass clippings, rake mulch, and gather debris for the final cleaning in a planting bed. When selecting from the many styles available, choose one that feels comfortable to you. A model with a reinforcement bar keeps the tines from bending.

■ A **hoe** is indispensable for making hills and rows in a vegetable garden, but it's also useful for leveling soil, preparing spots in the lawn for reseeding or sodding, and weeding. The best, longest lasting hoes will have the blade and shank forged from one piece of steel. Welded hoes may eventually come apart.

■ There's nothing like a **bow rake** to smooth soil for planting vegetables, flowers, or grass seed. It pulls out clods of soil, stones, and seedling weeds. You can also use it to work fertilizer

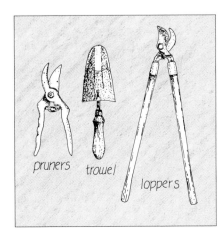

into the soil and to level a planting bed. Look for a bow rake that has the tines and bow forged from one piece of steel.

■ A **trowel** is probably the most used of all garden tools. It loosens and chops soil, digs small holes for bulbs and transplants, carves out small furrows for seeds, uproots weeds, and acts like a large spoon to mix potting soil. Choose one with a comfortable grip and sturdy construction to avoid bending or breaking.

■ Finally, a pair of **pruners** is a must for keeping plants groomed and clipping foliage and flowers to bring indoors. It's a good idea to have both a pair of hand-held pruners and a pair of long-handled ones called **loppers.** Loppers are good for pruning fruit trees, cutting nandinas and other plants with fat woody canes, and for clipping large branches for arrangements. Hand-held pruners are good for lighter cuts, such as pruning leggy impatiens, cutting back dead perennials, harvesting eggplant, and gathering flowers for arrangements. Look for loppers and pruners with sharp steel blades that operate smoothly. Scissors types make cleaner cuts than anvil types.

Watering the Garden

The green lawns and lush gardens of the South boast of frequent rains and plentiful water. But in recent years, there have been periods of drought when irrigation was required. That's when knowing how much and how often to water can mean a lot.

Regular watering is essential to plant health, whether you're watering a tree, shrub, or lawn. Plants under stress are more susceptible to insects and diseases. So for a hardier garden, apply about 1 inch of water each rainless week to average garden soil.

You'll see a big difference in growth between plants that have sufficient water and those that are occasionally stressed. Lawns that are growing vigorously will withstand foot traffic much better. However, too much water is as bad as too little; either will kill the plant. Roots need air to breathe, but saturated soil has no air spaces; if overwatered, roots will rot. So be judicious in your watering and be sure your soil is well drained.

The time of day and the amount of water you apply will vary with the type of soil in your garden. Whenever you water, you should apply enough to wet the soil 4 to 6 inches deep. That's about an inch of water. But how do you know when you've applied an inch? Set out empty 6½-ounce cans under your sprinkler. When they are full, you've watered enough. Note how long it took for the cans to fill so you can time your watering in the future.

If your soil is heavy clay, you'll find the excess running off or standing in puddles because the water needs time to soak in. To solve this problem, move the sprinkler to another area; then bring it back after several hours. If your soil is sandy, it will require less water to moisten it deeply, but the soil will also dry out more quickly. Therefore, with sandy soils, apply about ½ inch of water every three to four days.

If you water during the day, much of the moisture will be lost to evaporation or wind. So the best time to water is morning or late afternoon.

The Hardware

The most recent innovation in watering is a **water timer**. It can vary from a simple device measuring either time or quantity of water to a more complex computer that turns water on and off several times a week. Even the sim-

Water is essential to a healthy lawn, but knowing how to water is the key.

plest of these devices will enable you to go to bed or to work with the water running and know that it will turn itself off at the proper time. Those timers that turn the water on are ideal for keeping the garden watered while you are on vacation.

With all the variations in **sprinklers**, you will surely find one that suits your garden. Keep the approximate dimensions of your garden in mind as you shop for a sprinkler. If you have a large garden, look for one that will either cover the garden from one position or allow you to move it a minimal number of times. Oscillating, rotary, and pulse sprinklers usually cover the largest area. However, if you have a small plot, a large sprinkler pattern will probably water paving or the neighbor's yard. Stationary sprinklers are available in a variety of patterns to suit the shape of most small gardens.

Having the right **nozzle** allows you to get the job done right with the least amount of time and effort. There are high-pressure nozzles for cleaning paving, breaker nozzles for gently water-

ing plants, adjustable nozzles that let you vary the pressure, even soaker nozzles that can be left beneath a plant for slow watering. And having to change nozzles is much more convenient if you buy snap-on adapters.

You even have a choice of **hoses**. A ⅝-inch-diameter hose will deliver the most water to your garden, providing you have sufficient water pressure. However, whether you get a ½-inch- or ⅝-inch-diameter hose, fittings are all standard. If you have one of each, connect the ⅝-inch one to the faucet; then connect the smaller hose to the larger one. Rubber hoses are the most durable, followed by the reinforced type. Always drain and store your hose during severely cold weather to avoid splitting.

However, if your hose should split or one of the couplings should break, you can repair it with a hose-mending kit. If you have a leak in the middle of the hose, buy a kit with both the male and female ends (these parts are also available individually to repair broken couplings).

Container Gardening

Whatever the style, size, or type of garden, plants in containers make a delightful addition.

One of their greatest advantages is simply that they can be moved about to suit a particular need. Pots of colorful annuals are ideal for decorating the edge of a pool, where permanent flowerbeds are often messy and inappropriate. From welcoming guests at the front door to defining areas of the garden, their uses are nearly endless.

Flexibility is another asset of containers. With the exception of pots that hold trees and shrubs, most containers can be replanted seasonally, bringing variety to your garden and keeping plants at their best.

Containers offer an easy way to add color while keeping time and cost at a minimum. Plus, they can guarantee something will always be in bloom. For example, plant a mix of daffodils and pansies in fall. In the Middle and Lower South the pansies will bloom through winter. Then in spring, the daffodil buds will work their way through the pansies, yielding two layers of color. After these blooms fade, replace them with summer annuals, such as Madagascar periwinkle, impatiens, caladiums, or whatever conforms to your taste and climate.

In the cooler reaches of the South or extremely shady gardens, your choice of winter flowers may be limited. One solution is to use an evergreen shrub year-round and then add containers of flowers in spring. Japanese andromeda and leatherleaf mahonia are good choices because they bloom in early spring. However, if these are not hardy in your area, choose yew or a low-growing juniper.

Planting

It's especially important to use good soil when growing plants in containers. Not only must the soil drain well but it must also be free of insects and fungi. Sterilized potting soil is recommended over dirt from the garden.

When purchasing commercial potting soils, be aware of the variation in quality. As a general rule, a good potting soil consists of a mixture of sphagnum peat moss, sand or bark, and perlite or vermiculite. Many times it's hard to determine what ingredients a product has. You might consider experimenting with several brands until you find one that suits.

Or you may prefer to create your own mix. A multipurpose blend includes small wheelbarrow loads of each of the following: sphagnum peat moss, coarse sand, and finely ground bark. To each batch add 2 pounds of lime and ⅓ pound of iron sulfate. Then add either 2 pounds of slow-release fertilizer or 6 pounds of cottonseed meal.

Cover the drainage hole with a piece of window screen or other fine mesh to allow excess water to drain while keeping soil from leaking out. Fill the pot with potting soil to within an inch of the rim, pressing the soil firmly around the plants. Don't add any more soil than this as it may wash out when you water. Space vegetable, herb, or flower transplants about one-third closer than you would in the garden. That way they'll fill the pot completely yet won't invite disease problems.

Watering

Plants in containers don't have the soil insulation most plants have. As a result, they dry out quickly. Don't let plants wilt to the point of no return. Pay particular attention in summer, when daily watering may be required.

You can simplify the task of watering by setting up a drip irrigation system with tubes running to each pot. These systems supply a slow, steady trickle of moisture and can be run by an automatic timer.

Fertilizing

Plants in containers depend solely on you for nutrients. The easiest way to feed them is to incorporate a long-lasting, slow-release fertilizer, such as Osmocote, into the soil when planting. Because of the frequent watering potted plants require, count on the fertilizers to last from one-half to two-thirds of the specified time. A monthly feeding of water-soluble 20-20-20 fertilizer applied throughout the growing season should supply any additional food required.

With a seemingly endless selection of plants and containers to choose from, there's a combination to suit any setting.   Photograph: Mary-Gray Hunter

A lush green lawn draws the viewer's eye to this freestanding gate—a feature in itself.   Photographs: Van Chaplin, Mary-Gray Hunter, Sylvia Martin

PLAIN OR FANCY, GATES MAKE THE GARDEN

A gate reflects the thought and care that went into a garden's planning.
Few other features can be so practical yet so appealing.

by RITA W. STRICKLAND

At first glance, a garden gate seems a simple thing—a doorway to the garden. But a closer look reveals that a well-designed and thoughtfully placed gate can do a lot more than let people come and go.

As a start, it helps set a mood and adds interest. Approaching a gate, you must pause, which gives you a moment to appreciate the subtle colors or sweet fragrance of nearby blossoms. A see-through-style gate piques your curiosity by allowing a teasing glimpse of what lies ahead. A gate tucked into an out-of-the-way corner seems mysterious. Where will it lead? And a solid gate can lend extra emphasis to a garden feature suddenly revealed when the gate is opened.

A gate can even be a focal point in itself. If a bright white gate leads through an evergreen hedge or a light, delicate pattern graces a strong brick wall, it will stand out because it contrasts so sharply with its background. Set at one end of a garden, such a gate will draw your eye across the entire length of the space. If the gate can be opened to frame a vista, then the surrounding landscape becomes a part

(Left) *Lattice panels offer a view into this garden, yet the gate's height leaves no doubt that the space behind it is private. Landscape Architect: Dan Sears, ASLA, Raleigh.* (Right) *A gate doesn't have to be part of a fence. This one, of 1 x 4 pickets, marks the opening in a low hedge.*

(Left) *The geometric lines of this entry gate contrast with the intricate design of the doorway.* (Right) *This low double gate, anchored securely by heavy posts, leads guests to the front door.*

Here's a gate with dual assets: slender pickets on top offer a view; a solid panel below suggests privacy.

of the garden design as well.

Clues to the character of the space beyond can be revealed in a gate's design. For example, a low gate seems friendly and bids welcome. You might choose a gate less than waist high to lead visitors into an entry garden at the front door. On the other hand, a gate several feet tall may be more appropriate in your backyard or near the pool to indicate that the area is private and just for invited guests.

Of course, architectural harmony is a top priority. Frequently, details employed elsewhere are repeated in the gate's design to create a sense of continuity. If the doors that open onto your garden from inside the home feature an unusual molding, you might use that same molding on the gate. Or the pattern in a porch rail could be worked into the gate's design.

Whatever the style, be aware that quality building materials and hardware are essential. Use pressure-treated or other rot-resistant lumber for wooden gates, and select hinges and fasteners that won't rust or stain. Make sure the gate is solidly constructed. The best-looking design won't make up for a gate that buckles after it's installed. Don't forget practical considerations, too. If the gate is meant simply to admit people, then a 3-foot width is sufficient. But if the gate is also the sole access to an area, it should be wide enough to accommodate a garden cart or any other equipment you may need inside.

(**Left**) *At the University of Virginia, this gate offers a contrast between its delicate pattern and the brick wall.* (**Center**) *This open design allows a visual link between a lawn and pool area while also maintaining a sense of separation. Landscape Architect: Robert Chesnut, ASLA, Charleston, South Carolina.* (**Right**) *Detailing at the top of the wall is repeated in this gate. Architect: Barry Fox, AIA, New Orleans.*

(**Left**) *Graceful lines on this iron gate echo the cascades of the liriope. Landscape Architect: Rick Anderson, ASLA, Atlanta.*
(**Center**) *Crafted to reflect a Colonial style, this low gate opens into a formal garden. Architect: G. John Baxter, Atlanta.*
(**Right**) *In an urban courtyard, entry is gained through an iron gate. Landscape Architect: Sheila Wertimer, ASLA, Charleston, South Carolina.*

May

THE SOUTHERN GARDEN®

WHY NOT WEIGELA?

This old, familiar shrub has faded from view in recent years. But there's nothing wrong with being showy in spring and easy to grow.

It's paradoxical, but many plants that stand the test of time lose favor as a result. The common weigela (pronounced wy-JEEL-uh) is a case in point. It's easy to grow, never needs spraying, and blooms dependably. And that's precisely why many gardeners disdain it—because it doesn't offer enough of a challenge.

Of course, there are those who, after a long day at the office, don't want to do battle in the backyard. For these harried souls, a plant such as weigela may be the answer to their prayers.

Weigela (*Weigela florida*) hails from China and Japan but has been around so long that most Southerners think it's native. A large, dense shrub, weigela grows 8 to 10 feet tall and wide, with arching branches that reach for the ground. The trumpet-shaped flowers may be red, rose, pink, white, or even purple. Mid- to late-spring sees the heaviest bloom, when 1-inch flowers appear all along the branches on the previous year's growth. The shrub also blooms sporadically throughout the summer months, offering a few scattered blossoms on the current season's growth.

Fall color isn't weigela's strong suit. The autumn leaves may turn maroon but usually fall off green. Some weigelas atone for this with red- or purple-tinged summer foliage, while others flaunt variegated leaves.

SOME WEIGELAS TO TRY

Probably the most popular weigela today is Bristol Ruby, whose blossoms are rich, ruby red. Other recommended selections include Candida (pure-white blooms), Conquerant (deep rose), and Mont Blanc (fragrant white). If a slightly smaller shrub is more to your liking, consider one of the compact selections. Eva Supreme grows 5 feet tall with bright-red flowers. Variegata Nana grows 3 to 4 feet tall with light-pink flowers and cream-edged leaves. Minuet is about the smallest of all, reaching only 2 to 3 feet. It sports purple blossoms and purplish-green foliage.

Many gardeners use weigela in the shrub border, where it functions the same as a spirea, forsythia, or mock-orange. Others plant a row of weigelas to serve as an informal hedge. A well-groomed shrub also makes an attractive, freestanding specimen or seasonal accent.

To take advantage of weigela's cascading form, try planting the shrub at

the top of a low garden wall. In spring, the limbs tumbling over the edge of the wall will mingle their white flowers with any perennials and bulbs blooming below.

TIPS ON CARE

Weigela grows well in all areas of the South, except for the Coastal region. Give it full sun or light shade and fertile, well-drained soil. This shrub is a good choice for urban areas, as it tolerates pollution. A cup or two of a balanced shrub fertilizer, sprinkled around the base of the plant in spring, will go a long way toward producing

vigorous, handsome foliage.

But the real key to keeping a weigela looking good is proper pruning. Use hand pruners—never hedge trimmers—to prune the shrub back heavily after it flowers in spring, removing most of the growth that's more than a few years old. This will encourage plenty of young, healthy shoots to spring from the base. If you happen to inherit an old, greatly overgrown shrub, renew it by cutting off one-third of the canes at ground level each year over a period of three years. At the end of this time, the plant should be much more vigorous and attractive.

WEIGELA AT A GLANCE

Light: Sun or light shade
Soil: Loose, fertile, well drained
Water: During summer droughts
Pests: None serious
Propagation: Root softwood; take tip cuttings in June

For sources of weigela, send a stamped, self-addressed, business-size envelope to Weigela Editor, *Southern Living,* Box C-119, Birmingham, Alabama 35282.

(**Above**) *Weigela's flower-laden branches are spectacular in late spring.* (**Below**) *Some selections bear pink blossoms.*

Photographs: Van Chaplin, Mary-Gray Hunter

(**Above**) *At the center of this suburban garden stands* Pegasus *from Wheeler Williams's series "Childhood of the Gods."*
(**Right**) *The little glade of ferns and azaleas offers a quiet retreat.*

A Shaded Glade of Green

by LINDA ASKEY WEATHERS / photography MARY-GRAY HUNTER

Lush with ferns and fragrant flowers, a small retreat sits quietly, just a part of a large suburban garden. The pea gravel path makes a soft scrunch underfoot, scattering chipmunks and robins when it's time for morning coffee or afternoon refreshment. This is far from a place to toil with weeds and insects; it is a solace for the soul—an imagined Eden brought to reality in Atlanta.

The Garden Evolved

Soon after the current owners moved in, they discovered this intimate glade beneath a tangle of ivy. The stone bench was the first clue, then they found beds of ferns and azaleas, all beneath a tall canopy of trees.

Just as nature created the beauty of the garden, so a storm took away several large trees that shaded it, and the large camellias died in a hard winter. But what seemed a devastation was actually an opportunity for change and improvement.

Garden Designer Ryan Gainey was asked to renew the entire garden. He recommended moving the pink Gumpo azaleas from another portion of the property into the center bed of this small garden. A skirt of mondo grass offered a soft edge as well as textural interest.

All of the ferns are original to the garden. Huge cinnamon ferns and sensitive ferns unfurl in shaded beds. Resurrection fern, which is planted

along the stone wall, revives itself with every rain.

The old mountain laurel, leaning across the path toward a statue of *Pegasus,* had been reaching for the only spot of light left by the overhanging trees. Now with the open canopy, it's growing upward again, twisted like a living sculpture.

Though smaller than before, the camellias have grown back from their roots. They bloom in profusion and offer a link to what the garden was in the past.

However, gone is the seclusion, the comfortable security of a dense canopy. Gainey explains, "What's in the garden is one thing, but what makes it really intimate is its surround-

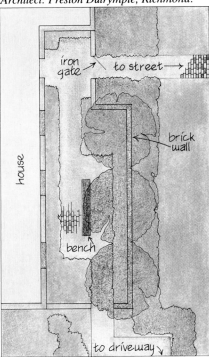

A low bench offers a pleasant place to stop in this Richmond garden. Landscape Architect: Preston Dalrymple, Richmond.

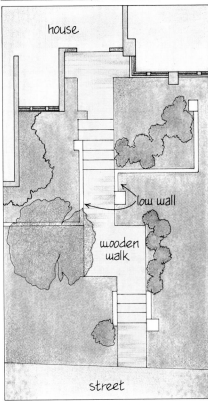

A series of steps and platforms leads down a slope to the front door of this Florida home. Landscape Architect: Tom Wallis, FASLA, Winter Park, Florida.

A Trail
Of Little Hands and Feet

*Concrete stepping pads make a garden path, but with little handprints, they become
a memento of playful days past.*   Photographs: Mary-Gray Hunter

Stepping pads are less expensive than a paved garden path, and in some cases they may be even more appropriate. But the best feature of these stepping pads is that they hold a record of the little hands and feet that have played there.

You can make them one weekend and set them in the garden the next. All you need are some building materials and wet concrete; the kids can do the rest.

Your first step is to construct a form. This one is held together by screws so it can be taken apart to release the pads. Don't nail or glue any of the joints except the lap joint on the 1 x 2 divider. Sheetrock screws are a good

choice because they are longer and more slender than ordinary screws and come with a rust-resistant coating.

Start with ½-inch, exterior-grade plywood. You only need half of a sheet to make a 48- x 48-inch square. Many lumber centers will make this cut for you. Next, cut three 2 x 4's into 48-inch braces. Using 4-penny nails, fasten the braces flat side down to the bottom of the plywood as shown at right.

The plywood will fit into a 1 x 4 frame, so cut two 1 x 4 sides to fit exactly. (They should be 48 inches long, but you may want to hold a board to the edge of the plywood and mark it.) Cut the other two sides 1½ inches longer. The pieces should meet flush at

the corners. Use two screws at each corner to hold adjacent sides of the frame together (see sketch). Always drill a hole for each screw to avoid splitting the wood.

Set the plywood platform on a level surface, and slide the 1 x 4 frame over it. Fasten the frame with one screw at each corner.

To make a divider for the four concrete pads, cut two 48-inch lengths of 1 x 2 lumber. Use a handsaw and wood chisel (or radial arm saw) to cut a lap joint in the center of each piece. Set the pieces in place on top of the plywood, and fasten them to the 1 x 4 frame with screws from the outside (see sketch).

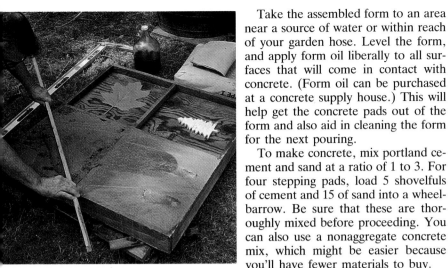

... a scrap piece of lumber as a screed ... smooth and level the concrete paver.

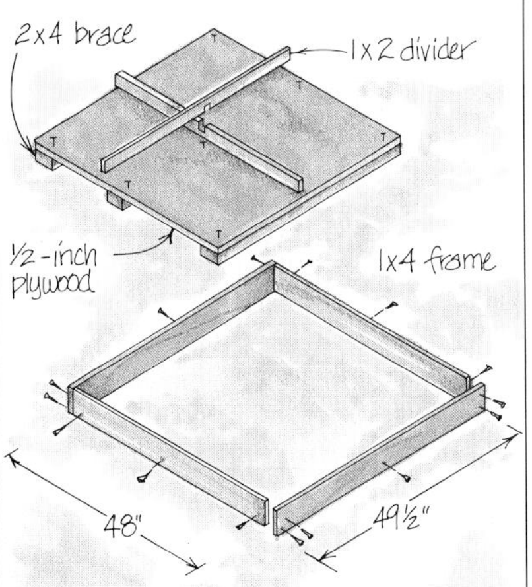

Take the assembled form to an area near a source of water or within reach of your garden hose. Level the form, and apply form oil liberally to all surfaces that will come in contact with concrete. (Form oil can be purchased at a concrete supply house.) This will help get the concrete pads out of the form and also aid in cleaning the form for the next pouring.

To make concrete, mix portland cement and sand at a ratio of 1 to 3. For four stepping pads, load 5 shovelfuls of cement and 15 of sand into a wheelbarrow. Be sure that these are thoroughly mixed before proceeding. You can also use a nonaggregate concrete mix, which might be easier because you'll have fewer materials to buy.

Add water, but the secret is to use only a little, work it in, and then add a little more. That way, you don't add too much. When you are finished, the concrete should be thoroughly wet but thick.

Trowel the concrete into each quadrant of the form, paying particular attention to the corners. Use the corner of your concrete trowel to cut vertically into the wet concrete at the corners and eliminate any air pockets. Get the concrete as smooth as you can using the trowel, and then finish leveling it with a screed (a straight piece of scrap lumber), working it across the form in a side to side motion.

Now the fun begins. Press hands or feet into the concrete, and use a stick to write a name and the date. Other ideas include pressing a leaf into the concrete or putting a wooden inlay in the bottom of the form.

Allow the pads to set up at least three days, spraying them lightly with water each day so that they cure slowly. On the third day, unscrew the edges of the form. Take it apart gently, letting the sides fall away. (You might want to number the sides so you can get them back together again.) Then remove the 1 x 2 dividers.

Let the stepping pads cure at least another two days before setting them in the garden. Rub any rough edges with a brick to smooth them out.

Diagram labels

2x4 brace
1 x 2 divider
½-inch plywood
1x4 frame
48"
49½"

MATERIALS
½-inch, exterior-grade plywood (½ sheet of 4x4)
1x4 (two 48" lengths and two 49½" lengths)
1x2 (two 48" lengths)
2x4 (three 48" lengths)
18 sheetrock screws
9 4-penny nails
portland cement
sand
form oil
water

TOOLS
drill   shovel
screwdriver   wheelbarrow
hand saw   concrete trowel
chisel   screed
level

The fun comes naturally. The wet concrete washes off easily without skin irritation.

Drop by drop, drip irrigation gives plants a deep, even watering.   Photograph: Mary-Gray Hunter

Irrigation–Drop by Drop

During the last couple of summers, most of us have had two choices: either watch our gardens perish in the drought or pay a fortune in water bills. Yet we often waste both water and money through inefficient irrigation.

Traditional sprinkler irrigation systems lose a great deal of water to evaporation. Still more is lost to runoff if water is applied too fast or over-sprayed onto pavement.

Although sprinklers are still perhaps the best way to water lawns, drip irrigation provides an alternative for the rest of the garden. "The whole idea behind drip is to put exactly the amount of water you need exactly where you need it," says Glenn Clonts, Jr., an irrigation specialist with W. P. Law, Inc., in Columbia, South Carolina. With a drip system, small emitters apply water slowly to individual plants. Evaporation is negligible, and runoff is all but eliminated. As a bonus, weed problems are lessened as well, because the spaces between plants aren't watered. "There's no point wasting water on weeds," Clonts says.

The best drip system is one tailor-made to suit each space or type of plant in your garden. "As with any other irrigation system, different areas need to be treated differently. As shrubs and trees mature and their roots get deeper and deeper, they won't need much supplemental water," says Clonts, "but a vegetable garden, for instance, needs water on a regular basis." Designing a custom system can be a big job unless you're familiar with the principles involved and the parts required. Before tackling it, you should get some professional advice.

On a smaller scale, however, you could begin by installing a drip irrigation kit in a small vegetable plot or flowerbed to help you get started thinking "drip." Several manufacturers market kits that contain almost everything you'll need. Most simply hook up to your outdoor water faucet.

Before you begin installation, connect a dual shut-off valve to your faucet. This valve will allow you to leave the drip system hooked to one side and still use the other side for hoses.

Next come the filter, pressure regulator, and backflow preventer or vacuum breaker. If your kit doesn't have all three components in some form, you will need to purchase them.

A filter keeps the minute deposits that exist in tap water from clogging the system. A pressure regulator reduces the pressure of your water after it leaves the tap. Normal water pressure is much greater than the 10 to 20 pounds needed for drip systems and could cause parts to blow out. Many local ordinances require backflow preventers to keep irrigation water from siphoning into home water lines. This is especially important if you're adding fertilizers to the system.

Use the hose fitting included in most kits to connect the polyethylene supply line. Usually, the main line is laid down one side of the garden, and lateral lines are run down each row. Depending on the kit you purchase, you may also have small "spaghetti" tubing that carries the water directly to individual plants. T's, elbows, and end caps, which simply slip into the pipe, are provided.

Emitters actually drip the water onto the soil. They may be installed in the lines or placed at the end of "spaghetti" tubes, again depending on the system you have. Some emitters are factory installed at regular intervals; some you must install yourself. The first system is easier, but the latter gives more flexibility. "Homeowners need to make sure they are buying pressure-compensating emitters," Clonts cautions, "or they may end up with all the water coming out at the beginning of the lines and none at the ends." Some emitters are self-cleaning as well, which makes maintenance easier.

Drip irrigation encourages root growth in a small area, so plants can become very dependent on regular watering. Check your system at least once a week to make sure it's functioning properly. "With a sprinkler system, it's obvious whether it's working right or not. If you don't keep a close eye on your drip system, however, plants can begin to die before you realize there's a problem," Clonts adds. Filters should be inspected several times a year. Open the end caps, and flush all the lines periodically.

For mail-order sources, send a self-addressed, stamped, business-size envelope to Drip Irrigation Editor, *Southern Living,* Box C-119, Birmingham, Alabama 35282.

A small courtyard is a welcome retreat in an urban setting. For Van Tribble, it's like having a little bit of Charleston at his Greenville home. Photographs: Van Chaplin

Bringing the Low Country Home

Van Tribble loves a Charleston courtyard as much as anyone, but he lives in the rolling terrain of the South Carolina Piedmont. So when he dreamed of a garden for his Greenville home, he longed for "a little bit of the Low Country." He called on the landscape architects at Arbor Engineering, Inc., to help make that dream a reality.

His home and business are on separate floors of an older house, which is located on a busy thoroughfare. Because of traffic, the entrances to both the home and business are off an alley that connects parking areas for adjacent businesses. That's where Van wanted his garden.

Landscape Architect J. D. Martin remembers that the design had to serve three purposes. "Because Van's guests and the majority of his clients come to the rear of the house, he wanted to create a gracious entrance there. Secondly, he wanted a good view from

inside his shop. We needed to hide the parking lot and the back of the shop next door. Finally, he was looking for a place to entertain."

Although Van's situation is unique, many people who live in townhouses and condominiums face similar challenges. The trick is to pack a lot of interest into a small space—a courtyard garden proved to be ideal. It offers a cozy, secure feeling as well as an outdoor retreat.

The garden was designed as two rooms. Martin explains that the first room is like an outdoor foyer, a gracious entry to the home. But if you turn and enter the garden, the path narrows and then expands into the second room, a brick terrace where Van and his guests can dine outdoors.

To screen the view from neighboring houses, river birches and tea olives were chosen to grow above the height of the angled brick wall. "We put in

river birch because it grows real fast," Van explains. "Now there's an umbrella of shade out there. It was delightful in the morning; now it's delightful in the afternoon as well."

Both a wall fountain and a small pool keep the city sounds at bay while making the garden feel a little cooler. The pool also serves as a focal point. By day, the arched wall and statue behind it draw visitors for a closer look. At night, lights shine up from the pool onto the statue, making streaks of light with every ripple of water.

The garden is a personal delight to Van. "I enjoy working in the yard, and now I can go out there and not be in the middle of the street or parking lot like I was before. I take my indoor plants out in the summer and put them on the glass porch in the wintertime." In addition to foliage plants, shade-loving caladiums and impatiens are set out for color.

FLOWERS THROUGH THICK AND THIN

When, day after day, the merciless sun stares down from a cloudless sky, a garden needs plants that can tough it out. Here's a collection of colorful annuals that will stick by you in bad times and good.

by STEVE BENDER

Blame last summer's drought on the greenhouse effect. Blame it on the destruction of the rain forests. Blame it on whatever you want. No matter the cause, the drought changed a lot of people's minds about how they garden—or more specifically, about how they water the garden. For when the well runs dry and water restrictions go into effect, only those plants that sip instead of gulp can keep summer gardens looking good.

Because water reserves continue to dwindle as demand increases, it makes sense to select plants that give maximum show for minimum moisture. A good place to start is with your choice of annual bedding plants. You'll be glad to know that many accept heat and drought without batting an eye. Some are old standbys; others are new to the garden scene.

Wax begonia (*Begonia* x *semperflorens-cultorum*) has to be about the most familiar heat- and drought-tolerant annual of all. It's also one of the few that bloom well in both sun and shade. Flowers of red, pink, rose, or white appear continuously above the green or bronze leaves. Some gardeners criticize the tightly rounded, dwarf selections for looking like flowering Ping-Pong balls, but taller, looser growing selections, such as Avalanche, Charm, and Wings, easily surmount this problem.

Anyone who's been gardening for long knows **spider flower** (*Cleome hasslerana*). It reseeds readily, so once you plant it, it'll be with you forever. The flowers may be rose, pink, white, lavender, or purple. The plant can reach 4 feet tall, but if you pinch it back early before it starts blooming, you'll get a shorter, stockier specimen with more blossoms.

Up to now, **narrowleaf zinnia** (*Zinnia linearis*—which is also listed as *Z. angustifolia*) has been a greatly underappreciated annual. But it won't be much longer, if Sara Groves has her way. A garden designer and horticultural consultant in Oxford, Georgia, she's been spreading the word about this zinnia throughout the Southeast. "It's an excellent plant," she states, "that blooms over a very long period. It's heat and drought tolerant and even takes overwatering." Moreover, it never needs spraying for insects and disease. Thanks to its searing, golden-orange flower color, it also makes an effective substitute for many mite- and fungus-prone types of marigolds.

Talk about tough and you're talking about **verbena**. Among the slew of selections, hybrids, and species, two of the better forms for Southerners are rose verbena (*Verbena canadensis*) and

Wax begonias fill these planters with blooms all summer in Houston.

(**Left**) *Most verbenas have prostrate, trailing, or mounding forms. Here rose verbena cascades over a wall in Birmingham.* (**Below**) *Tall stalks of spider flower blend well with perennials and shorter annuals.*
Photographs: Van Chaplin, Mary-Gray Hunter

moss verbena (*V. tenuisecta*). The former features trusses of bright-rose blossoms; the latter has mosslike foliage and violet-blue flowers. Both flourish in heat and drought, as well as the most nutrient-starved soil imaginable. "Verbena grows all along the state roads here," says Ralph Graham, director of landscape operations for Sea Island Properties in Sea Island, Georgia. "Many times, we won't have had a rain for months and there it is blooming."

Lantana (*Lantana* sp.) is another rugged plant you won't lie awake nights worrying about. One of the favorite nectar sources of butterflies and hummingbirds, its flowers may be red, orange, pink, yellow, peach, or lavender. Depending on the species, the growth habit may be mounding or trailing. About the only thing that bothers lantana is whitefly; other than that, it's completely care free. At Monticello in Virginia, the gardeners plant it in a south-facing bed at the foot of a large tree that sucks up moisture by the

You can use narrowleaf zinnia for edging, as a ground cover, or to fill gaps between other plants in a border. Garden design: Edith Eddleman, Durham, North Carolina.

Yellow lantana and mealy-cup sage give a striking show at Thomas Jefferson's Monticello.

it bears golden, star-shaped flowers all summer. The only care it requires is a little pruning in late summer.

Several other ironclad annuals deserve mention. **Globe amaranth** (*Gomphrena globosa*) is extremely drought tolerant. Once it's established, forget about watering. Look for a compact selection named Buddy, which grows 6 inches tall and bears purple, cloverlike blooms. **Madagascar periwinkle** (*Catharanthus roseus*), also known as annual vinca, is "the toughest annual of all," according to Armitage. Its white, pink, or rose blossoms rest atop glossy, deep-green foliage. For blue in the garden, you can't do better than the splendid navy spikes of **Victoria mealy-cup sage** (*Salvia farinacea* Victoria). And Wilkerson sings the praises of **moss rose** (*Portulaca grandiflora*) for the dry Southwest.

Some of the plants discussed here are really half-hardy perennials, rather than true annuals. This means that these particular plants are usually hardy in the Lower and Coastal South, but not the Middle and Upper South. But even where they're hardy, they often decline after several years.

All of these plants need well-drained soil. Except for wax begonia, full sun is the rule. Fertilizer is appreciated but not absolutely required. Lantana, moss rose, and Madagascar periwinkle tolerate salt spray, which is good news for coastal gardeners.

gallon. "That bed isn't covered by our irrigation system, and we have to water by hand," explains Peter Hatch, superintendant of grounds. "So we select low-maintenance plants that will thrive in the dry conditions there."

Drawing rave reviews from test gardens across the South is **melampodium** (*Melampodium paludosum*), a new kid on the block. According to the experts, the only trouble you'll have with it is pronouncing its name. "It's a Gold Medal Winner in our test gardens," says Allan Armitage, professor of horticulture at The University of Georgia in Athens. "It's just dynamite in hot weather," adds Don Wilkerson, Extension floriculturist with the Texas Agricultural Extension Service in College Station. From a distance, melampodium resembles yellow lantana. Growing into an 18-inch mound,

For sources of these plants, send a stamped, self-addressed, business-size envelope to Drought-Tolerant Annuals Editor, *Southern Living*, Box C-119, Birmingham, Alabama 35282.

(**Left**) *A green-and-gold skirt of melampodium decorates an Atlanta mailbox.*
(**Right**) *Buddy, a compact selection of globe amaranth, has purple, cloverlike blooms.*

LETTERS

TO OUR GARDEN EDITORS

Iris: The leaves, stems, and rhizomes of my irises have been rotting. What is the cause, and what can I do to save these plants? *R. M. S., Cheverly, Maryland.*
Your trouble is probably caused by the iris borer. This large caterpillar bores into iris rhizomes, providing easy access for fungi that cause rot. To control this pest, spray the new foliage in spring with Cygon or lindane according to label directions. Also rake up and destroy any dead iris leaves left from last winter, as they will often harbor borer eggs.

Oleander: Something strange is happening to my oleander. Bunches of new shoots appear in spring just below the branch tips. Then the shoots turn brown and die. Please recommend a solution. *W. U., Pontotoc, Mississippi.*
Oleander is usually a lovely, care-free shrub, but occasionally it is attacked by fungi. In the case of your plant, a fungus is causing a peculiar condition called witch's broom. Unfortunately, there is nothing you can spray to cure the problem. The best answer is to prune out the witch's broom, cutting 6 inches below it on the stem. Be sure that you sterilize your pruning shears after each cut by dipping them in rubbing alcohol.

Southern magnolia: I planted three Southern magnolias last spring. All three did well through summer and winter, but this spring, they lost many of their leaves. Only a few small leaves from last summer's growth now remain. Do you think I am going to lose my trees? *J. W. B., Woodville, Virginia.*
Southern magnolias (*Magnolia grandiflora*) normally drop some leaves in spring and, indeed, throughout the year. But we suspect that your trees are reacting to last winter's cold. These broadleaf evergreens will grow in your part of the Upper South, but sometimes severe winters defoliate them. There is little you can do to prevent this, except to plant in protected locations out of strong winter sun and wind. If the leafbuds on your trees still appear green and healthy, the plants will probably begin to leaf out very shortly.

Crabapple: About five years ago, I planted a purple-leaved crabapple in my backyard. It appears healthy, but it's barely 5 feet tall. How can I make it grow faster? *D. M., Bessemer City, North Carolina.*
You probably have a crabapple selection called Royalty, which is noted for its purple foliage and moderate growth rate. Yours is growing a little slowly. To grow its best, the tree needs full sun and fertile, well-drained soil. If your soil is poor, try feeding the crabapple this fall after it has gone dormant by spreading 5 pounds of 10-10-10 fertilizer around its dripline.

There are a couple of other things you might check. First, make sure the tree isn't growing on top of buried stones or concrete. Second, inspect the base of the tree to see if the bark has been damaged by a lawnmower or chewing rodents. Applying a plastic tree guard around the base of the trunk will prevent injury to the bark.

Japanese persimmon: In May, all the fruit on my Japanese persimmon dropped for no apparent reason. What might be the cause? *E. T. W., Monroe, Louisiana.*
Overfertilization often causes Japanese persimmons to prematurely drop their fruit. The primary culprit is excess nitrogen. If you are feeding with a fertilizer containing 10% or more of nitrogen (such as 10-10-10), switch to 5-10-5. If the annual growth in the terminal branches is 10 inches or more, stop feeding altogether.

Bulbs: Given my first shot at flower gardening last year, I planted nothing but spring bulbs in a small garden bed. The garden was lovely in early spring but now contains only unsightly foliage. What would you suggest I do? *E. T., Petersburg, Virginia.*
The problem you describe is one that many novice gardeners face when they devote an area entirely to spring bulbs. One thing you might consider is planting annual bedding plants, such as Madagascar periwinkle, marigolds, wax begonias, or salvia, in the garden as soon as the bulbs' foliage dies down. Then in fall, replace these flowers with pansies, which will bloom in autumn, go dormant in winter, and bloom again the following spring. Your spring bulbs will come up right through the pansies, and the pansies will help disguise the bulbs' foliage. When the weather gets too warm for the pansies in late May or June, replace them with warm-weather annuals. This way, you can have a colorful garden nearly year-round.

Snakes: Do you know of anything that will keep blacksnakes off our property? A friend said that putting lye or sulphur along the boundaries will keep snakes from crossing. *B. P., Darlington, South Carolina.*
We've never heard of lye or sulphur repelling snakes. The question you really need to ask is why these reptiles are attracted to your property in the first place. They're probably looking for food—most likely rodents, including rats and mice. Rodents need cover, such as tall grass, weeds, and thick brush, in which to hide. If you eliminate the cover, the rodents will go elsewhere, and so will the snakes. Resist the impulse to kill the snakes. The vast majority are harmless to people and do an excellent job controlling the rodent population.

TIP OF THE MONTH

When planting caladium bulbs in heavy clay soil, fill the holes with potting soil or vermiculite. Not only will the bulbs flourish but they will also be easier to find and dig up in the fall because of the different soil color and texture. *Charlene C. Papale, Covington, Louisiana.*

Editor's note: We'd like to have your ideas—the ones that have worked for you. We're especially interested in vegetables, houseplants, shrubs, trees, and garden care. For each tip that is published, we will pay $10 and send you one of our garden books.

Submit as many ideas as you wish, but each must be on a separate sheet or card, along with your name, address, and telephone number. We may need to edit the tips, and none will be acknowledged or returned. Send to Gardening Tips, *Southern Living*, Box 523, Birmingham, Alabama 35201.

CHECKLIST
For May

☐ **Bedding plants**—Set out transplants of bedding plants now for a summer full of color. Garden centers are well stocked, so buy early for the best selection. Choose annuals that will perform well in your particular garden situation. If you have full sun, plant verbena, Madagascar periwinkle, ageratum, marigolds, zinnias, petunias, celosia, or wax begonias. (In Florida, however, ageratum and zinnias are recommended for spring rather than summer.) In shaded beds, plant impatiens, caladiums, and coleus. If you have a northern or eastern exposure that gets only partial sun or if you live in one of the cooler regions of the South, some of the early-flowering annuals, such as sweet alyssum, lobelia, and annual dianthus, will continue all summer.

☐ **Bees**—The common honeybee pollinates the majority of fruits and vegetables, so be careful when applying insecticides poisonous to them. Carbaryl, Diazinon, and malathion are just a few that pose a risk. Apply these chemicals late in the afternoon when bees are less active. Also use sprays instead of dusts, as the bees are more likely to pick up the dusts.

☐ **Chrysanthemums**—Set out new plants in late spring or root cuttings from the new growth of your old plants. If last year's plants showed no signs of disease, dig the old clumps, divide, and reset in well-prepared soil. As plants become established, begin pinching out terminal buds every 10 days to promote branching and increase flower production.

☐ **Cut flowers**—If you're interested in growing flowers to use for indoor arrangements, choose selections with long-lasting blooms and strong stems. Try gladioli, zinnias, roses, baby's-breath, pinks, daisies, purple salvia, black-eyed Susans, tiger lilies, or strawflowers. Early morning is the best time to cut garden flowers; that's when blooms are freshest. Carry a pail of water into the garden, and put the stems in water the moment they are cut. Once indoors, snip the ends of the stems again as you arrange them, and add a floral preservative to the water to lengthen the life of the arrangement.

☐ **Fertilizer**—You may have noticed little beads in the soil of plants bought at a nursery. These are slow-release fertilizers. Unlike other fertilizer pellets, these have been coated so that they release nutrients slowly, giving plants a steady supply throughout the growing season. In addition to saving labor in nurseries, slow-release pellets are also ideal for the busy gardener. When planting, include slow-release fertilizer in the soil, not just on top. After the pellets have had time to dissolve, you can apply more to the soil surface.

☐ **Junipers**—Bagworms are some of junipers' worst pests. These tiny caterpillars live in bags made from the juniper's needles. They come out to feed on the plants at night. Bagworms are easiest to kill in early summer because they are still small; spray or dust the plants with Dipel or Thuricide. Mites are another serious pest. The tiny, spiderlike mites feed under and between the needles. Infested branches turn pale green and eventually brown as the mites increase. To control, spray the plants with insecticidal soap at the first sign of infestation.

☐ **Ornamental vegetables**—Flower enthusiasts may be pleased to find that inexpensive, fast-growing vegetable plants may be just what they need in a flower border. Squash plants have coarse-textured foliage and big yellow flowers. Be sure to choose a bush type rather than a vining one that runs over the garden. Zucchini plants have silver mottling on the leaves that can be particularly attractive. Although squash plants will not last all summer, you can plant seeds again and have a replacement in only a few weeks. Swiss chard also offers a lot of color and lasts all summer. Unlike other plants, it's not the flowers or the leaves that give the color; it's the midrib of the leaves. Vulcan is a selection with red veins, Lucullus Light Green offers contrast to darker-green foliage, and Swiss Chard of Geneva brings white veins with deep-green leaves. Curly leaved parsley is lovely and low growing in the front of the border. During cool months, lettuce offers quick color, varying from lime green to red, depending upon the selection. Use caution if you plan to harvest any of these edibles from your flower border. Many pesticides approved for use on ornamentals should not be used on vegetables—read the label carefully before you apply.

☐ **Screening**—As the summerlike weather allows us to spend time outdoors, the need for privacy screening becomes evident. Walls and fences produce an immediate effect, but their cost is relatively high. A planted screen or hedge may be less expensive, but it could take years for some selections to fill out completely and will take up much more room than a fence. A third alternative is to grow vines on a framework of wood and wire. This combination won't require a lot of space, and many vines grow quite rapidly. Check with your local Extension office for selections recommended in your part of the state.

☐ **Slugs**—These slimy little creatures are a menace to bedding plants and young vegetables during warm, wet weather. They climb on plants during the night, often stripping whole stems of leaves. You can control slugs with a metaldehyde slug bait scattered around the base of victimized plants. However, metaldehyde is toxic and should be used with caution if children, pets, and wildlife visit the garden. Another way to deal with slugs is to trap them. They will congregate under cantaloupe rinds turned upside down in the garden. They are also attracted to beer. Set a shallow pan of beer in the garden, or sink a margarine tub or other container into the ground near the plants so its rim is at ground level. Fill with at least an inch of beer. In the morning, you can dispose of drowned slugs.

☐ **Spider flower**—This is a good month for direct seeding spider flower (cleome) in your garden. Sprinkle seeds lightly on a well-prepared seedbed. Then rake the soil gently. If the seedbed is kept moist, germination will occur in about two weeks. Once the true leaves are present, thin the seedlings to about 10 inches apart. Remember, spider flower plants are generally 3 to 4 feet tall by midsummer, so plant them as a background to other flowers. The seeds are usually available in mixed colors, ranging from white to pink.

☐ **Staking**—Use stakes to support tall flowers, such as lilies, dahlias, and gladioli, so they will not bend and break in storms. In the vegetable garden, tomatoes are usually staked or caged to keep ripening fruit off the ground. When you tie plants to their supports, use nylon hosiery, twist ties made of covered wire, or other soft material. Never bind the stem to the support; attach it loosely to allow the stem to grow and bend. If you live in an area with a prevailing wind, place the stake so that the plant can lean against it.

☐ **Storing seeds**—Flower and vegetable seeds left exposed to humidity and warm temperatures will lose their viability. Instead, store them in an airtight container, and place in the freezer or refrigerator. To be sure the seeds stay dry, add a tablespoon of powdered milk or silica gel to each container.

☐ **Watering**—As the days get hotter, newly planted trees and shrubs will be under stress. You need to water each week that it doesn't rain, and water deeply to encourage deep rooting. Sprinkling the surface of the soil will do more harm than good, training young roots to find their water in the top 2 inches of soil. Then when you fail to water, they dry out. New plants should have a collar of soil 1 to 2 feet away from the trunk. Water until this collar holds a puddle. Let it seep slowly into the soil, and repeat two to three times. If your soil is sandy, it may never form a puddle. However, you will have to water well and twice as often until plants become established.

A 3-inch mulch of shredded leaves or pine straw will help retain moisture and keep soil temperatures cooler. In addition, it will reduce the number of weeds competing for water.

SPECIAL TIPS FOR THE SOUTHEAST

☐ **Raspberries**—Pruning will prevent your raspberry patch from becoming a mass of thorny canes. Remove all but the heaviest five or six shoots on each plant; these will bear fruit next year. Remove year-old canes this summer after they have fruited. Limit the width of a row to 2½ to 3 feet. You can dig up suckers that have strayed too far and transplant them to begin new rows.

☐ **Vegetables**—Gardeners in the Upper South can start planting warm-weather vegetables as soon as the danger of frost has passed. These include snap beans, tomatoes, corn, peppers, squash, and cucumbers. Gardeners in all areas should try to make the most of their garden space by replanting as soon as a crop is harvested. For example, in the Middle South, lettuce and spinach are beginning to bolt. Pull these out, and plant bush beans in their place. It takes some planning to have the seeds on hand, but your forethought will pay off.

SPECIAL TIPS FOR FLORIDA

☐ **Lawn**—Adjust the height of your mower so the lawn is cut at the proper height. Mowing too short invites weeds and makes the lawn more apt to die during hot, dry weather. Mow Bitterblue St. Augustine at 2½ to 3 inches and newer varieties, such as Floratam and Floralawn, at 1½ to 2½ inches. Cut centipede at 1½ to 2 inches, Bahia at 1½ to 2½ inches, Zoysia at 1 to 2 inches.

☐ **Vegetables**—There are a few vegetables you can plant now that don't mind the heat and humidity. These include cherry tomatoes, New Zealand spinach, okra, and eggplant. They will continue fruiting through fall until nighttime temperatures cool to the 50's. Tried-and-true varieties of cherry tomatoes include Patio, Florida Lanai, Florida Petite, Florida Basket, and Cherry. You can choose nearly any variety of okra, but those recommended by the University of Florida include Clemson Spineless, Perkins Long Pod, Emerald, and Blondy. Successful eggplant varieties include Black Beauty, Dusky, Ichiban, Florida Market, and Long Tom.

SPECIAL TIPS FOR TEXAS

☐ **Sesame**—This easy-to-grow herb thrives during hot Texas weather. Sesame reaches 3 feet in height, producing white bell-shaped flowers and large quantities of seeds. Sow sesame in a sunny area of well-drained soil. When seedlings are 2 to 3 inches tall, thin to 12 inches apart. Throughout the growing season, water only when soil becomes dry to the touch. Begin harvesting when the lower seedpods have ripened but the upper ones are still green. Cut off the entire stalk, and place in a paper bag. As the seeds become completely dry, they will fall out of the pods into the bag.

☐ **Vegetables**—When soil temperatures climb above 65 degrees, it's time to plant okra, Southern peas, and sweet potatoes. Choose a sunny spot with well-drained soil. Keep okra to the north end of the garden so it won't shade lower growing plants. Recommended okra selections include Clemson Spineless, Emerald, Burgundy, and Lee. Among Southern peas, try Blackeye No. 5, Purple Hull, Mississippi Silver, and Cream. Puerto Rico is a compact selection of sweet potato; Centennial is a good choice for larger gardens.

IRON DEFICIENCY

If plants can't obtain sufficient iron, they can't produce chlorophyll. As a result, their leaves begin to turn yellow. This condition, known as chlorosis, may be caused by various factors, but iron deficiency is the most common.

Symptoms first appear on new growth. New leaves will be small, and plants may become stunted. In the early stages, the veins of leaves remain green, but in severe cases, they turn yellow as well. Leaves may even turn white and eventually die.

Azaleas, camellias, gardenias, hollies, and other acid-loving plants are most likely to be affected. When the

Yellow leaves and green leaf veins indicate chlorosis, a condition most often caused by iron deficiency.
Photograph: Mary-Gray Hunter

soil is alkaline, as it is in regions with limestone, most of the iron is in a form that plants can't absorb.

To alleviate chlorosis, liquid iron can be sprayed directly onto the leaves of affected plants for quick but short-lived results. For a long-term solution, apply a soil acidifier, such as sulfur or ferrous sulfate, to lower the pH and make existing iron more acid. Chelated iron, which can be absorbed even in alkaline soils, may also be added. Follow all label directions carefully when applying soil amendments or fertilizers.

Your local office of the Agricultural Extension Service can give you valuable information on kits and soil tests.

June

fountain

lawn

brick
edging

IMPATIENS: FIT FOR SHADE

by LOIS B. TRIGG

Familiar yet treasured, impatiens have long been a first choice for shade. Today's plants sport some new looks.

In shaded neighborhoods all over the South, impatiens are a friendly and familiar flower. Proof that there is strength in numbers, these annuals bloom profusely and tirelessly from spring until frost. Their flowers range from a fluorescent-like luster to pastel tints, offering as many colors as any flower for full sun—and probably more uses. A single plant fills a pot or hanging basket for a spot of color on a shady terrace or porch. In mass, impatiens blanket a flowerbed like ground cover. They also mix graciously with ferns, caladiums, and other shade lovers. If left on their own in a wooded setting, impatiens often act like wildflowers, coming back from seed every spring. However, the new flowers will be different colors—the lineage of the ones originally planted.

You see, all impatiens, or sultanas as they are sometimes called, are hybrid descendants of the wild ones introduced from their native Africa. These first plants had blossoms below the leaves instead of above them. In fact,

until the mid-1950's, impatiens were primarily houseplants grown as much for their glossy leaves as their flowers. Then the first garden hybrids appeared. We've been enjoying new selections ever since.

WHAT'S THE LATEST?

Truly short ones. Have you ever bought impatiens with a tag stating they'd get 12 inches tall, then three months later discovered they actually grew to twice that size? They might grow only 12 inches tall up North or in California but not in the South, where warm nights encourage more growth. Now, a new series of selections called Minis keeps our climate in mind. They grow about a foot tall and stay there.

The Super Elfins, another new

(**Above**)*A border of flower-laden impatiens colors and unites the edges of this lawn and pool deck.* (**Right**) *Sweeping through the garden, this mass of impatiens works like a ground cover, one more colorful than most.* Photographs: Van Chaplin, Mary-Gray Hunter

(Left) *Because of their large flowers and upright, bushy form, New Guinea hybrids are well suited for pots.* **(Right)** *Soft-pink impatiens cascade gently, forming a pleasant contrast with the surrounding angular architecture.*

group, are dwarf versions of the old but ever-popular Elfins. These plants grow to about 14 inches in the South. They are very full and spill nicely over the edge of a pot.

Different ones from New Guinea. In 1970, plant explorers from the USDA and Longwood Gardens in Pennsylvania discovered a different type of impatiens while on an expedition to New Guinea. These have bigger flowers and more colorful leaves than the popular sultana types—many with red or variegated foliage. Not surprisingly, they tolerate more sun so they are especially welcome in the South.

New Guinea hybrids may still be hard to find locally but are likely to be more available in the future. Look for them in the same colors as sultana types but with leaves that are plum colored, green, or variegated. They range from 18 to 26 inches tall.

STILL TIME TO PLANT

Many of us planted impatiens in March or April, when transplants first appeared in nurseries. However, it's still not too late. You can set out transplants now everywhere except South Florida, where impatiens are grown in fall and winter. If you can't find transplants, you can start most impatiens from seed. The exceptions are the New Guinea types. Only two of them—Tango and Sweet Sue—are available from seed. Most New Guinea impa-

tiens are patented and can't be propagated without permission. Look for them in local nurseries.

Contrary to their reputation of being difficult to germinate, impatiens seeds sprout quickly if you do things right. As tiny as ground black pepper, the seeds need light to germinate, so never cover. Instead, pat them gently into contact with the soil. Keep the seeds moist so they don't dry out; seedlings will sprout in a week or 10 days at a temperature between 70 and 75 de-

Tango is a bright-orange New Guinea hybrid that can be started from seed.

grees. Transfer the seedlings to small pots. When they are about 3 inches tall, you can set them in the garden.

GIVE THEM WATER AND A PEEK AT THE SUN

Ron Adams, Technical Services Manager at Ball Seed Company, shares the following tips for keeping impatiens at their best.

■ Water regularly. In hot weather, plants may need watering every day. Leaves may droop during the hottest part of the day, but plants perk up in the afternoon.

■ Give them some sun. About two hours of sunlight (morning sun) per day helps keep sultana types low and blooming profusely. Plants growing in full shade and with plenty of water may get twice as tall as the same variety that gets a couple of hours of sun per day and less water. Keep this in mind when you choose your selections and planting locations—a 16-inch plant in shade getting plenty of water might be nearly 3 feet tall by late summer. New Guinea types do best with a half-day of sun, preferably in morning.

■ Don't overfeed. Too much fertilizer encourages lots of leaves and not enough flowers. Fertilize once at planting time and again only if the leaves start to turn light green. New Guinea types need a tablespoon of slow-release fertilizer once per month per plant to keep the leaves colorful.

Staggered layers of sandstone stop erosion on this steep slope.

(Left) The lush, coarse foliage of staghorn ferns adds a tropical touch to this Florida garden. (Right) These young ferns are growing in a wire pocket filled with damp sphagnum moss attached to a wooden plaque.

Stunning Staghorn Ferns

Whether growing outside in the gardens of the Coastal South or adorning well-lit indoor spots farther north, staghorn ferns always command attention. Their lush growth and coarse texture add a tropical feeling to any setting.

One look at their extraordinary antler-like foliage explains why the botanical name of the genus is Platycerium, which literally means "broad horn." In addition to these fertile, spore-producing leaves, however, staghorns also have sterile fan-shaped leaves at their base, which collect moisture and nutrients.

Like most other plants, staghorns grow best under conditions that imitate their natural environment. Native to the humid Australian tropics, staghorns are epiphytes, attaching themselves to the bark of trees and living on the leaf mold and water they catch there. For this reason, they flourish when grown in sphagnum moss attached to a piece of wood.

Although staghorn ferns can be grown successfully in conventional containers, it's simple to devise a more naturalistic home for these stately plants. First select an appropriate wooden support. Any piece of wood will do, but sculptural driftwood, a cypress knee, or a carved plaque will add

interest. If there's no natural hollow for the plant to rest in, you can chisel an indentation into the wood, or staple a chicken wire "pocket" to the board. Wrap the root ball of your staghorn with enough damp sphagnum moss to fill the hollow or pocket. Then insert the ball, and attach it firmly with wire or nylon string.

An essential factor to success with staghorn ferns is perfect drainage, but this shouldn't be a problem if your plant is growing on a wooden support. Always water thoroughly and never allow the sphagnum moss around the root ball to dry out completely. Staghorns need good light, but shade them from direct sun. Because they come from the tropics, they appreciate frequent misting. The barren back leaves, which are green at first and later turn brown, should not be removed until they show signs of decay and are ready to fall off naturally.

Most staghorns can be propagated from spores, but that's a technique best left to experts. Home gardeners can simply remove the rooted offsets that develop at the base of the plants. Cut the plantlets away carefully with a sharp knife, and replant as directed. Cover the new fern for a few days with plastic to ensure high humidity until it's over the shock of transplanting.

Hackett, Arkansas, is a small town near the Oklahoma border that is known for the beautiful brown sandstone quarried there. The stone has a unique quality that makes it invaluable for landscape construction. "It isn't cut like a lot of stone, yet it breaks out in strips of very uniform thickness and width," says Landscape Architect Jim Culberson of Creative Landscapes in Little Rock. "Because the stones are so regular, you can stack them on very steep surfaces," he says. For that reason, Culberson finds them ideal for tackling the difficult slope problems he frequently faces, especially in areas of the city where high bluffs rise sharply from the Arkansas River.

Here, Culberson designed a dry-laid Hackett stone retaining wall to prevent erosion on a slope that resulted when the homesite was graded. "You just lay the stones parallel to the contours of the slope," he explains, "then place successive layers so that the joints are staggered like bricks." Culberson kept the front surface of each layer even by filling or excavating behind the stones as necessary to make them fit.

To add extra interest, Culberson created planting pockets in the wall. A number of stones in selected areas were simply left out, then one long stone was placed over the top of each gap. "The long stones work the same way as a lintel over a door or window," he says. Junipers are his favorite choice for the planting pockets because their fine texture contrasts so well with the rough stone. But he adds, "Phlox and Carolina jessamine also work well, and they give you color in the springtime."

Pots brimming with petunias and verbena stand atop brick pedestals.

ONE GARDEN, MANY MOODS

This New Orleans garden is made up of several outdoor rooms. Sunny or shaded, large or small, each has its own purpose and personality.

by RITA W. STRICKLAND / photography VAN CHAPLIN

Changes in light and shadow give each garden space a different feeling.

Just as a house is made up of individual rooms, Carl and Peggy Gulotta's garden is composed of separate spaces, each with its own distinct character. Together they turn the lot into an open-air extension of the home. "It isn't a big lot, but the spaces are so well designed I've entertained 150 people out here," Peggy says.

An old plum tree keeps the lower terrace cool and shady during the hot summer. "We were going to take that plum tree out," says Landscape Architect Fritz Von Ostoff, "but Dr. Gulotta suggested we taste the fruit first. One bite did it. The plum tree stayed."

Two brick steps connect this area with the larger garden above. Originally, the lot sloped upward slightly, so the steps were designed to emphasize this difference in elevation. "One foot in New Orleans can have as much impact as three feet in other cities," says Von Ostoff.

Featured in the upper garden is a vine-covered pergola. Its elegant white columns are a striking contrast to the wild tangle of wisteria that grows on the arbor's rustic beams. The floor of the pergola is slate, edged with old brick; a dining table, chairs, and tea-cart are permanent furnishings. "We use this spot for meals when we have company," Peggy says.

Farther on, there's a raised pool that's home to water lilies and colorful fish. Because the garden winds around the corner of the Gulottas' house, this pool is the focal point of the view from either direction. The sound of gently splashing water makes even the hottest days seem cooler. A big open space to the left of the pool is the center of

This pergola makes a delightful, sheltered outdoor room.

activity when the Gulottas entertain.

Beyond this bright, sunny area, there's a small, quiet courtyard decorated with statues depicting the four seasons. These sculptures seem to underline the pleasant fact that in New Orleans, the outdoors is meant to be enjoyed year-round. Holly ferns, Japanese ardisia, and other shade-loving plants give the courtyard a lush, tropical feeling.

A high brick wall had enclosed the original garden but was almost hidden by several huge camellias. Von Ostoff wanted to preserve the camellias and also call attention to the old wall, so he designed several low pedestals to accent the brick edging used throughout. These pedestals echo the materials and color of the wall and the design of its piers. "Because they pick up these details, the pedestals make you more conscious of the wall in the background," he says. Each one holds a huge pot of bright flowers that are Peggy's special joy.

"She wanted a backdrop against which to display these annuals," explains Von Ostoff. For that reason, most of the plants in the garden are evergreen. In addition to the existing camellias, there are low-growing azaleas, hollies, cape jasmine, dwarf gardenias, and ground covers.

Seen through the garden gate, a plum tree provides both shade and delicious fruit.

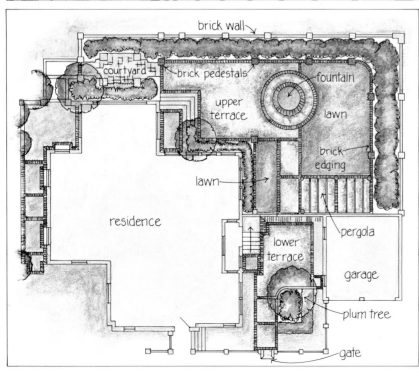

Pruning Climbing Roses

Wonder why your climbing rose didn't bloom this year? There may be several reasons, but chances are you didn't prune it properly. Here are some guidelines to help you have a beautiful plant next year.

Most climbing roses fall into one of two categories: large-flowered climbers or ramblers. **Large-flowered climbers** have a hybrid tea, grandiflora, or floribunda rose grafted onto a climbing understock. They bloom throughout the summer primarily on shoots that are 2 years old. When you plant a new large-flowered climber, it will look like any other rose. Shortly, however, it will send out long, arching canes that will not bloom the first year. *It is important not to prune these canes back for at least the first two years.* If you do, you won't get any flowers. Train the canes to a trellis or fence, using twist ties or strips of nylon hose.

After the first bloom period, it's

time to begin regular maintenance (see Pruning a Large-Flowered Climber). June is a good month to do this. First, remove weak or dead shoots. Then cut the stems that flowered back to two or three leafbuds. These stems will send out new growth, which will bloom next year. If any of the main canes have become woody and unproductive, cut them off at the base. This encourages the formation of new, vigorous canes, which you can distinguish by their bright-green color. Finally, should any suckers rise from below the graft union (the notch near the base of the plant), prune them off immediately.

Ramblers are not usually grafted, so you don't have to worry about basal suckers. They bloom heavily in spring on growth made the previous year. When you plant a new rambler, select the three strongest canes, train them to a fence or trellis, and remove the others. Following the next spring's bloom, remove any canes that flowered, and select three more young canes to take their place (see Pruning a Rambler). May and early June are good months to prune.

(**Right**) *To prune a large-flowered climber, remove weak or dead shoots (see A); cut stems that flowered back to two or three leafbuds (see B); remove old, woody canes (see C); remove suckers from below the graft (see D); allow a few young canes to grow every year (see E).* (**Below**) *After a rambler finishes blooming in spring, remove the canes that flowered, and allow new canes to grow from the base.*

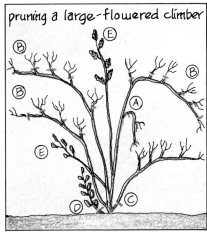

pruning a large-flowered climber

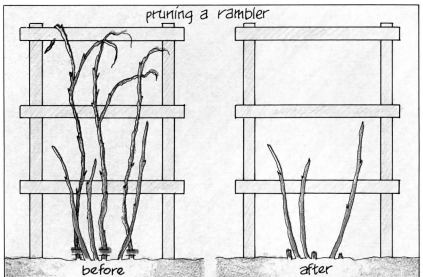

pruning a rambler

before   after

Letters to Our Garden Editors

Red maple seed: I would like to grow a red maple from seed. Can you tell me when to collect the seeds and how to plant? *W. J. B., Birmingham, Alabama.*
Collect the ripened seeds of red maple (*Acer rubrum*) in early summer. You'll know they're ripe when they turn red or reddish brown. Soak them in water for two days; then plant 1 inch deep.

Morning glories: This spring, I planted seed for five groupings of big, blue morning glories. Of the five, only one has large, blue blooms. Why didn't I get the flowers I wanted? *J. W., Murfreesboro, Tennessee.*
The seed company may have mixed up your seed. Or, perhaps you saved seed produced by hybrid plants from the previous year. Second-generation seed usually doesn't come true; the flower color of morning glories grown from it often reverts to the color of one of the parents. The only way to guarantee a color is to plant new hybrid seed each year.

Azaleas: Can you tell me how to start new azalea bushes? *C. L., Gallagher, West Virginia.*
The easiest way to propagate most azaleas is by layering. Simply bend a lower branch to the ground, weight it down, and cover the stem, but not the leaves, with soil. In six to eight months, the branch will have rooted and you can separate it from the mother plant.

You can also root cuttings. Take tip cuttings about 3 to 4 inches long in June and July. Dust the cut ends with rooting powder, then stick them in moist potting soil. Keep the soil moist and the plants out of direct sun. They should root in 8 to 10 weeks.

Leaf rollers: Leaf rollers nearly destroyed my cannas last year. Please tell me how to control them. *V. G. O., Austin, Texas.*
Spraying with either *Bacillus thuringiensis* or carbaryl, according to label directions, should take care of this problem. Begin spraying when the leaves unfurl, and spray once a week while the leaf rollers are present.

LETTERS

UPPER SOUTH
MIDDLE SOUTH
LOWER SOUTH
COASTAL SOUTH

TO OUR GARDEN EDITORS

Fuchsia: I live on the Gulf Coast and recently bought a fuchsia plant. A friend told me that it will die in hot weather. Is there anything I can do to stop this from happening? *C. T., Long Beach, Mississippi.*
We're afraid your friend is essentially correct. Common fuchsias don't like the South's hot, humid summers and often drop their flowers. In extreme heat, they may die. Try keeping your fuchsia in a pot or hanging basket in the shade. During the summer, give it plenty of water. It will likely look its best during spring and fall.

Cherry laurel: In return for the seeds from my feeder, the birds leave me cherry laurels. I'd like to know more about this plant, such as size and growth rate. *R. L., Kenner, Louisiana.*
Your plants are most likely Carolina cherry laurels (*Prunus caroliniana*). They quickly grow to be small, evergreen trees about 20 to 30 feet high. Small, white flowers appear in March and April, followed by black fruits that the birds favor. Carolina cherry laurel grows in sun or shade, tolerates heavy pruning, and will grow in most well-drained soils.

Banana shrub: I recently moved from Louisiana to Texas and miss my banana shrub and sweet olive. Will they grow here? *E. R., Robert Lee, Texas.*
To grow either banana shrub (*Michelia figo*) or sweet olive (*Osmanthus fragrans*) in your area of Central Texas, you'll need to do something about your alkaline soil because both plants like acid soil. We suggest you dig a large hole about 2 feet deep and wide for each one. Discard the original soil, and backfill with a half-and-half mixture of sphagnum peat moss and topsoil. Sprinkle a few handfuls of garden sul-

fur around the base of each plant in spring to help keep the soil acid. With the soils amended, the plants should do just fine.

Cascading shrubs: I'm looking for shrubs to cascade down a steep bank that is difficult to mow. Would some form of jasmine be a good choice? *S. S., Sharon, South Carolina.*
It would, as long as you choose the proper species. Gardeners in the Lower and Coastal South should consider showy jasmine (*Jasminum floridum*), an evergreen shrub that grows 3 to 4 feet high and spreads even wider. It bears small, yellow flowers for several months, beginning in April, but the floral display is never spectacular. Gardeners in the Upper and Middle South should choose the hardier winter jasmine (*J. nudiflorum*). Although it's deciduous, its green stems make it ap-

Showy jasmine bears yellow, star-shaped flowers for several months each year.
Photograph: Mary-Gray Hunter

pear evergreen. The bright-yellow flowers, which appear from January to March, are quite a bit showier than those of the misnamed showy jasmine. Both shrubs take full sun or part shade and grow in just about any well-drained soil.

Abelia: I have several abelia shrubs in my yard. I would like a few more, but none of the nurseries in my area have them. Can cuttings of this shrub be rooted? *J. K. C., Kenbridge, Virginia.*

Yes, you'll need to take tip cuttings about 3 inches long in summer or fall. Strip away the lower leaves of each cutting, then dip the cut end in rooting powder. Stick the cuttings in moist potting soil out of direct sun. They should root in several weeks. Glossy abelia (*Abelia* x *grandiflora*) is one of the longest blooming shrubs around, flowering from spring until fall.

Hibiscus: I have a beautiful hibiscus plant that I set outside this spring. It has healthy green leaves but hasn't bloomed. What is wrong? *M. B., Hartford, Kentucky.*
Chinese hibiscus (*Hibiscus rosa-sinensis*) blooms best in the long, hot days of summer. Place yours in full sun, and give it plenty of water. Make sure the container drains freely. Feed monthly during periods of active growth with water-soluble 20-20-20 fertilizer.

Daylilies: Help! My daylilies are in bloom, but the foliage is dying from the bottom. Can you tell me why? *J. R. D., Nashville, Tennessee.*
The problem with your daylilies seems to occur most frequently on plants grown in full sun. However, the underlying cause is as yet unknown. You might try moving your plants to partial shade. And be sure to pick off and destroy any browning leaves.

TIP OF THE MONTH

Here's an easy way to get two heads of cabbage from one plant. When you cut the first head, leave the large leaves closest to the ground intact. In about a week, you'll notice several small heads forming in a circle around the stem of the plant. Wait a few days, then remove all but the largest little head. This second head won't grow quite as large as the first, but will be just as tasty. *Marcella White, Lake Worth, Florida.*
Editor's note: We'd like to have your ideas—the ones that have worked for you. We're especially interested in vegetables, houseplants, shrubs, trees, and garden care. For each tip that is published, we will pay $10 and send you one of our garden books.

Submit as many ideas as you wish, but each must be on a separate sheet or card, along with your name, address, and telephone number. We may need to edit the tips, and none will be acknowledged or returned. Send to Gardening Tips, *Southern Living,* Box 523, Birmingham, Alabama 35201.

Squash Vine Borers

Squash vine borers feed inside the stem.
Photograph: Mary-Gray Hunter

Every year, squash vine borers invade gardens, causing squash plants to wilt and die. The culprit is a white caterpillar about 1 inch long, with a stocky, accordion-like body and a brown head. It feeds inside the stem, cutting off the supply of food and water to the rest of the plant.

The most effective way to deal with this problem is prevention. First, check plants regularly for tiny, oval-shaped borer eggs. They are mahogany colored, shiny, and slightly flat and are usually found on the stem, but may be on any part of the plant. Look closely; eggs may appear to be specks of dirt. Simply crush any that you find.

Secondly, when plants have developed three to four leaves, begin regular applications of a pesticide containing malathion, endosulfan, or methoxychlor. Apply pesticides thoroughly, especially to the base of the stem where most eggs are laid. After plants begin to bloom, spray only in the late afternoon, when bees are less active. The pollination of squash and many other crops depends on bees.

If your squash plants have already been attacked, split the infested stems with a knife and destroy the borers. A yellow excrement will indicate their approximate location. Cover the split stem with dirt to encourage new root growth.

To delay infestations next year, be sure you destroy all affected vines so the pests can't overwinter in your garden or compost pile. And plant squash as soon as the danger of frost has passed next spring. That way you can harvest a crop before the borers come out in abundance.

Lubber Grasshoppers Love Your Plants

It's easiest to control lubber grasshoppers when they're young.
Photograph: Mary Carolyn Pindar

If you've been a Florida resident for even one summer, you're probably all too familiar with the notorious eastern lubber grasshoppers. They often appear like armies near marshes and on roadsides. These colorful pests invade a yard by the dozens, their little jaws constantly working to eat up your plants. They are particularly fond of flowers and plants with succulent leaves, such as young ferns, ginger lilies, and begonias.

Young eastern lubbers are black with red or yellow markings that look like seams on their torso and legs. These are the ones you are likely to first see feeding in your garden. The adults are large (up to 3 inches long) and yellow with black markings; they cannot fly.

The pests feed during summer, laying their eggs in your garden to ensure their progeny a good place to feed next year. The best time to control them is when they first appear. You can kill the young by dusting carbaryl on the plants they feed on. However, the adult grasshoppers are nearly impossible to poison. The best way to kill them is to crush them with an item harder than they are—a foot, for example, works fine.

In North Florida, working the soil during the winter in order to expose their eggs to frost will also help control them.

Dealing with Japanese Beetles

Hungry Japanese beetles can make a mess of garden roses.
Photograph: Mary-Gray Hunter

You may have seen these pretty, metallic-green beetles in your garden. If so, you have also noticed that the damage they leave behind is not so lovely. These are Japanese beetles, a hungry horde of insects that is moving steadily south and west, gobbling gardens as they go.

At a rate of 10 to 15 miles per year, Japanese beetles have steadily spread through the Southeastern states. Their favorite fare consists of tender leaves and flowers. They feed in masses, leaving a skeleton of veins where a leaf used to be. Roses, in particular, are fodder for these ravenous creatures.

Adult females lay their eggs in the soil in midsummer. Hatching into white grubs that feed on roots, the larvae can severely damage turf as well as ornamentals and vegetables.

The most effective chemical control is carbaryl, an old garden standby. Applied as either a dust or a spray, it will kill the insects, although they will probably continue to feed until they die. Reapply carbaryl as directed on the label and after any rain.

Another method is to use traps, which are readily available in garden centers. Traps are effective in reducing populations, and thereby controlling next year's problem. The bait is either a floral-scented or synthetic sex attractant that lures the beetles into the trap. Place traps at least 30 feet away from the plants to be protected.

To control the white grubs that feed on plant roots, treat with milky disease spore. Although it may take two to three years to become fully effective, it will provide permanent control in turf areas.

CHECKLIST
For June

☐ **Ajuga**—If a whole bed of ajuga suddenly seems to melt into the ground, the culprit is crown rot. This disease is brought on by warm, wet weather. To protect a planting, you can drench the soil with Terraclor or another soil fungicide that controls crown rot. If the disease is already present, dig up the infested plants, and then treat the entire planting with the fungicide.

☐ **Annuals**—Remove faded blooms to prevent annuals from going to seed and to encourage continued flowering. Side-dress plants with 2 pounds of balanced fertilizer per 100 square feet of bed about once every four to six weeks. Remove weeds, which compete with annuals for food and moisture, and check beds periodically for signs of insects or diseases. Early detection will lead to the best control.

☐ **Crepe myrtles**—Using a pole pruner, clip the seedpods from the tips of the branches and you'll get a second crop of flowers in about six weeks. If suckers have sprouted at the base of the tree, remove them. Flowering saps energy from the trees, so fertilize with a slow-release fertilizer to keep the foliage dark green and vigorous. You may also spot the white, powderlike growth of powdery mildew on the foliage now. Usually the trees tolerate this fungus without too much damage, but if your trees are victims year after year, the disease might be keeping them from growing as vigorously or blooming as well as they should. You can kill the fungus by spraying with Daconil 2787 according to label directions.

☐ **Fruit trees**—Limbs of apple, pear, and peach trees producing large crops of fruit may need support. Use a piece of 2 x 4 lumber with a V-shape notch cut into one end. Lift the limb slightly, and wedge the brace in place. Be sure to place it closer to the tip of the limb than to the trunk.

☐ **Houseplants**—Don't put houseplants in direct sun. Leaves that are accustomed to being indoors will burn in sunlight. Keep them in the shade this summer, and they will have less of a shock when you move them back indoors in fall.

☐ **Mulch**—Apply pine needles, ground bark, or other organic material to garden beds to hold moisture in the soil and to prevent weeds. If weeds have been a problem in the past, you might consider using some sort of barrier beneath the mulch. Several layers of newspaper will let water soak through to the soil and keep the weeds from growing. The newspaper will last for a season and then decompose into the soil. (There is no danger of lead from the ink.) You can also buy fabric made for this purpose at your local garden center. It will last for several seasons.

☐ **Peppers**—Peppers that develop brown, translucent spots on leaves and fruit may be plagued by bacterial leaf spot, a disease brought on by humid weather. Symptoms first appear as water-soaked spots on the lower leaves. Later the spots turn brown and enlarge up to ¼ inch in diameter. Sometimes the leaves become twisted and curly; later they may yellow and drop. Spots on the fruit also start as water-soaked areas that become raised and scabby. To control the disease, apply a copper spray, such as copper sulfate, at the first sign of infection. If the disease is present in the garden every summer, begin spraying during rainy weather so you can stop it before it has a chance to take hold.

☐ **Pest management**—Good cultural practices can help reduce pest problems before they get started. Pick up and remove fallen leaves, limbs, and other debris, and keep weeds under control. Weeds and debris often harbor insects and diseases. Make sure plants are properly fertilized and watered; plants under stress are more susceptible to attack. Prune away all dead wood from trees and shrubs, and treat pruning scars and other wounds to prevent the entry of fungi and borers. Larger insects, such as bagworms, can often be removed by hand. Be sure to wear gloves. If spraying becomes necessary, read the warning label and follow all directions exactly.

☐ **Roses**—Healthy blooms in fall require summer care. Remove old flowers as they fade to prevent seed production and allow more energy for flower production. Cut the flowers off just above the first five-leaflet leaf. Add about 1 cup of 10-10-10 fertilizer to each plant monthly through August, watering well after each application. Be sure to continue spraying every 7 to 10 days with Benlate or Funginex to help control black spot and powdery mildew. Removing spent flowers from around the base of the plant will help reduce disease problems.

☐ **Seed Savers Exchange**—This nonprofit organization, dedicated to preserving *heirloom* seeds, is looking for gardeners who have seeds of vegetable selections that have been passed down in the family and are not available commercially. They are also interested in traditional crops of the American Indian, garden selections of the Mennonite and Amish, outstanding foreign selections, and mutations and selections that are extremely tolerant of cold, drought, diseases, or insects. To be a member, you must be willing to multiply the seeds. Each year the exchange publishes a yearbook listing members and the seeds they have to offer. The exchange has also compiled The Garden Seed Inventory, a computer inventory of all nonhybrid vegetable seed still being offered by seed companies. For a free brochure, send a long, self-addressed, stamped envelope to Rural Route 3, Box 239, Decorah, Iowa 52101.

☐ **Shade trees**—Do not hesitate to plant an oak or other large tree just because you think it grows too slowly. Some trees that are thought to be very slow growers aren't really so slow when given a good location, adequate water, and fertilizer. Live oaks, white oaks, and Southern magnolias will grow 1 to 2 feet per year if planted in full sun in an area where there is no root competition from other trees. Feed the trees in spring and fall with a slow-release fertilizer, and keep them well watered throughout the year, even in winter.

☐ **Summer greens**—Even if your spinach has bolted and the mustard has gone to seed, you don't have to live without greens. Plant those that can take the heat. Swiss chard is an excellent choice for the summer garden, and it will continue even after the first frosts of autumn. Soak seeds overnight to speed germination, and sow them directly into the garden soil. Thin seedlings to stand 3 to 4 inches apart. Then when the plants are touching, thin them to a 9- to 12-inch spacing.

Another good choice is climbing spinach, offered by seed companies as basella or Malabar spinach. Because it is climbing, it will need support, such as a fence or trellis. Harvest by cutting 3 to 5 inches off each vine. This will encourage tender new growth for future harvests. New Zealand spinach is a spreading plant with upright shoots. Harvest the tips as you would for climbing spinach. Use either of these plants in any recipe that calls for spinach.

☐ **Weeds**—It is important to keep weeds out of the vegetable garden because they will compete for water, nutrients, and light. A small hoe is good for removing weeds between rows, but for those growing close to vegetable plants, you'll need to wet the soil and then hand pull the weeds, roots and all. Mulch will prevent most weed seeds from germinating. Those that do will be easy to pull.

SPECIAL TIPS FOR THE SOUTHEAST

☐ **Bramble fruit**—Allow blackberries and raspberries to fully ripen on the plant before picking; they do not sweeten after harvest. Ripe fruit will separate easily from the stem; fruit that is not ready will cling to the stem. When the harvest is over, cut canes that bore fruit down to the ground.

☐ **Chives**—Each time you need a few chives from the garden, cut generously, as that will encourage new growth. Snip the extras into short segments, put them into a plastic container, and keep in the freezer. By the time frost kills back your plants, you will have frozen enough to last through the winter.

☐ **Chrysanthemums**—If you depend on mums for fall color, it will be a disappointment if all you get are soil-splashed flowers—victims of weak stems that bent over in the rain. Avoid this problem by pinching off the tip of each stem repeatedly during the early part of the season. This will give you shorter, stronger stems with more flowers. Pinching should begin early. Cut plants back to 3 to 4 inches now, and feed with soluble 20-20-20 or similar fertilizer. Continue pinching just the tip of the stems whenever the new growth exceeds 3 inches. Stop pinching on the first of August in the Upper South, the middle of August in the Middle South, and the first of September in the Lower South. Fertilize monthly throughout the season.

☐ **Lawns**—The spring fertilizer application has been used up or washed away by now, so warm-season grasses in the Middle and Lower South are probably ready for a second feeding (except for centipede, which should only be fed in spring). Buy a good quality fertilizer recommended for your type of grass. Follow label directions, or use this rule of thumb: 1 pound of nitrogen per 1,000 square feet of lawn. Remember, if the fertilizer is 25% nitrogen, you will need to apply 4 pounds of fertilizer to get 1 pound of nitrogen.

☐ **Perennials**—Remove faded flowers from perennials for a tidy garden; often your effort will be rewarded with additional blooms. Plants that will respond well to this extra attention include golden marguerite, foxgloves, coreopsis, coralbells, garden phlox, and stokesia.

This is also the time to cut back perennials that will grow too tall for their spot in the garden. Use your clippers to cut back the stalks of sneezeweed (*Helenium* sp.), joe-pye weed, narrow-leaved sunflower (*Helianthus* sp.), and tall asters. Remove as much as half of their current height. The result will be compact plants with even more flowers.

SPECIAL TIPS FOR FLORIDA

☐ **Bougainvillea**—If your bougainvillea has outgrown its bounds, prune it after it blooms to allow the new growth to mature and produce flowerbuds for next year. Fertilize after pruning with 1 cup of slow-release 6-6-6 fertilizer per vine. Also watch for bougainvillea caterpillars. You don't always see them because they drop to the ground quickly when the plant is disturbed; however, you can't miss the holes they chew in the leaves and blossoms. To kill these pests, dust the plants with carbaryl or rotenone. (Be sure not to use rotenone near a goldfish pond or other water feature as it is poisonous to fish.)

☐ **Big vegetables**—Gardeners who grow vegetables of record size or weight can now have them officially registered with the Extension service. You can get information on how to register your possible champion from your local Extension office.

☐ **Fruit drop**—Avocados and mangoes may drop fruit this month but don't be alarmed; this is part of a natural shedding that ends by the first of July. The trees are dropping excess fruit that they can't sustain; healthy trees retain plenty for harvest later in the summer.

☐ **Palms**—Feed palms with a fertilizer containing minor elements, such as iron, to keep the foliage a healthy, dark green. Palms that are yellowing may also need an extra dose of manganese, an element lacking in some soils. Queen palms and Royal palms are particularly quick to develop the typical symptoms of manganese and iron deficiency, which include yellowing of the leaves between the midribs and new fronds that don't grow as large as they should. To correct the deficiency, apply manganese sulfate to the ground around the plants at the rate recommended on the label. It takes from two to six months for plants to turn green again, depending on the severity of the problem.

☐ **Planting**—June usually brings rain to Florida, making this a good time to plant trees and shrubs. Select healthy specimens from your nursery, and set them in a shady place while preparing planting holes. If you must delay planting, water daily if it doesn't rain; otherwise, plants could easily dry out. To get plants off to a good start, incorporate a slow-release fertilizer into the planting hole at the recommended rate.

SPECIAL TIPS FOR TEXAS

☐ **Palms**—Summer is the time to plant palms. Texas palmetto, cabbage palmetto, dwarf palmetto, and windmill palm are among selections hardy in the southern half of the state. Because their root systems are fairly small, stake palms until they become established.

☐ **Tarragon**—You may find both French and Russian tarragon for sale at garden centers, but for best flavor, choose the French. Because it never flowers, it cannot be grown from seeds; it can be propagated only by division. If you have any doubt about the plant you are buying, pinch the end of a leaf. French tarragon has a scent like licorice. Russian tarragon smells like a lawn that has just been mowed. Although French tarragon has a reputation for being temperamental, once you've found the right spot to grow it, it will thrive. Its primary requirement is good drainage. If your beds retain too much water, grow tarragon in a raised bed or in a container.

☐ **"Texas grown"**—By identifying plants produced within the state, the Texas Department of Agriculture hopes to promote the nursery industry in Texas. You can encourage the state's agricultural development if you look for and purchase plants bearing the "Texas Grown" label.

July

Combining two selections of caladiums requires imagination and planning.

DELIGHTFUL, DEPENDABLE CALADIUMS

When it's hot and muggy, not many plants show off. Caladiums do, however, and with flying colors.

by TODD A. STEADMAN / photography VAN CHAPLIN

Caladiums. The word may not roll off your tongue with the cadence of the words "camellias" or "azaleas," but caladiums are right up at the top of the list of favorite Southern plants. Why? They thrive in summer heat, grow in sun and shade, and come in a staggering array of colors and patterns. And the fact that they are relatively easy to grow certainly adds to their popularity. The

many purposes they serve also contribute to their value. Besides being ideal for containers, they are strong visual elements in a planting bed or along a garden path. Striking in color and texture, they can effectively draw attention to a certain feature or even become an accent themselves. On the other hand, because they grow up to 18 inches tall, they can be used en masse to fill large areas.

WHICH TO CHOOSE

There are two basic categories of caladiums: fancy leaved and lance leaved. Don't be alarmed if you're unfamiliar with the lance-leaved types. They aren't as common as the fancy leaved. The only real difference between the two is the shape—the fancy leaved is more heart shaped; lance leaved is more arrow shaped.

Included within these two basic types are dozens of colors, patterns, and combinations. The range extends from the almost pure white of Candidum to the burgundies of Irene Dank and Postman Joyner, and a host of variegated selections in between. Should you be tempted to try several different colors in one spot, resist the urge. Usually they will clash, and you'll lose the beauty of the plant. Instead, try masses of a single type or limit yourself to two carefully selected colors.

When purchasing the tubers, be aware of the difference in sizes. Diameters range from 1 inch to 3½ inches, and prices increase with size. The larger tubers typically produce the greater amounts of foliage. A couple of

Like a low-lying cloud, this mass planting of a selection called Candidum fills a shady bed.

large ones create much the same effect as six smaller ones.

TIME TO PLANT

You can plant caladiums in the garden after all danger of frost has passed and soil temperature has reached 70 degrees. If you plant too early in the season, you stand a good chance of having the tubers rot in the ground.

It used to be that caladiums were considered suitable only for areas that had at least partial shade. Recent studies by Bob Brackman, director of horticulture at the Dallas Arboretum and Botanic Garden, indicate that some caladiums will also do quite well in full sun. "Aaron, Lance Whorton, Red Frill, Pink Cloud, and others had tremendous success. And we were growing them right out in the open in full Texas sun," Brackman explains. Candidum Jr., Pink Symphony, Gypsy Rose, and several others were found to have a low tolerance to full sun and do best when planted in a shady location. For best results, check with your local garden center when choosing colors and selections.

Wherever you plant, make sure the soil is rich, moist, and well drained. Place tubers on their side about 3 inches deep and 18 inches apart. If planting in full sun, space them about 8 inches apart. This helps keep the soil

cool and shades the tender new growth. Pack the soil firmly around the tubers. Add 2 teaspoons of 5-10-10 fertilizer to the soil at the time of planting, and continue feeding with 1 teaspoon per plant each month during the growing season.

Caladiums need a lot of water. They wilt quickly and will die if left too long without water. It is a good idea to mulch the soil around them to help retain moisture. Plants growing in full sun will need water frequently—early-morning watering is best. Bright sunlight shining through water on the leaves can scorch the plant.

Keep an eye out for the insignificant flowers that may shoot up on stalks, and pinch them off. This prevents the plant from wasting nutrients needed for colorful, healthy foliage.

If you'd like to save caladiums for another year, the process is simple. In early fall, withhold water until the leaves start to die back. Once leaves are brown, but before the first frost, dig up the tubers, clean off the soil, and air-dry them in a shaded, well-ventilated area several days. Dust with a fungicide, pack them in dry sphagnum peat moss, and store at a temperature between 65 and 70 degrees until next year. Never refrigerate; they are almost sure to rot if you do. You can leave caladiums in the ground if you are living in a frost-free region of the South. But whether you dig and store or leave them in the ground, don't expect quite the same foliage show the next year. Each season seems to take a little something out of the plant. That's why many gardeners buy new tubers each year.

The selection White Christmas forms an interesting backdrop for garden sculpture.

Tucked-Away Treasures

Discovering the unanticipated is one of the pleasures of a garden. And small garden ornaments are treats wherever you find them.

by RITA W. STRICKLAND

Unexpected garden features are often the most delightful. "I like to incorporate small ornaments as surprises," says Charleston landscape architect Robert Chesnut, ASLA. Landscape Architect Tay Breene of Gardenworks Design in Lexington, Kentucky, agrees: "Unless an ornament is a focal point, I usually tuck it away so it's revealed as you pass through the garden, rather than at the moment you step outside."

Turning a corner, for instance, you might happen upon a statue of Pan playing a silent tune while perched on a rock. Or you may spot a terra-cotta bunny, partly concealed under a bush, its ears erect as if startled. Beside a path, a little girl, cast in lead, stands amid the flowers. "Small details like this give a garden personality," Chesnut says.

Garden shops across the South, as well as mail-order outlets, feature a vast selection of outdoor ornaments—urns, fountains, plaques, statuary, birdbaths, finials, wind chimes, and more. You're sure to find delightful pieces that suit both your garden and your budget.

Just remember that restraint is the key to success with ornaments. "It's easy to get carried away," Breene cautions. "Then before you know it, you've got little bunnies everywhere. These pieces lose their effect if you use too many."

Be careful about combining ornaments made from different materials. "It's difficult to mix lead pieces with concrete, for example, or stone with terra-cotta," she says. "In most cases, I wouldn't recommend grouping different types."

Many inexpensive garden ornaments are made of concrete. Although somewhat stark when new, concrete will

(**Above, right**) *A shaft of light penetrates the canopy of trees to accent this statue of Pan.* (**Right**) *This urn, a souvenir of a vacation abroad, gives distinction to an out-of-the-way spot in this garden.*

(**Above, left**) *Sheltered beneath an umbrella, a little girl stops to admire the flowers.* (**Above, right**) *Concrete ornaments take on a weathered appearance over time.* (**Left**) *Climbing fig and a terra-cotta plaque add interest to a previously blank garden wall.*

weather to a mellow gray. And there are techniques for speeding up this process (see "Letters to Our Garden Editors," page 79.)

Hand-carved stone ornaments are extremely durable but can be expensive. More reasonably priced are stone pieces made through casting. Marble, limestone, or other rock is finely ground, mixed with a cement, then poured into molds. "It looks and weathers very much like natural stone, and holds up extremely well," according to Breene.

Beautiful terra-cotta pieces, whether imported or made of Southern clays, can add much to a garden. Because terra-cotta is porous, it's subject to cracking in cold, wet weather and so is probably best suited to the Lower South. The most popular metals used for ornaments are iron, lead, copper, and bronze. Iron stands up well to variations in heat and cold, but it will rust if you don't keep it painted. Lead pieces are practically maintenance free, but they soften in the hot sun and could be damaged. Copper develops a light-green film of verdigris over time, which contrasts beautifully with the darker green of many plants. And sunlight striking the surface of a bronze seems to throw sparks into the landscape.

Even though Breene owns a shop specializing in garden ornaments, she's quick to suggest commonly used items that work as well. "An old wheelbarrow full of flowers or an attractive watering can placed in the right spot can be a wonderful substitute for an item purchased simply as an ornament."

Photographs: Van Chaplin, Mary-Gray Hunter, Sylvia Martin

Curving planters and low, wide steps lend visual interest to this tile terrace.
Photograph: Sylvia Martin

Charleston Charm, Minimal Maintenance

These days, Morton and Tricia Ellison enjoy spending time in their garden, but that wasn't the case when they purchased their Charleston, South Carolina, home. "The backyard was awful," Tricia explains. "A brick patio with a huge barbecue pit took up almost all the space. And the brick wasn't mortared so it was messy and hard to keep clean." In addition, the prior owner collected camellias, which were scattered randomly throughout the garden. "We didn't think we'd ever be able to do anything with that backyard," she says.

Tricia is the first to admit that gardening isn't one of her strongest talents, so she and Morton called Landscape Architect Sheila Wertimer, ASLA. "They wanted a functional, visual garden—a pretty setting where they could sit and enjoy the view without having to spend a lot of time on maintenance," Wertimer explains. The plan she developed combines easy upkeep with an elegance that befits the Charleston tradition.

Adjacent to the house, Wertimer designed a raised, curving terrace that's accessible from the kitchen and dining room. Unlike the brick that had been there, the tile used for this terrace is easy to clean, and its surface is slip-resistant even when wet.

One feature of the new terrace taught Tricia the value of listening to the advice of a professional. Wertimer's design called for two planter boxes to be built into the terrace—a long one near the parking court and a shorter one next to the house. Steps leading down to the lawn separated the two. "I didn't think I wanted a planter next to the house," Tricia says, so she suggested the smaller box be omitted. "Sheila felt that would be too stark looking, but how could she argue with a homeowner who wants something a certain way? She had them build it like I wanted." As soon as the installation was complete, however, Tricia realized that Wertimer had been right. The smaller planter was needed for continuity and to give some visual weight to that side of the terrace. "So a year later, we had them rebuild it like she had it to begin with."

Wax myrtles are native to the Low Country and require little care, so Wertimer used these evergreens to create a sense of enclosure around one side of the terrace. The built-in planters are filled with dwarf yaupons, a low, slow-growing selection of a coastal native holly.

Beyond the wax myrtles stands a large oak underplanted with azaleas. "This was the one part of the garden that was doing well, so we left it the way it was," Wertimer says.

A high wall painted to complement the color of the tile encloses the garden. In front of the wall are beds of ground cover, evergreen shrubs, and small deciduous trees. At night, landscape lights accent the dogwoods, Savannah hollies, and Bloodgood Japanese maples, and create intricate shadow patterns on the surface of the wall.

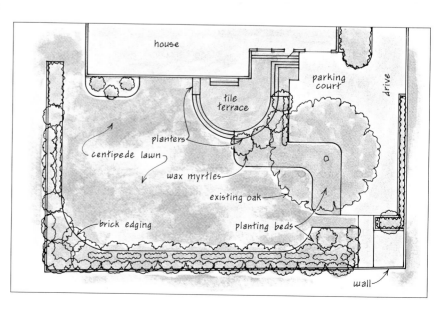

The garden occupies a narrow space between the house and adjacent property.   Photographs: Van Chaplin

A Narrow Escape in Houston

Landscape Architect David Foresman, ASLA, had much to consider when he was called to design the garden of this Houston home. The owners wanted a pool, sitting area, lawn, and planting beds. But the backyard was quite small with just a narrow space between the house and adjacent property. The challenge: develop an outdoor "room" accommodating all of the desired amenities.

A pool, tucked neatly between a terrace and privacy wall, is one element of Foresman's solution. Black marble dust mixed into the plaster gives the pool a charcoal color, the

Relaxing on the terrace is a pleasure.

look of a natural pond. The dark color also reduces glare when the pool is lit at night. Pencil-thin water jets along the back rim serve as a fountain.

Family and friends can exit from the house's living room onto a small upper terrace, which is connected by steps to a larger poolside terrace. Foresman carefully matched the brick of the terraces to that used in the house. Moreover, the gray of the flagstones used for the pool coping matches the color of the pool.

A predominantly evergreen planting, featuring hollies, azaleas, topiary boxwoods, Texas mountain laurel, and mondo grass, lends the garden a distinctly formal look. "The planting scheme goes hand in hand with the architectural style of the house, which is that of a classical English manor," says Foresman. Most of the trees and shrubs stand

in front of the gray-brick privacy wall, helping to soften it. "I didn't want people in the garden feeling like they were sitting in a big shoebox," he explains.

Today, the owners enjoy a very private place. While the garden may be small, it encompasses a lot.

CHECKLIST
For July

☐ **Bearded irises**—If irises have been in place three to five years, you probably need to divide them. Cut leaf blades back to 6 to 8 inches. Then carefully dig up the clumps, and thoroughly wash dirt from the roots and rhizomes. Cut off any damaged, soft, or leafless rhizomes, and discard them. Cut remaining pieces into 2- to 4-inch-wide divisions consisting of a rhizome, roots, and leaves. Dust cuts with sulfur to prevent rot. Replant so that the rhizomes are just below the soil surface and at least 6 inches apart in well-prepared soil.

☐ **Container gardening**—Try superabsorbent gels, recommended for use in potting soil. They are available in garden centers and are ideal for foliage plants, hanging baskets, window boxes, or any plant with restricted root space that may dry out quickly. Because these gels hold more water than potting soil and release it to plant roots as needed, you don't have to water as often. This is particularly helpful when you are planning to be away for several days. Follow rates recommended on the label, mixing the powdered gel into the potting soil before you plant.

☐ **Daylilies**—These perennials can be divided and transplanted as soon as they stop flowering. Transplanting now still gives them plenty of time to become established before winter. Dig up the clumps, and separate them into individual plants. Cut the foliage back to 8 or 10 inches; then replant in well-drained soil. Be sure to water during hot, dry weather.

☐ **Deadheading**—Snipping off faded flowers will encourage many plants to continue blooming. Annuals that will benefit from this extra care include zinnias and marigolds. Perennials such as coneflowers (*Rudbeckia* sp.), purple coneflowers (*Echinacea purpurea*), and coreopsis will bloom far longer if you do not let the flowers mature into seeds. It even works for crepe myrtles; trim the fading clusters to get a second bloom.

☐ **Figs**—Sometimes fig trees don't fruit well because of a disease called fig rust. The rust causes the leaves to become distorted and develop pinpoint-size brown spots. Eventually the leaves yellow, then brown, and drop. On severely affected trees fruit may also drop off or ripen while undersized. To control fig rust, spray affected trees with a copper spray, such as Bordeaux mixture.

☐ **Fleas**—Fleas love the warm, usually moist conditions that exist in lawns. If fleas indoors or on your pets are a problem, your control program should include treatment of turf areas. Apply Dursban, Diazinon, or carbaryl to the lawn, according to label directions. Insecticides containing growth regulators are available for use inside and on pets. Insect growth regulators prevent fleas from reaching maturity, thus interrupting their life cycle.

☐ **Herbicides**—If your weeds are so intertwined with desirable plants that you are unable to spray with herbicide, use a wick-type applicator. It will take more time to apply, but you won't accidentally damage nearby plants. You can also use an old paintbrush to spot treat the garden; be sure to wear gloves.

☐ **Herbs**—Any excess from your herb garden can be successfully dried in a frost-free refrigerator. Lay the herbs on a cookie sheet, and place in the refrigerator for 24 hours or until completely dry.

☐ **Lawns**—Now is the best time to renovate a lawn or plant anew. First determine which areas are too shaded, too wet, or walked on too much to sustain healthy grass. Plan an alternative such as ground cover or paving. For more information on lawn care, see pages 38-54.

☐ **Mower maintenance**—If you've noticed that your mower leaves ragged, brown edges on the grass, the blade probably needs sharpening. Although you could sharpen it yourself, you risk getting the blade out of balance, which will cause the mower to vibrate. Having a professional do the job is not expensive. Your owner's manual should tell you how to safely remove and reinstall the blade so you won't have to take the mower to the shop.

☐ **Pesticide safety**—When using pesticides, always read label directions completely to be sure the pesticide is safe for the particular plant you're applying it to. Never use pesticides in greater rates or more frequently than recommended. Wash hands thoroughly after applying, and store pesticides out of the reach of children and pets. Dispose of empty containers as recommended on the label.

A QUICK CURE FOR ROTTING TOMATOES

When you've waited months for homegrown tomatoes, it's disappointing if they rot before they ripen. The problem is usually blossom-end rot. Without any apparent cause or warning, a dark sunken spot appears on the blossom end (the side of the tomato opposite the stem) and grows larger. Peppers may also be affected. Fortunately, the cure is quick, simple, and certain.

Unlike other rots caused by bacteria or fungi, this one is the result of a calcium deficiency. Supply the needed calcium, and the problem is solved.

The quickest method is to spray foliage and developing fruit with Stop-Rot, a solution of calcium chloride, according to label directions. It is available from your local garden center.

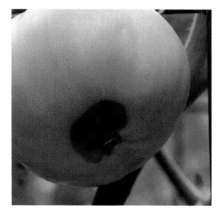

Blossom-end rot can ruin your summer tomato harvest. Calcium deficiency is the problem. Photograph: Mary-Gray Hunter

Because this treatment will not cure any fruit already affected, discard any tomatoes that have begun to rot. Those remaining on the plant should develop normally.

Fluctuations in soil moisture and growth rate can aggravate the problem. Keep the garden evenly moist, and apply calcium chloride sprays when tomatoes are growing rapidly, as they are after a heavy rain.

Before planting tomatoes again, have the soil tested. Amend the soil with lime or gypsum as the test results recommend. If you live in an area with acid soil, use lime. It will add the needed calcium while raising the soil pH. However, if your soil is alkaline, or the pH needs no adjustment, use gypsum (calcium sulfate) to supply the necessary calcium.

☐ **Soil solarization**—You can help get rid of nematodes by covering the soil with a sheet of clear plastic to trap heat from the sun. The process is simple and free of chemicals. Before laying the plastic, be sure to dig up all weeds, as nematodes may live in their roots. Cover the area with clear plastic, weighting it down with bricks or boards along all sides so it won't blow off. Leave the plastic in place until fall.

☐ **Trees**—Be careful not to nick trees when mowing or using a nylon-string trimmer around their base. Mower blades and string trimmers cut through bark and the thin layer of live wood just below. A tree continually subjected to this punishment may die slowly, as the wounds girdle the tree and cut off the flow of sap from the roots. Protect your trees by trimming grass at their base carefully with a pair of hand-held grass shears.

☐ **Vacation**—Take care of gardening chores before you go. Cut the lawn, water all plants thoroughly, and make sure they have adequate mulch. Ask a neighbor to keep vegetables harvested to encourage continued production. Make sure insect problems are under control.

☐ **Vegetables**—After squash, bush beans, and corn are harvested, pull out declining plants and replant for a late-summer harvest. Discard any plants that harbor insects or diseases, and put the others on the compost pile. Fertilize other crops to keep them producing all summer long. Side-dress pole beans with ¼ cup of 5-10-10 per 20 feet of row after the first harvest. Give peppers ¼ cup per 10 feet of row.

Cucumbers will continue to produce if you keep them picked. Oversize cucumbers should be removed and discarded or they'll slow production. For a fall harvest of tomatoes, set out a few plants now. If they are no longer available at your garden center, root cuttings from the ones in your garden.

☐ **Water**—Always water well before applying any pesticide or fertilizer to your trees, shrubs, flowers, or lawn. Water about 24 hours before treatment to allow time for the plants to absorb water and for the foliage to dry. Moisture on the leaves will dilute the concentration of the spray.

☐ **Zinnias**—If you have noticed powdery mildew beginning on the foliage of zinnias, spray now with benomyl. Because you cannot clear up foliage that is already infected, you should pull out and destroy plants that have a severe problem. You still have time to replant by sowing seeds directly into well-prepared beds. They'll be up and flowering in only a few weeks.

SPECIAL TIPS FOR THE SOUTHEAST

☐ **Perennials**—This is a good time to start the seeds of perennials for transplanting in fall. You can have sizable clumps of stokesia, columbine, butterfly weed, hollyhocks, and gloriosa daisies by starting them now. All you need are a few flowerpots and fine-textured potting soil. Sow one kind of seed in each pot, following the directions on the seed packets for planting depth and spacing. After the seedlings have their first leaves, transplant into flats (trays) or individual pots. Feed monthly with soluble 20-20-20, and they'll be ready to transplant into garden beds this fall.

☐ **Succession planting**—To get the most from your garden, be ready to plant the next crop as soon as one is harvested. For example, plant seeds of bush beans when the corn is finished, plant pumpkins after squash, and set out new tomato plants for fall as soon as the cucumbers have been harvested. Gardeners in the Middle and Upper South should begin growing transplants of cole crops for the fall vegetable garden; Lower South gardeners can wait until next month. In the Upper South, gardeners can also begin sowing lettuce, beets, carrots, Chinese cabbage, Swiss chard, turnips, and rutabagas directly in the garden.

SPECIAL TIPS FOR FLORIDA

☐ **Bananas**—Feed and water fast-growing banana plants regularly during the summer. Apply about 2 pounds of slow-release 6-6-6 per full-grown plant every six to eight weeks. Broadcast the fertilizer under the plant canopy, and water it in. Also remove suckers from plants that are bearing fruit, as the suckers will sap energy needed to ripen the bananas. When the fruit is nearly ripe, leave any new suckers that appear in order to start a new plant for next year.

☐ **Geraniums**—Geraniums set out in spring may be tall and spindly by now. Rejuvenate the plants by cutting their leggy stems back 3 to 6 inches; then fertilize with a soluble houseplant fertilizer such as 18-18-18 or 20-20-20 diluted according to label directions. In South Florida, geraniums are grown through winter and spring, but they don't like hot weather and should be removed from the garden in summer. Start again with fresh plants in November.

☐ **Pennywort**—Also called dollar-weed, pennywort invades lawns and flowerbeds with circular leaves that range from the size of a nickel to that of a silver dollar. Because the leaves are round, they act like little umbrellas casting shade, which weakens grass. To kill pennywort in the lawn, you can treat with Weed-B-Gon; it may take several applications two to three weeks apart to kill all of it. To treat weeds growing among flowers and the lower branches of shrubs or ground covers, use a sponge to dab a little Roundup or Kleenup on each leaf. Wearing gloves, apply a ready-to-use formula, or dilute a concentrate according to label directions.

SPECIAL TIPS FOR TEXAS

☐ **Palms**—Summer is the time to plant palm trees. Since these plants suffer in severe winters, you might want to consider planting only the most cold-hardy species in areas other than the Gulf Coast and Rio Grande Valley. The following grow well in protected locations as far north as Dallas: Texas palmetto (*Sabal mexicana*), windmill palm (*Trachycarpus fortunei*), jelly palm (*Butia capitata*), and the desert fan palm (*Washingtonia filifera*).

☐ **Peppers**—It's not too late to plant ornamental peppers. Selections of this colorful, heat-tolerant plant suited to Texas include Holiday Cheer, a bright-red pepper; Holiday Flame, with fruit that ranges from yellow to red; and Midnight Special, which starts out purple and turns to red. Set out transplants 18 to 24 inches apart. In two weeks, add 2 tablespoons of 10-10-10 or similar fertilizer per plant and repeat every three weeks. Be sure to keep the peppers well watered.

☐ **Water conservation**—Most Texas lawns, trees, and shrubs require 2 inches of water each rainless week to avoid heat stress. Reduce waste by watering only in the early morning or evening to minimize evaporation losses, and avoid watering on windy days. Remember that it's better to have one prolonged watering than several light ones.

August

Double-flowered annual types resemble zinnias or dahlias.

CONEFLOWERS
At Home in the Garden

*Commonly found in the countryside,
coneflowers don't need a warranty to do well in the
garden. They're used to making it on their own.*

by LOIS B. TRIGG

Thriving next to burning asphalt, in ditches, and around abandoned homes, coneflowers tempt you to grab a shovel and head for the countryside. But keep your shovel at home. You can buy seeds or plants that will give you bigger and more colorful flowers than those in the wild.

The ones you'll find in seed packets are annual coneflowers (*Rudbeckia hirta*), commonly called black-eyed Susans and Gloriosa daisies. They include flowers with pinwheel-like markings of mahogany and double blossoms of gold; most are about 3 feet tall. Popular selections include Goldilocks, Rustic Colors, and Marmalade. Annual coneflowers bloom all summer, beginning in June. To help keep them blooming, you need to remove the flowers as they fade. Although they're

annual, sometimes the plants come back from their roots for a year or two, but the best thing to do is replant. If some come back, consider it a bonus.

If you'd rather not replant, try perennial coneflowers (*Rudbeckia fulgida*). These look like black-eyed Susans, grow about 3 feet tall, and come back dutifully every August. Goldsturm is the most popular selection. You can buy Goldsturm plants from mail-order sources or a local garden center that carries perennials. You can also start them from seed. No matter how you start the plants, be sure to give them plenty of room. Because Goldsturm spreads by rhizomes, a clump will get bigger each year.

Coneflowers do well by themselves or in a flower border. You can scatter seeds of the annual type at the edge of

Perennial Goldsturm coneflowers combine with verbena and asters for a fresh breath of color in this late-summer border.
Photographs: Van Chaplin

a wooded lot where they'll grow randomly like wildflowers. In this case, leave faded flowers on their stems so the plants will reseed.

The vivid color and open form of Goldsturm make it a versatile addition to the garden. You can plant it with

other perennials or alone in a large mass for fresh, bright color in late summer when other blossoms often look tired. Just remember to leave about 3 feet on each side of the plant to give it room to spread.

ON THEIR OWN

When you first sow seeds or set out plants, keep them watered until they begin blooming. After the plants are established, they'll be fine on their own. "Coneflowers are real winners," claims Jane Bath, a garden designer from Stone Mountain, Georgia. "They stand erect without staking, grow in sun to partial shade, from bogs to dry spots, and rarely have any pests. They're wonderful." Bath recommends them for gardeners who are just starting out, and for those wanting low-maintenance designs.

If you're starting coneflowers from seed, follow the directions on the seed packet. You can sow them directly into the garden or in a flat to grow as transplants. Whichever you choose, the secret is to keep the seeds watered daily so they won't dry out. There's still plenty of time to sow seeds or set out plants of the perennial Goldsturm, but if you want to grow the annual types, wait until after frost next spring.

A STREETSIDE RETREAT

Some say this garden's in back of the house; others think it's out front. But everyone agrees on one thing—it's delightful!

by RITA W. STRICKLAND / photography VAN CHAPLIN

With characteristic Southern graciousness, Diana and Mickey Palmer accept the compliments that guests lavish upon their New Orleans garden. But they have to smile when they hear the question that first-time visitors invariably ask: "Is this the front yard or the back?"

The confusion is understandable. The Palmers live in the Lake Vista area, an older planned community that wasn't designed the way most subdivisions are today. Instead of facing the street, homes in Lake Vista were turned in the opposite direction to overlook the large park spaces that form the core of the neighborhood. Access streets run along the back side of the lots.

"The area was developed before people became so very dependent on their cars," Diana explains. "The idea was that visitors would park down at the end of the street, then walk back through the park to the front door." Over the years, this arrangement proved inconvenient, so the back entries began to be used more frequently. "Now people come in through what was the rear service area," says Landscape Architect René Fransen, ASLA, who designed the garden. "So this actually is the backyard, but people think it's the front because it faces the street."

Fortunately, the controversy in no way detracts from the garden's beauty. It's a carefully planned and beautifully executed composition of water, plants, and stone—a wonderful example of what happens when a dedicated gardener and a talented designer work together.

A canopy of tall trees, splashing water, and shades of blue, green, and violet make the garden seem cool and inviting, even when the New Orleans summer is hottest. The pool itself is in the sunshine, but there's always a spot of shade to be found on the terrace. A hedge of cherry laurel screens the view from the street.

In contrast to the cool colors that predominate, Diana uses pots of bright red and yellow portulaca to call attention to the elegantly curving steps that lead into the pool. "The shape of these steps repeats the lines of a terrace that already existed near the house," Fransen says. This is just one of many instances where the repetition of a single design element, such as a recurring line or color, gives the garden a sense of continuity.

The pool, which is tinted a deep, dark blue, is surrounded by a terrace of lilac-colored flagstone. This color combination is repeated in an everchanging display of flowering plants, including French hydrangea, plumbago, agapanthus, heather, and princess flower.

Pale-blue ceramic plaques decorate a low wall and house jets that stream water into the pool. "The plaques were made by John Hodge, a local artist, and each one features a different type of iris," Diana says. In spring the living counterparts of these sculptures, all in shades of blue, come to life in the garden. "In addition to the more common irises," Fransen adds, "we also have butterfly irises [*Dietes vegeta*],

(**Above**) *Dark water, cool colors, and spots of shade make this garden inviting even on the hottest days.* (**Above, left**) *The iris plaques that stream water into the pool were made by artist John Hodge of Covington, Louisiana. Each one depicts a different iris.* (**Right**) *Plumbago cascades over a low wall as if trying to dip its branches in the water.*

which have foliage similar in color to the pineapple guavas."

The Palmers' garden isn't just for show, however; Diana grows herbs there as well. "I stick them in sunny spots between the flowers," she says. Rosemary, thyme, parsley, and oregano peak out between the heather and plumbago.

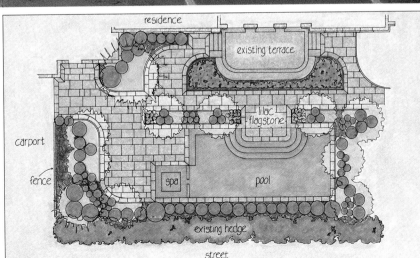

Photograph: Mary-Gray Hunter

Photograph courtesy of the Agecroft Association

(**Left**) *Horticulturist Beth Corker designed the annual display to reflect the large masses of color typical of American gardens in the 1920's. Here, impatiens, blue mealycup sage, marigolds, and santolina bloom at the foot of Agecroft Hall.* (**Right**) *Prior to the restoration of the garden, huge boxwoods claimed much of the space, reducing its allure.*

A Garden Grows Younger at Agecroft

Gardens aren't frozen in time. They grow, mature, then finally decline and need restoration. That's the story behind the wonderful Sunken Garden at Agecroft Hall in Richmond. Created in the 1920's by Landscape Architect Charles Gillette, the garden slowly outgrew its bounds, obscuring much of the original design. But thanks to the recent efforts of four dedicated gardeners, the site has recaptured the sparkle of yesteryear.

Of course, the garden never would have existed without the imposing presence of Agecroft Hall. Built in 15th-century England, this huge Tudor mansion was derelict by the time T. C. Williams, Jr., a prominent Richmond businessman, bought it in 1926. In an operation of staggering proportions, he had the house disassembled, shipped across the Atlantic, and reconstructed on his 26-acre estate overlooking the James River.

The first garden built near the house was the formal Sunken Garden, mod-eled after the one at Hampton Court in England. Gillette's garden featured long flowerbeds flanked by parallel re-taining walls. Because of concerns over maintenance, however, boxwoods soon supplanted the flowers. In the decades that followed, the boxwoods burgeoned, engulfing the outer walls and spreading over the lawn.

In 1987, Estate Manager Richard Moxley came to Agecroft. Formerly garden superintendent for the William Paca Garden in Annapolis, he was well-versed in the restoration of his-toric gardens. Together with Horticul-turist Beth Corker, Senior Gardener Marvin Mason, and Gardener David Land, he pored over old photographs of the grounds, using them to recon-struct the garden in its original 1920's style. The staff removed the central boxwoods, severely pruned the box-wood borders, and reinstated the flow-erbeds. Today, the Sunken Garden is like an aged fresco, from whose sur-face accumulated grime has been meticulously removed, revealing the true colors.

There's much more to see at Age-croft, however, than just the Sunken Garden. Visitors may also stroll though the Knot Garden, Formal Gar-den, and Herb Garden, which feature plants of the Elizabethan era. The house is itself a stellar attraction and is maintained by a trust as a museum.

The restoration at Agecroft contin-ues. Some gardens are currently being renovated, while others are just in the planning stage. So if you visit during the next few years, don't be surprised to see a tractor or two hidden behind a hedge. For the gardens at Agecroft aren't static—like the seasons, they're always changing.

Agecroft Hall, located at 4305 Sul-grave Road in Richmond, is open Tuesday through Saturday 10 a.m. to 4 p.m. and Sunday 2 to 5 p.m. Admis-sion is charged. For more information, call (804) 353-4241.

LETTERS

TO OUR GARDEN EDITORS

Evergreens for espalier: I am looking for an attractive, fast-growing evergreen that can be trained against a brick wall. The mature height must be at least 6 feet. The location receives five hours of sun per day and has heavy, moist soil. What do you suggest we use? *S. A. W., Florence, South Carolina.*
The practice of training plants against a flat surface is known as espalier. Probably the fastest growing evergreen used for this is firethorn (pyracantha). However, it will need well-drained soil. For heavy soil, try one of the upright hollies, such as Burford, yaupon, or Savannah holly. If you can improve soil drainage by either regrading, building raised beds, or adding organic matter, you could also try Japanese cleyera (*Ternstroemia gymnanthera*), sweet olive (*Osmanthus fragrans*), Chinese fringe (*Loropetalum chinense*), leatherleaf viburnum (*Viburnum rhytidophyllum*), or Southern cherry laurel (*Prunus caroliniana*).

Rhododendron: Can you recommend a technique for successfully propagating a rhododendron? *D. B., McKenney, Virginia.*
Rhododendrons are usually propagated by cuttings. However, success depends greatly on the particular selection—some are easy; others are difficult. Here is a method that works for most. First, take a tip cutting about 3 inches long in mid-August. Use a razor blade to score the bark around the cut end; then dip the cut end in rooting powder. Place the cutting in a moist rooting medium consisting of half sphagnum peat moss and half perlite. Cut all of the cutting's leaves in half to reduce transpiration. Mist the cutting several times per day, and keep it out of direct sun. Rooting should occur in two to four months. When the cutting has developed a thick network of roots, transfer it to its own pot. Place the plant in a well-ventilated cold frame for the winter before planting it in the ground next spring.

Elm: We have a large elm tree, and its roots sit on top of the ground. Would it cause a problem if we covered the roots with topsoil? *V. D. W., Lilburn, Georgia.*
It's generally not a good idea to spread soil over the roots of any established tree. This blocks the passage of soil oxygen and other gases and can severely injure the tree. However, elms are more tolerant of soil filling than most trees, as long as the soil is porous, gravelly, and doesn't contain a lot of clay. Spread the soil no deeper than 3 inches over the roots. But realize that the tree will probably send new surface roots into the soil within a few years, and you'll be faced with the same problem all over again.

Cape primrose: While in Boston, I purchased three cape primrose plants. I brought them home and placed them outside in a screened room that received no direct sun. The temperature varied from about 93 degrees in the

Cape primrose needs cool temperatures and bright, indirect light to do its best.
Photograph: Mary-Gray Hunter

daytime to 73 degrees at night. One by one, the plants began to die. What did I do wrong? *H. C., Fort Myers, Florida.*
Cape primrose (*Streptocarpus hybridus*), a close relative of the African violet, is very difficult to grow outdoors in Florida because it likes cool temperatures. You'll have to grow it indoors in an air-conditioned room. Give it bright, indirect light and moist, well-drained soil. To increase humidity around the plant, place its container atop a gravel-lined saucer filled with water. Feed once a month with African violet fertilizer.

Roses: All of our rose bushes have quite a lot of new growth, but the flowers are very small. Can you help us with this problem? *A. W., Ridge, Maryland.*
The first thing to do is make sure your roses receive plenty of water. During the summer, they are very thirsty. They're also heavy feeders, so give each plant a half-gallon of water-soluble 30-15-30 or 20-20-20 fertilizer each week throughout the growing season. Finally, pinch out all but two or three flowerbuds from each cluster. Fewer buds mean larger flowers.

Understory plants: Several years ago, we planted loblolly pines as a windbreak around our home. What shrubs should we plant at the bases of these trees to create a thicker screen? *M. W., Cleveland, Tennessee.*
Good understory plants for this purpose include mountain laurel (*Kalmia latifolia*), wintergreen barberry (*Berberis julianae*), Japanese aucuba (*Aucuba japonica*), nandina, mahonia, holly, and many of the taller growing azaleas.

TIP OF THE MONTH

Here's a good use for those wild onions that grow in your lawn. Dig them up, cut them into small pieces, and soak them overnight in a jug of water. Strain the solution, and pour into a hand sprayer. Spray this liquid onto your chrysanthemums and other flowers. It's very effective for ridding them of aphids and other pests.
Rodney Petty, Sr., Marietta, Georgia
Editor's note: We'd like to have your ideas—the ones that have worked for you. We're especially interested in vegetables, houseplants, shrubs, trees, and garden care. For each tip that is published, we will pay $10 and send you one of our garden books.

Submit as many ideas as you wish, but each must be on a separate sheet or card, along with your name, address, and telephone number. We may need to edit the tips, and none will be acknowledged or returned. Send to Gardening Tips, *Southern Living,* Box 523, Birmingham, Alabama 35201.

CHECKLIST
For August

☐ **Annuals**—Cut back leggy petunias, verbena, and spider flowers now and you'll have compact plants with lots of blooms this fall. Pinch long stems back to a point just above a short side shoot to stimulate new growth, and feed the plants with a water-soluble 20-20-20 or similar analysis fertilizer. Use the rate recommended on the label.

☐ **Chrysanthemums**—Begin setting out mums for dependable color this fall. Hardy mums will rebloom each year if you plant in full sun and in a spot where the soil drains well. Sprinkle a tablespoon of slow-release fertilizer into each planting hole when you set out the plants, and water during dry weather. Plants purchased in 4- to 6-inch pots should be almost full grown and ready to bloom. Do not cut them back or you will remove the flowerbuds.

☐ **Crepe myrtles**—To encourage a fall crop of blossoms, remove spent flower heads. If the leaves of your crepe myrtles are sticky and blackened, aphids are probably to blame. Apply insecticidal soap following label directions.

☐ **Dried flowers**—Prepare to add winter color to your home by cutting and drying flowers while they are plentiful. The easiest method is to cut them and then hang them upside down in a dry, well-ventilated location, such as an attic or an air-conditioned room. Dampness and humidity will cause the flowers to brown. If you want to make a wreath of dried flowers, do so while the flowers are still fresh; otherwise, they will be too brittle to handle. Then leave the wreath on a horizontal surface until the flowers are dry.

☐ **Garlic**—It's about time to harvest garlic that was planted in spring. You'll know it's ready when the tops have yellowed and withered. Dig the bulbs, and dry them for several days in a well-ventilated location out of direct sun. You can also replant now for a spring harvest. Separate a bulb into individual cloves. Set the cloves in a shallow furrow 4 to 6 inches apart with the pointed end up. Cover with 3 inches of soil. The leaves that sprout will stay green through winter.

☐ **Geraniums**—Take cuttings from your geraniums now for use in next year's garden. Cut pieces 3 or 4 inches long from the ends of vigorously growing stems. Remove the leaves from the bottom third of the cuttings; then stick them in a container of sand, vermiculite, or perlite potting soil. Water thoroughly; then place the container in a clear plastic bag. Use short stakes or a wire frame to keep the plastic off the cuttings, close the bag securely, and place your "mini greenhouse" in a well-lit spot away from direct sun. Check the soil periodically to make sure it remains moist. After cuttings have rooted (in about two to three weeks), plant them in 3-inch pots. Give them plenty of light, water regularly, and feed with a soluble plant food according to label directions. By spring you'll have geraniums ready for planting.

☐ **Hanging baskets**—Annuals and vines purchased in spring may need a trim now to keep the top full and flowering. Trim back trailing plants, such as lobelia, verbena, and purslane, one-third to one-half their length. Some shoots may need to be cut all the way back to the top of the pot to encourage fullness. After pruning, fertilize with a couple of tablespoons of slow-release houseplant food or a solution of 20-20-20. New growth will appear in time for a good fall show. You can also root the trimmings to start new baskets for next year.

☐ **Hydrangeas**—Prune and shape French hydrangeas (*Hydrangea macrophylla* Hortensia) as soon as they finish blooming. If pruning is postponed, next year's flowerbuds could be removed. Also, if the flowers were either a pale pink or pale blue this year and you want a richer color next year, amend your soil. For a deeper pink, apply 1 tablespoon of hydrated lime per plant, and fertilize monthly until frost with ¾ cup of 5-20-10 per plant. For rich blue, dissolve 1 pound of aluminum sulfate in 5 gallons of water, and drench the soil with 1 gallon of the mixed solution per plant. Repeat every two weeks from now until frost.

☐ **Landscape design**—Even though woody ornamentals can be set out successfully this month, August is a better time for planning than planting. The first step is to identify existing problems and opportunities on your lot. Are there unsightly views that need screening or good views that need framing? Do outdoor living areas have ample shade in summer? Consider how you use the garden. Do you have adequate room for outdoor entertaining? Should you plant ground covers to reduce lawn maintenance? If you don't feel confident about your skills as a designer, consult a local landscape architect who can devise a plan tailored to the conditions on your lot and the requirements of your lifestyle.

☐ **Lawns**—Bag grass clippings if your lawn is prone to heavy thatch or if the clippings exceed 2½ inches in length. Otherwise, leaving clippings on the lawn will provide nutrients as they decompose. If you plan to let the clippings remain, be sure the grass is dry before you mow. Wet clippings will form clumps that are unsightly and detrimental to your lawn.

☐ **Perennials**—This is a good time to start seeds of butterfly weed, purple coneflower, coreopsis, and other perennials for fall planting. Fill a flat with potting soil, and moisten it. Make shallow furrows in the soil with a wooden ice-cream stick or pencil. Sprinkle seeds into the furrows, and cover gently. Label each row with the name of the plant and the date sown. Cover the flat with clear plastic wrap to prevent moisture loss. As soon as seedlings appear, uncover and place the flat in bright, indirect light. The first two leaves to appear will be the seed leaves, but as soon as true leaves sprout, use the stick or pencil to gently lift the seedlings; then plant them in individual containers. Fertilize every two weeks with soluble 20-20-20. In a couple of months, they should be large enough to transplant into the garden.

☐ **Pruning**—Although you usually think of pruning fruit trees in late winter and early spring, trees that have been espaliered will benefit from a summer trimming. However, this should be done early this month so any new growth will have matured before the first freeze of autumn.

☐ **Sooty mold**—You may find a black coating on the leaves of gardenias, azaleas, and crepe myrtles. Oddly enough, this is not a leaf disease but a mold that harms the plant indirectly by blocking light to the leaves. This mold grows on the sweet honeydew secreted by aphids and whiteflies that feed on the plants or the trees above. To control these pests, spray with insecticidal soap as recommended on the label. If temperatures will permit, apply a summer oil spray. This will control the insects and help dislodge some of the black coating on the leaves.

☐ **Watering**—Even watering is essential to avoid dry spots in the lawn. To measure your sprinkler's coverage, place several small containers at equal distances throughout the coverage area. All should fill with an inch of water in the same amount of time. If not, adjust your watering pattern or consider purchasing a more accurate sprinkler.

SPECIAL TIPS FOR THE SOUTHEAST

☐ **Rosemary**—In the Upper South, this herb must be brought indoors for the winter. Although rosemary is usually hardy in the Lower South, gardeners in the Middle South should take some precautions against winterkill. Dorothy Bonitz, an herb gardener in Hampstead, North Carolina, suggests layering rosemary. Layering is a method of propagation where cuttings are rooted while they are still attached to the parent plant. Even if the parent plant is killed, the young plants around it will probably live because they are closer to the ground and better insulated. Simply bend a stem over until it touches the ground, and anchor it with a small stone several inches from the tip; in a few months it will take root. You'll find that it roots faster if you wound the stem where it touches the soil. To prepare for cold weather, mulch the plant and the layered stems. By spring, enough roots will have grown to support the young plant. Just clip the stem to the parent plant.

☐ **Vegetables**—As soon as summer vegetables have been harvested, gardeners in the Upper South can set out transplants of cabbage, broccoli, collards, and kale. They can also sow seeds of Chinese cabbage, lettuce, spinach, beets, edible-podded peas, kohlrabi, English peas, and turnips. Gardeners in the Middle South should wait until later this month; gardeners in the Lower South should plant in September.

SPECIAL TIPS FOR FLORIDA

☐ **Mulch**—Renew decaying mulch in flowerbeds, vegetable beds, and under shrubs. Mulch keeps the soil from drying out and stops many weeds from coming up. The most popular mulches are organic because they add nutrients to the soil as they decompose. Pine straw and pine bark are two common ones in North Florida. Cypress mulch, which often comes from virgin trees cut for making mulch, is popular throughout the state, but pine bark is a better choice because it is a by-product of the timber industry. New alternatives include mulches made from melaleuca and eucalyptus trees. Ask your favorite garden center to stock them.

☐ **Vegetables**—Begin planning for the fall garden now. Order seeds or start transplants to set out late this month and throughout the fall. Fall is the best time to garden in Florida because the weather is milder and some of the insects begin to retreat. Gardeners in northeast and northwest Florida can set out tomato trans-

plants for a fall crop now. To lengthen the harvest, choose early-bearing selections, such as Quick Pick, Early Girl, and Champion.

SPECIAL TIPS FOR TEXAS

☐ **Lettuce**—Gardeners in Dallas and northward should have lettuce seed planted by midmonth for harvest in the fall. Gardeners in the rest of the state except for Coastal Texas and the valley can wait until the end of the month. Along the coast and in the valley, wait until November to plant lettuce seed. Using window screen or shade cloth supported about 6 inches above the seedbed will help lower soil temperature thus encouraging germination. Keep the seedbed moist until seedlings sprout; then water regularly. Don't wait for the plants to mature; the young leaves are tender and delicious.

☐ **Palms**—This is the last call this year for planting palms in Coastal and South Texas. Choose a sunny location with well-drained soil rich in organic matter. To improve their chances of surviving the first winter, purchase larger, more mature plants. Those over 5 feet tall will need to be staked for the first two years to protect them from wind damage. If you live away from the coast, use cold-hardy palms, such as Texas palmetto (*Sabal mexicana*), cabbage palmetto (*S. palmetto*), windmill palm (*Trachycarpus fortunei*), and jelly palm (*Butia capitata*). These palms will do well as far north as Dallas.

BAGWORMS EARNED THEIR NAME

Bagworms are like snails and turtles in that they produce their own house and carry it around with them. Resembling a dead twig or leaf, they often go unnoticed until the thinning foliage signals that there is a problem. Like other caterpillar pests, they are hungry and damaging.

Although they can infest all deciduous and evergreen trees, they are particularly common on junipers and arborvitae. Ranging from ¼ inch to 1½ inches, the bags hang down like dead twigs, but look carefully—they move.

A seemingly dead twig is actually the home of hungry bagworms that can defoliate your plants. Photograph: Mary-Gray Hunter

In fact, they move along branches, eating as they go, consuming enough foliage to seriously weaken a plant. In addition, the silken bands that attach overwintering bags to a plant may gir-

dle and kill young branches.

Bagworms overwinter as eggs in their mothers' bags. Hatching in late spring, they crawl out, feed, and form their own bags. Males pupate and emerge as moths; females, however, remain in their bags, lay their eggs there, and die.

At this time of year, the best method of control is handpicking and burning or collecting them in a trash bag and throwing it away. Do not toss bagworms on the ground, as they will multiply and be a problem again next year. In the case of severe infestations, you may want to follow up with a spray of *Bacillus thuringiensis* in late spring when the eggs are hatching. This bacterium attacks the larvae without harming humans or the environment.

September

GERBERAS
ARE WORTH THE PRICE

by STEPHEN P. BENDER

*The blossoms of this exotic perennial shine
like no other. You'll want to have them both
indoors and out, even if they don't come cheap.*

It's said that in this world there's no free lunch. A prime example of this maxim is the gerbera daisy (*Gerbera jamesonii*), a plant that bears long-stemmed blossoms of the most astonishing colors, from solar yellows and reds to the softest pastels. In the garden, the show continues as long as the weather stays warm, often bringing a welcome spark to fading, late-summer borders. And as a cut flower indoors, a gerbera is unsurpassed. So what's the catch?

Put simply, the price. Many seed catalogs will charge $2.50 or more for only five gerbera seeds. That makes them practically worth their weight in gold. Why so expensive? Because current demand exceeds supply. Gerberas just don't set many seeds. Says one grower in South Carolina, "Of the 10,000 plants I've grown in the last 10 years, I haven't seen seed one." The seeds Southerners do get come from Holland and Japan and command top dollar.

Now for some good news. Gardeners in the Coastal South, Lower South, and the lower half of the Middle South can overwinter gerberas in the garden and not have to replant each year. Those living farther north can bring their plants inside for the winter. And even though you can't count on getting more plants from seed, you can propagate gerberas by division in spring.

You'll sometimes see gerberas listed as Transvaal daisies in garden books because the plants originated in the Transvaal region of South Africa. But at the garden center, ask for gerberas; that's the name gardeners know.

You can choose from a wide range of flower shapes and colors. Blossoms up to 4 inches across may be single, double, scarlet, orange, yellow, pink, white, salmon, or cream. They stand atop sturdy stems 8 to 18 inches tall. Many garden centers carry established plants for those who want instant color. But if you're one of those intrepid souls who enjoy the challenge of germinating seeds, here's how.

Fill a seed flat with commercial seed-starting mix. Sprinkle the seeds over the surface, cover lightly with ¼ inch of mix, and water gently. Cover the flat with a sheet of clear plastic to retain soil moisture. Place a heating cable beneath the flat to provide bottom heat of approximately 70 degrees. The seeds should germinate in one to three weeks.

When the seedlings sport two to three sets of true leaves, transplant them to individual 3-inch pots. Give the plants bright light, either from the sun or a special grow light. Feed weekly with liquid 20-20-20 fertilizer diluted to half-strength. In about 10 weeks, the plants will be big enough to set into the garden.

Select a sunny spot. The soil should be well drained and contain lots of organic matter. If you can, plant in a raised bed. Set each plant in the ground so that its crown is exactly even with the soil surface.

According to Horticulturist Cynthia White of Savannah, gerberas are heavy

(**Left**) *Spot gerberas throughout the border to add bursts of color.* (**Below**) *You can bring gerberas inside for the winter, but they'll need very bright light.* (**Bottom**) *Flower colors range from pastels to electric pinks and reds.* Photographs: Van Chaplin, Mary-Gray Hunter

feeders. So give each a tablespoon of slow-release fertilizer in spring, followed by monthly feedings of liquid 20-20-20. She also recommends that gardeners with acid soil give each plant a yearly teaspoon of lime. Don't skimp on water—when gerberas are blooming, they can use a good, stiff drink every day.

In areas where the ground doesn't freeze, you can overwinter gerberas. Just cover them in early winter with 1 to 2 inches of pine straw or dry leaves. In colder areas, you'll need to bring

them indoors to a *very* sunny window for the winter. Mist daily in order to maintain humidity.

Compared to most perennials, gerberas are rather short-lived and may need replacing after several years. So don't make your flower border dependent upon them. Instead, spot them in groups here and there to add bursts of intense color throughout the season. Their warm shades blend especially well with blues, purples, yellows, whites, and silvers.

Should you wish to cut gerberas for

arrangements, here are some tips from Maloy Love of the Mountain Brook Flower Shop in Mountain Brook, Alabama. Cut the stems just as the flowers fully open, and place in very clean water to which you've added chlorine bleach (1 teaspoon per quart) and floral preservative. Keep the cut flowers out of drafts and hot sun and they may last for a week or more.

Gerberas do exact a price. But as their popularity attests, many Southerners think they certainly are well worth it.

The Pleasures of Potpourri

Elizabeth Harris makes her rose potpourri from the flowers that grow on the grounds of the Georgia Governor's Mansion.
Photographs: Mary-Gray Hunter

Elizabeth Harris loves roses. "It really hurts me when they die," she laments. To make the beauty and fragrance of the roses last, she dries the petals and blends them into potpourri, using recipes that she develops herself.

As the First Lady of Georgia, she gives her potpourri to special guests and official visitors and takes it as a gift when she travels abroad. "It's become a way to say 'This is part of us; this is Georgia,' " she says.

"We design our own lace sachet bags and stuff them with potpourri. I also have some cross-stitch bags with a little rose on them. The Dogwood

Petals are dried on screened trays; quick drying yields the best color.

potpourri. Its title makes you wonder whether it was named for an English queen or a certain Georgia lady.

Sweet Elizabethan Rose

4 cups dried rose petals and
   small buds
1 cup dried rose leaves
1 cup dried rose geranium leaves
2 tablespoons dried citrus peel
1 tablespoon whole allspice
1 teaspoon anise seed, crushed
1 whole nutmeg, crushed
1 bay leaf, finely broken
4 cinnamon sticks, broken into 1-inch
   pieces
1 tablespoon powdered orris root
Several drops each: jasmine oil, rose
   geranium oil, and tuberose oil
10 drops Elizabethan rose oil

Place rose petals, rose leaves, and rose geranium leaves in a large container. Add spices, and mix thoroughly with your hands.

In a separate container, combine the orris root powder with the oils, working them together with your fingers. [Wear gloves because some people are allergic to orris root.] Then sprinkle the powder over the rose petals, and stir thoroughly.

Place the potpourri in a tightly closed container, and leave it in a dark, cool place for about six weeks, stirring the mixture occasionally.

For sources of potpourri ingredients, send a stamped, self-addressed, business-size envelope to Potpourri Editor, *Southern Living*, Box C-119, Birmingham, Alabama 35282.

Chapter of the Embroiderer's Guild of Georgia helped create those."

When the Harrises moved into the mansion, there were only a few diseased rose bushes. A local nursery helped develop a rose garden, now dedicated to the one who cuts and tends the roses—Mrs. Harris.

"Cutting roses is a great way to get rid of frustrations," she explains. "There's something about the cutting away of the old and the anticipation of the new that makes pruning roses so rewarding."

The fresh blooms are cut for arrangements in the house, and she sends roses to the governor's office twice each week. "Now isn't that a reverse?" she laughs.

When the arrangements begin to look tired, the roses are pulled apart and the petals are spread onto screened trays in a drying rack. The rack is kept in a corner of the boiler room in the basement of the mansion, where the ventilation is good and the air is warm and dry.

"Fast drying preserves the color," she explains. "That's why the boiler room is the best place. You see, in a day and a half I can have potpourri petals. When they become the consistency of corn flakes, I know that they are dry enough to use.

"You can dry petals outside, but sometimes the humidity here in the South is too much. Perhaps when I move back home I can dry them over the hot water heater."

After the rose petals are dry, Mrs. Harris advises, "Put them in glass jars, and freeze them for a week. This kills any bugs. It keeps all those little critters from enjoying my potpourri after I give it to someone."

In addition to herbs, spices, and scented oils, she includes orris root powder in the mixture. It contributes no scent but serves as a fixative to help hold the fragrance.

Although Mrs. Harris has given her potpourri to people around the world, she is the one who gets the most pleasure from it. She explains, "Roses do take time, but the joy you get from them is worth it. Like any relationship in life, you just have to maintain it."

The following is her recipe for rose

Sachets filled with sweet-scented potpourri make memorable gifts.

Side Yards: Useful Places, Not Wasted Spaces

If your garden were a fairy tale, would your side yard be the neglected stepdaughter?
You don't need a magic wand or a fairy godmother to transform it into a vision.

by RITA W. STRICKLAND

Consider the poor side yard, ignored and abused while her sisters in front and back gobble up our time and attention. After all, who among us doesn't enter that friendly competition for the greenest front lawn in the neighborhood? And we work hard to make our backyards pleasant as well, because we spend so much of our leisure time there. But too often the lowly side yard sits forlornly between the two, uncared-for and unsightly.

These days, however, the status of side yards is rising. More and more homeowners have realized their importance as the connecting link between garden spaces in front of and behind our houses. No matter how stunning these larger areas are, guests who have to negotiate an obstacle course of garbage cans, firewood, or just plain junk to get from one to the other will fail to be impressed. "If your side yard isn't attractive," says Landscape Architect Dan Franklin, ASLA, of Atlanta, "it can destroy the whole effect of your garden."

Many of the most appealing side yards are composed of a simple walkway leading from the front yard to the back, with well-designed planting areas on either side. At his own home, Franklin built a gracefully curving walk of brick laid on sand. This is the major entrance to his back garden, so it serves to whet a visitor's appetite for what lies ahead. Along

A statue raised high on a pedestal provides a focal point in the center of a long, narrow space. Landscape Architect: Robert Chesnut, ASLA, Charleston, South Carolina.

the walk, evergreens, flowering shrubs, bulbs, perennials, and ferns offer a combination of colors and textures that changes with every season.

In many cities, the increased attention that's devoted to side yards is simply the result of limited space. Land costs are high, so lots are small, but the houses are as big as ever. That leaves less and less usable area outdoors.

"Often, much of the front yard is taken up by off-street parking, and there may be a pool or garage in the back," says Landscape Architect Charles Godfrey, ASLA, of Spartanburg, South Carolina. The Converse Heights area of Spartanburg presents some real challenges, he says. "For the most part, the neighborhood was laid out in 50- x 100-foot lots. The side yard is extremely valuable simply because you don't have space anywhere else." For homeowners Judy and Leland Bowmar, he designed a deck off the kitchen for outdoor dining, a small lawn area where the children can play, and lovely beds of evergreens and annuals—all in a side yard about 10 feet wide. "It's amazing what you can do in these small areas," Godfrey says.

In Houston, Landscape Architect Richard Dawson, ASLA, is called on frequently to make the most of such spaces. "Especially in the River Oaks neighborhood," he says, "we have a lot of deep, narrow houses, and many of them go all the way to the back property line. That leaves a long, narrow space along one side, with many of the interior rooms looking out in that direction." Often, Dawson en-

(Right) Entering this side yard through an iron gate, guests follow a flagstone walkway that leads them to the backyard. Landscape design: Lambert's, Dallas. Photographs: Van Chaplin, Mary-Gray Hunter

Nestled into the lowest part of the garden is this secluded terrace. It collects and channels water off the property during heavy rains. Photographs: Van Chaplin

Handsome Terrace Solves a Tough Problem

Nestled between the house and property line, this inviting garden used to be nothing short of a quagmire after a rain. And in Metairie, Louisiana, it rains over a hundred days each year. When the owners got tired of the mud, they asked New Orleans landscape architect René Fransen to bail them out.

"Originally they had an herb garden in raised beds, but there was so much shade, nothing would grow. Plus they had this terrible drainage problem," Fransen says. "Water would stand there for days." Knowing a ground cover or lawn would be hard to establish, he decided to pave the area instead, turning a problem into an asset. Now the owners have a private terrace—a woodsy retreat that's as nice to be in as it is to look at.

"They have a huge window in the living room that looks out on the side yard," Fransen says, "so the garden is for viewing as much as anything else." And with a large, open lawn in both the front and back of the house, the owners wanted this space to be smaller and more enclosed.

To pave the terrace, Fransen chose Pennsylvania red stone for an aged, elegant appearance that blends with the stone on the house. The terrace was lowered two steps to add interest as well as to set it apart from surrounding areas. In addition, lowering it allows water to collect on the terrace during extremely heavy rains. This proved to be an easier way to solve the drainage problem than regrading. Water is collected in catch basins that feed into the city storm drainage system.

To one side of the terrace, Fransen added a small rectangular reflecting pool. Though only 18 inches deep, its dark sides and bottom give an illusion

The delicate light-green foliage of Australian tree fern stands out against the background of evergreens.

of depth. Two fountains in the pool can be varied from small, gurgling jets to splashing columns of water to drown out unwanted noises and form a haven of peace and quiet. Lush plantings give the terrace an intimate, enclosed feeling; several large oaks offer a high, shady canopy.

In a planting bed along the house, Fransen used a row of sasanqua camellias. Beneath these he added gold-dust plant (*Aucuba japonica* Variegata) and cast-iron plant (*Aspidistra elatior*) to fill in between the sasanquas. A mix of big blue liriope and impatiens covers the rest of the bed.

Across the terrace are more cast-iron plants in addition to Japanese fatsia (*Fatsia japonica*), crinum lily (*Crinum* sp.), and Florida anise (*Illicium floridanum*). The thick planting of evergreens forms a dark-green mass, a perfect stage for showing off ferns and annuals. Wood ferns (*Dryopteris* sp.) are found throughout the bed. They die back in winter but return in spring.

Large Australian tree ferns (*Alsophila australis*) are also used. Two of these are planted in large clay pots that can be moved to the garage when temperatures drop below freezing.

A table and chairs placed near the fountain offer the owners a chance to fully enjoy the terrace—that is, when they aren't enjoying it from the comfort of their living room. As Fransen says, "The window really does make you feel as if the garden is inside . . . or that the living room is outside. It just depends on where you are."

LETTERS

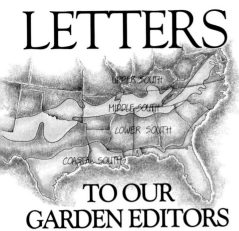

TO OUR GARDEN EDITORS

Black spot: Everyone in our area has considerable trouble with black spot on the leaves of roses. Can you tell me the cause and what to do about it?
W. J. G.,
Virginia Beach, Virginia.
Black spot is caused by the fungus *Diplocarpon rosae*. Its spores drift through the air, occasionally landing on rose leaves. There they sit, until a film of water coats the leaves for at least six hours, allowing the spores to germinate and penetrate the foliage. Once inside, the spores cannot be controlled.

The best way to handle this disease is by preventing it. First, pick up and destroy any fallen rose leaves, which often harbor overwintering spores. Then in late fall, strip off and destroy all foliage from your rose bushes. In late winter, apply a dormant spray of lime sulfur to the rose canes to kill any overwintering spores. When spring arrives, remove any old mulch around your bushes, and apply a fresh, 3-inch layer of shredded bark or pine straw. Finally, spray every 7 to 10 days throughout the growing season with Funginex or Phaltan. Be sure to follow label directions carefully.

Dogwood: Will cutting the lower branches off a dogwood make the top grow faster or fuller?
H. F.,
Aiken, South Carolina.
Trimming the lower branches off a dogwood may encourage it to grow taller, but it won't make it fuller. The biggest factor affecting the density of this tree is the amount of sunlight it receives. Trees planted in full sun become dense, low-branching, and rounded. Those growing in shade become loose, tall, and open. If your primary concern is to speed up the tree's growth, sprinkle about 3 pounds of 10-10-10 fertilizer per inch of trunk diameter around the dripline of the tree this fall. And keep the tree well watered next spring and summer.

Crinums: How can I divide and transplant crinum lilies?
T. C. W.,
Tuscaloosa, Alabama.
Fall is a good time to divide crinums. First, dig up the mature bulbs. This isn't as easy as it sounds, for the bulbs can be quite large. Then separate the offsets, and plant them several inches deep in a new location. They'll be too small to flower at first but will bloom after several years. Next, dig a hole about 1 foot wide and deep for each mature bulb. Set the bulb so that the "neck" protrudes about 1 to 2 inches above the soil surface. Backfill the hole with composted manure or compost from the garden. Space the bulbs 2 to 3 feet apart.

Yellow nandina: Have you ever heard of a yellow-fruited nandina? I saw one recently and would like to know where I could purchase one.
M. S.,
Waynesboro, Tennessee.
Yellow-fruited nandinas, while far from common, do exist. In fact, just about any species of tree or shrub that produces red fruit—holly, viburnum, crabapple, pyracantha—includes individual plants with yellow fruit. Unfortunately, we don't know of any commercial sources for a yellow-fruited nandina. The best way to obtain a plant is to ask a friend who already has one for a division. Or you could collect a handful of nandina berries, remove the seeds, and sow them about ½ inch deep into an empty garden bed in fall. They'll germinate sporadically during the next year. Most of the seedlings will produce red berries. However, other colors—yellow, cream, pink, or white—are possible.

Although nandina berries are usually red, they may be yellow, cream, white, or pink.

Lily-of-the-valley: Will I be able to grow lily-of-the-valley in a shallow pot on my balcony?
M. K.,
Jupiter, Florida.
A lovely ground cover for shade, lily-of-the-valley (*Convallaria majalis*) is, unfortunately, difficult to grow in South Florida. For one thing, unless you can refrigerate the roots for about three months each winter, the plant won't bloom. Moreover, growing it outside in a shallow container during the summer presents other problems. Lily-of-the-valley likes moist soil, so you'd have to water several times a day. If you forget one day, the leaves will scorch. All in all, you'd be better off growing plants suited to your area.

Trees and drain pipes: We removed a large flowering cherry from our front lawn this summer because its roots had clogged our pipes. What fast-growing shade tree with shallow roots could I plant instead?
M. E. B.,
Lutherville, Maryland.
It's not a good idea to plant a shallow-rooted tree near your pipes. Believe it or not, shallow-rooted trees, such as maples and poplars, cause the biggest problems in this regard. A deep-rooted tree, such as an oak, would be a better choice. We'd especially recommend red oak (*Quercus rubra*) because it grows quickly, makes a nice shade tree, and has good fall color. Don't plant directly on top of the pipes, however. Keeping all trees as far away from pipes as possible will minimize potential problems.

TIP OF THE MONTH

You can discourage a cat from digging in the soil around a potted plant by cutting a circle of thin mesh screening the same width as the pot. Slit the mesh to the center of the circle, and carefully fit it around the base of the plant.
Mary Ann Johnson,
Rocky Mount, Virginia.
Editor's note: We'd like to have your ideas—the ones that have worked for you. We're especially interested in vegetables, houseplants, shrubs, trees, and garden care. For each tip that is published, we will pay $10 and send you one of our garden books.

Submit as many ideas as you wish, but each must be on a separate sheet or card, along with your name, address, and telephone number. We may need to edit the tips, and none will be acknowledged or returned. Send to Gardening Tips, *Southern Living,* Box 523, Birmingham, Alabama 35201.

CHECKLIST
For September

☐ **Cabbage loopers**—These garden pests can destroy broccoli, cabbage, cauliflower, and other cole crops. Apply *Bacillus thuringiensis* as soon as the first small worms are sighted. Follow label directions exactly, and reapply as indicated.

☐ **Camellias**—Disbudding camellias now will result in larger blooms this winter. Camellias produce two types of buds: flowerbuds, which are fat and rounded, and leafbuds, which are pointed and slim. To get the biggest flowers, remove most of the flowerbuds in each cluster, allowing only the largest one on a shoot to remain.

☐ **Compost**—You can build a simple compost bin by shaping a piece of wire mesh 4 to 5 feet wide and 9 feet long into a circle and fastening the ends securely. Place it in a partially shaded site, and use stakes to hold it in the ground. Begin by adding a 2-foot layer of leaves, grass clippings, pine needles, etc., to the bin. Tamp the material down to a height of 6 to 8 inches, and sprinkle a thin covering of soil over the top; then add 2 pounds of 20% superphosphate and ¼ pound of ammonium nitrate. Repeat with additional 2-foot layers until the bin is full. Make a slight depression in the center to trap rainwater, and sprinkle lightly during periods of drought. Turn the pile every three months, moving uncomposted material into the center of the pile.

☐ **Garden tools**—Prevent rust by cleaning tools after every use; knock or rinse away clinging soil, and store the tools in a dry location. An occasional rubbing with oil is also beneficial. Don't leave fertilizer in your spreader or wheelbarrow; it will corrode the metal.

☐ **Hedges**—Pruning hedges now will allow time for new growth to conceal cut leaves and twigs and then harden off before cold weather arrives. Trim out dead wood, and remove seedlings that do not belong, such as privet and honeysuckle. Remember, to keep the lower portion of the hedge thick, it has to get plenty of light. This is done by keeping the top of the hedge narrower than the base.

☐ **Hummingbirds**—To attract hummingbirds to your garden, try planting these flowers. Scarlet sage (*Salvia splendens*) is a popular annual that grows in full sun or partial shade and flowers from summer through fall over most of the South. In coastal areas, it's best for spring and summer bloom; in South Florida, it flowers in fall and spring. Cardinal flower (*Lobelia cardinalis*) is a native Southern perennial that loves partial shade and is a perfect choice for the edge of the woods. In the Southeast it adapts to both moist and dry areas, but along the coast it prefers wet spots. Trumpet honeysuckle (*Lonicera sempervirens*), unlike the pesky Japanese species, provides summer-long nectar for hummingbirds, and they, in turn, provide entertainment for the gardener. Florida gardeners can plant fountain plant (*Russelia equisetiformis*), also known as firecracker plant. This is a low, spreading plant with arching branches and a feathery texture. Small red flowers appear throughout the year, making it a popular ground cover for sunny areas. You will find that hummingbirds do visit other flowers, but to ensure plenty of activity in your garden, keep a feeder in the garden from spring through October. Refill the feeder weekly with fresh sugar solution. By the way, you'll probably have only one pair of these tiny birds because they guard their territories.

☐ **Landscape design**—If you are building a new home, consider consulting a landscape architect to help you locate the house on the site, allow for circulation of cars and people, and plan outdoor living areas. If you intend to save existing trees, safeguard them during construction. Keep heavy equipment away from the trunks and off the roots, as compacted soil will cause the trees to decline. Subtle but deadly damage is done by filling and grading around a tree. You cannot replace a mature tree, so be sure that you consult an arborist before work begins.

☐ **Mail-order plants**—As by-products in the manufacture of plastic foam, chlorofluorocarbons are partially responsible for the depletion of the ozone layer. Some environmentally conscious companies have stopped using plastic foam "peanuts" to pack mail-order plants. Instead, they use shredded paper or other renewable, recyclable materials. You may want to follow suit by starting your seeds in peat pots or reusing clay or plastic pots rather than buying plastic foam cups.

☐ **Perennials**—Yarrow, spider lilies, Shasta daisies, coreopsis, coneflowers, gaillardia, and daylilies are some of the perennials that can be divided and replanted in early fall. Plan beds carefully, considering each plant's height and color. Before replanting divisions, amend the beds with plenty of organic material, and work in 1½ pounds of 5-10-10 fertilizer per square yard of bed. Water every few days until the divisions become established.

☐ **Propagation**—An easy way to propagate shrubs that weep, such as azaleas, forsythia, lantana, honeysuckle, and winter jasmine, is by layering. This is a technique of rooting a stem while it is still attached to the parent plant. Choose a new shoot on the side of the plant that receives the most sun, and scrape a narrow band of bark from around the stem. Bend the injured stem so that it touches the ground, cover with soil, and anchor in place with a forked stick, brick, or rock. In spring, cut the rooted stem free, and transplant it to the garden.

☐ **Shade**—If you need shade immediately for an outdoor living area, such as a patio or deck, consider building an arbor. First, study the angle of the sun during those times of day when you use the area most; then locate the arbor accordingly. An open, lath-type structure overhead will usually provide adequate shade and allow maximum air circulation. Vines can be grown on the arbor to provide color or fragrance. The arbor should fit in with the style of your house and with surrounding garden spaces. If you have any doubts about location, design, or construction, consult a landscape architect.

☐ **Spider mites**—These pinpoint-size pests can cause damage you don't notice until it's nearly too late. Spider mites breed on the underside of leaves where you can't see them and then seem to appear overnight. When it gets too crowded on leaves, they move to new growth and flowerbuds, where their feeding stunts growth. To control mites, apply insecticidal soap according to directions on the label. It may take several applications to control them all, so be on the lookout for them to come back as long as the weather is dry.

SPECIAL TIPS FOR THE SOUTHEAST

☐ **Bulbs**—It's time to plant, and the rewards may be sooner than you think. Fall-flowering bulbs should be set out immediately. If you wait too long, these eager bulbs may flower unnoticed in a paper bag. Good choices for autumn color include colchicums, crocuses, red spider lilies, baby cyclamen, and white swamp lilies. Delay planting spring-flowering bulbs until next month in the Upper South and until November in the Middle and Lower South.

☐ **Conservation**—Most of us would never consider digging up an endangered plant from a natural area. However, if you buy a plant or bulb that has been dug, you are supporting those who do. To be sure you buy from a reputable firm, read the catalog and look for phrases such as "nursery propagated." Be wary of catalogs offering native orchids and trilliums inexpensively; they are almost surely dug.

☐ **Herbs**—Plant perennial herbs now to fill bare spots in beds. Sage, oregano, lemon balm, thyme, and winter savory may not grow much this fall, but they will develop a good root system that will support growth next spring. You can also set out cloves of garlic for harvest in late spring and early summer. Allow 4 to 6 inches between plants. Clip off the flower stalk when it appears next spring to divert energy to the bulbs. This is also a good time to sow seeds of biennials and hardy annuals. Caraway, coriander, and chervil can be sown in well-prepared soil. While caraway and coriander need exposure to full sun, chervil requires partial shade.

SPECIAL TIPS FOR FLORIDA

☐ **Flowers**—Hardy annuals and perennials to plant this month for winter and spring color include browallia, gaillardia, lupine, pansies, petunias, pinks, poppies, Shasta daisies, and sweet alyssum. Either set out transplants or start seeds indoors in flats for later transplanting. Before setting out transplants, improve the soil by working in a 4-inch layer of compost, finely ground bark or sphagnum moss.

☐ **Spider lilies**—Grasshoppers can ruin your spider lilies by chewing the young stems to the ground. At the first sign of infestation, dust the plants with Sevin according to label directions; if necessary, continue regular applications until flowering is complete.

SPECIAL TIPS FOR TEXAS

☐ **Bluebonnets**—September is bluebonnet planting time. Seed sown now will have time to germinate and form well-rooted rosettes that can survive the winter. Because bluebonnets have a tough seed coat, poor germination frequently results. In the past, many ways of softening or scarifying the seed coats have been recommended, including soaking them in water, scratching them with sandpaper, or rolling them in a rock tumbler. Now there are bluebonnet seeds available that have been pre-scarified with acid, thus greatly increasing germination rates. Bluebonnets aren't particular about soil, as long as it's well drained. Till the planting bed, and broadcast the seed; then cover with ¼ to ½ inch of soil. The soil should be kept moist until seedlings appear, usually in a week or 10 days. Once well established, stands of bluebonnets should reseed themselves annually.

☐ **Herbs**—Plant herbs now to fill bare spots in your winter landscape. Sage, thyme, and winter savory are hardy throughout the state. South Texas gardeners can also plant rosemary and dill. Transplants set out now will have plenty of time to become well established before cold weather arrives.

☐ **Tulips**—In the lower half of Texas, tulips and many other spring-flowering bulbs will need to be chilled 45 to 60 days before planting if they're to flower properly. For that reason, and to ensure the best selection, purchase bulbs now. Place them in a plastic or paper bag that has been punched with holes to allow air circulation, and store them in the vegetable drawer of your refrigerator. Don't put fruit in the drawer, since some fruits give off ethylene gas, which may cause blossoms to be malformed.

PLANT SPINACH IN FALL, HARVEST ALL WINTER

Although spinach can be grown in spring, fall planting is ideal. For a fall harvest, seed should be sown from four to eight weeks before the first frost is expected in your part of the South. Try to select a spot away from streetlights or floodlights; these artificial light sources can trigger bolting (flowering), which results in a strong, bitter taste.

Before planting, work in ¼ cup of 10-10-10 per 10 feet of row. Sow seeds in rows spaced 1½ feet apart, or scatter seeds over beds about 18 inches wide. Cover with ½ inch of soil. Thin seedlings to 4 to 6 inches apart after they sprout. When plants have four to five leaves, side-dress with ¼ cup of 10-10-10 per 10 feet of row.

Be sure to plant enough to last through winter. For fresh use, plant 5 to 10 feet of a single row or 1½ to 2½

Shorter days and cooler temperatures make fall the ideal time to grow spinach.
Photograph: Van Chaplin

feet of an 18-inch-wide row per person. If you want more for freezing or canning, double this amount.

Growth will stop when cold weather arrives, but the plants will survive, and their taste will improve after they're exposed to frost. Leave plants in the garden and harvest as needed. In the Upper South, you'll need to protect them from severe weather by covering with a light mulch, such as pine straw, or use floating row cover sold by garden equipment companies. Young plants that overwinter will begin growing again in spring as temperatures rise. Be sure to harvest early because the first warm spell will cause bolting.

There are two ways to harvest spinach. You can pinch off the large outer leaves when they are 3 to 6 inches long. This will allow the plant to produce new leaves from its center. Or cut the entire plant at soil level when it reaches 4 to 6 inches in diameter.

Often called a living fossil, the ginkgo may drop its leaves in a single day.

xanthophyll. What benefits these colors provide to the trees is unclear. But if their beauty causes a tree to be planted or propagated or saves it from being cut down, they've served their master well.

The Southern fall may not be as storied as that of New England, but it persists considerably longer. The first trees to change, those in the Appalachians, may do so in late August if the weather is right. Along the Gulf Coast, fall color lingers well into December. Some of the season's first yellows belong to the remarkable ginkgo (*Ginkgo biloba*), a survivor from prehistoric times. Its leaves change to a transcendent butter yellow and later drop in a single day.

In quick succession come the sulfur yellows of tulip poplar (*Liriodendron tulipifera*), the bright canaries of red maple (*Acer rubrum*), and the rich golds of sugar maple (*A. saccharum*).

White ash (*Fraxinus americana*) combines yellow and purple into a color that has no name. The foliage of the venerable American beech (*Fagus grandifolia*) assumes the golden-brown color of warm dinner rolls. And the aureate leaves of hickory (*Carya* sp.) shine like a beacon among Southern pines.

The golden fall ends with a grand procession of sturdy oaks— willow oak (*Quercus phellos*), chestnut oak (*Q. prinus*), bur oak (*Q. macrocarpa*), and water oak (*Q. nigra*)—that mix brown tannins into their yellow-stained mantles. When these last leaves have dropped, winter begins—and autumn lies resting on the ground.

A double row of sugar maples forms a gilded canopy above this country drive.

An attractive fence screens the front rooms of this Jackson, Mississippi, house from the street. Photographs: Mary-Gray Hunter

No Longer in a Fishbowl

Windows let you see out of a house, but they also let the neighbors see in. This was the dilemma facing Stan and Exie Pratt of Jackson, Mississippi. Two large windows in front of the living and dining rooms afforded very little privacy from the street. "We felt we were living in a fishbowl," recalls Exie.

The home had other problems, too. According to Landscape Architect Carter Brown, ASLA, of Green Oak Landscape, the brick and board-and-batten facade of the house "just shouted sixties." Moreover, access to the front door was limited to a narrow walk between the driveway and front steps. The Pratts

Before improvements, the front rooms had little privacy, and visitors had to cross the lawn to get to the door.

asked Brown to come up with a plan that would update the house's appearance, improve access, and provide the needed privacy.

Brown's design features a new, formal walk that allows visitors parked

out on the street to approach the house without crossing the lawn. He also added a handsome fence that encloses the front door and steps then extends to the side of the house. The fence's stuccoed posts consist of concrete-filled cinder blocks, while pressure-treated shutters comprise the wooden panels. These panels contribute a softer, more natural feeling than concrete or brick would. Stucco was also applied to the house's exterior, resulting in a more contemporary look.

Brown transformed the space between the house and fence into a charming courtyard garden. Visitors can either walk straight to the front door or detour down a meandering gravel path through the courtyard to a gate that opens to a side yard. A small fountain lends the refreshing sound of splashing water. Concealed light illuminates the courtyard at night.

In effect, the courtyard adds an extra room to the house. Whether the Pratts are dining, entertaining, or simply relaxing, they feel as if they're out among the plants, even though they're sitting inside.

Best of all, this garden room is very private. "Now we never draw the front window shades," says Exie.

This courtyard garden between the house and fence can be enjoyed from the path or from inside the house.

LETTERS

TO OUR GARDEN EDITORS

Lily-of-the-valley: I have lilies-of-the-valley planted in a shady area by our front porch. They have multiplied rapidly, but only one or two plants bloom each year. Can you tell me how to get more blooms? *A. L. M., Auburn, Alabama.*
Lily-of-the-valley (*Convallaria majalis*) is among the most attractive of shade-loving ground covers. It does best in a highly organic soil that retains moisture. Try top-dressing your lily bed this fall with a mixture of composted cow manure and finely chopped leaves. Also sprinkle a little slow-release fertilizer, such as blood meal, cottonseed meal, or fish emulsion, over the bed. If you repeat this procedure every fall and water the plants thoroughly during summer droughts, you should see more blooms in the future.

Pruning spirea: I have approximately 30 huge spireas across the front of my property. All are full of dead limbs. Would it be okay to cut the shrubs to within a foot or two of the ground? *W. C. P., Marianna, Florida.*
Although you could prune your spireas severely, such a drastic step would ruin the bloom for next spring. Here's what to do instead. This fall, after the shrubs have dropped their leaves, remove one-third of their canes at ground level. Cut out the oldest and woodiest canes first, along with any that are dead or diseased. Repeat this procedure the next fall and the next after that. At the end of three years, you will have completely rejuvenated plants.

Summer bulbs: This spring I planted a bed of summer bulbs that included gladioli, freesias, montbretias, and tuberous begonias. Will they survive the winter in the ground if given a heavy pine straw mulch? *R. E., Carrollton, Mississippi.*

Montbretias may survive in your area if mulched heavily in late fall. The other bulbs will have to be dug and stored. Dig them before the first freeze in your area. Allow the bulbs to air dry; then dust them with captan to prevent fungus and mold. Place them in mesh bags, and store until spring in a dark, dry place that stays above freezing.

Sneezeweed: A friend of mine gave me a plant called sneezeweed, but I'm afraid to plant it because of my allergies. Should I be concerned about this? *R. B., Albany, Georgia.*
Not at all. Sneezeweed (*Helenium* sp.) is a misnomer; the plant causes neither sneezing nor hay fever. In fact, it's one of the finest perennials for the fall garden. Growing 3 to 4 feet tall, it bears flowers in all colors of autumn—

Sneezeweed produces flowers of orange, bronze, or yellow in late summer and fall. Photograph: Mary-Gray Hunter

yellow, orange, bronze, and red. The blossoms open early in September in much of the South, and the show continues for six weeks or more. Sneezeweed prefers full sun and moist, well-drained organic soil. Sprinkle 1 tablespoon of slow-release fertilizer around each plant in spring. Divide clumps every three years in spring to keep the plants vigorous. Sneezeweed belongs in the rear of your perennial border for lots of bright color at a time when little else is blooming.

Grass: We're away from our house during the summer, and by the time we return in fall, our centipede grass has turned brown. Is there a grass we

could plant that would stay green through the winter? *S. C., Wilmington, North Carolina.*
Grasses that stay green in winter like cooler summers than the ones you have in your area. We suggest that you stick with your centipede, which is an excellent, low-maintenance grass that will pretty much take care of itself while you're away in summer. Then in the fall, overseed the centipede with either annual or perennial rye. The rye will give you a nice, green lawn from fall through spring. When warm weather returns, the rye will die, but the centipede will green up. Repeat this procedure each fall.

Gardenia: Recently, quite a few of the leaves of our two large gardenias have turned yellow. What is causing this, and how can I correct it? *A. C. C., Tuscaloosa, Alabama.*
Even though gardenias are evergreen, it's normal for their older leaves to turn yellow and drop periodically. This usually signals that the plants are going dormant. However, several other factors, such as unusually dry weather, may be causing the problem. Another possibility is a deficiency of iron in the soil, which will cause the leaves to turn yellow between the veins. You can correct this by applying iron chelate or iron sulphate to the soil around your plants. Both products are available at many local garden centers.

TIP OF THE MONTH

Just before the first frost, I pick all of the tomatoes in our garden that are large enough to save. Then I wrap them individually in newspaper, about two sheets for each, and store them in a loosely covered box in a cool, dark room. The tomatoes will slowly ripen and keep for weeks. Last year, I had fresh tomatoes for Thanksgiving and Christmas. *Janet A. Barbour, Smithfield, North Carolina.*
Editor's note: We'd like to have your ideas—the ones that have worked for you. We're especially interested in vegetables, houseplants, shrubs, trees, and garden care. For each tip that is published, we will pay $10 and send you one of our garden books.

Submit as many ideas as you wish, but each must be on a separate sheet or card, along with your name, address, and telephone number. We may need to edit the tips, and none will be acknowledged or returned. Send to Gardening Tips, *Southern Living,* Box 523, Birmingham, Alabama 35201.

CHECKLIST
For October

☐ **Caladiums**—It's time to dig up tubers when caladium foliage begins to yellow. If left in the ground, they will be killed by the cold. Use a shovel or fork to lift the tubers, being careful not to wound them. Spread them to dry, and then pack in sphagnum peat moss. Store in a cool, dry place until time to plant in spring.

☐ **Diamond-back moth**—Larvae that hatch from the eggs adult moths lay on cabbage, collards, broccoli, and cauliflower can devastate these cole crops. The adult moths are small and grayish, and the wings of the male form a row of diamond-shaped, yellow spots down the middle of the back. The eggs are tiny, yellowish white in color, and may be laid singly or in small groups, usually on the underside of leaves. Within a month, they'll be fully grown, yellow-green in color, less than ½ inch in length, and may be observed dropping from the plant on a silken thread. Apply *Bacillus thuringiensis* spray or dust, such as Dipel, according to label directions.

☐ **Fruit**—The catalog of catalogs has been published by the Seed Savers Exchange, a nonprofit organization of vegetable gardeners and fruit hobbyists. The *Fruit, Berry and Nut Inventory* is a 366-page compendium of all fruit selections currently offered for sale by 248 mail-order companies.

It is an excellent resource for hard-to-find items as well as for information. For each selection, you usually find a description of the fruit, hardiness, chilling requirement, earliness, and its history. To obtain a copy, write to Seed Savers Exchange, Rural Route 3, Box 239, Decorah, Iowa 52101. ($19 postpaid for softcover, $26 postpaid for hardcover.)

☐ **Garlic**—A 10-foot row of garlic can easily produce a year's supply, but you'll need to get started this month to have your first crop by next May or June. Break cloves from the bulbs, making sure there's a piece of the bulb's base on each one. Plant cloves upright with the base at the bottom in furrows 1 or 2 inches deep.

☐ **Landscaping**—Planting and transplanting trees and shrubs are good projects for fall. Cool weather makes it easier for the plants to establish their roots before topgrowth resumes in spring. Be sure to set containerized plants at the same depth as they were growing in the container. To do this, see that the top of the root ball is level with the ground. Then work a slow-release tree-and-shrub food into the backfill when refilling the planting hole. Apply at the rate recommended on the label. Water the plants thoroughly, and continue watering about twice a week through the fall and winter, skipping only when there is a rain.

☐ **Leaves**—Rake falling leaves from lawn areas before they mat down and suffocate the grass. Remove debris

from concrete sidewalks, driveways, and terraces because the decaying matter will stain paving. A leaf blower is handy for removing leaves in beds of ground cover, such as ivy, juniper, and pachysandra. These are difficult to rake around because it is so easy to snag the stems, tearing them out of the ground.

☐ **Overseeding**—Overseed Bermuda and centipede lawns as soon as possible with annual rye for a green lawn all winter long. Mow your lawn about an inch tall, and rake it deeply to scratch up the thatch. Using a fertilizer spreader or a seeder, broadcast the grass seed over the lawn at the rate of about 5 pounds per 1,000 square feet. Don't be tempted to scatter the seeds by hand because the results will be uneven. Drag the back of a rake over the entire area to work the seeds into the turf. Feed with a starter fertilizer, and water daily until the grass is about 3 inches tall. Continue watering once or twice each rainless week through winter.

☐ **Propagation**—Rather than rooting cuttings, you can propagate shrubs by layering, a technique of rooting a stem while it is still attached to the parent plant. Choose a new shoot that's long enough to touch the ground and that's on the side of the plant that receives the most sun. Use a sharp knife to cut an angled slit halfway through the stem or scrape off a narrow band of bark from around it. Make a depression in the soil near the plant; then bend the

FEED THE GARDEN IN FALL, TOO

Don't put away the plant food yet; fall may be the most critical season to fertilize.

In the Upper South, fescue and bluegrass lawns will benefit from a feeding of 1 pound of nitrogen per 1,000 square feet. Apply the same to overseeded lawns in the Middle South once the new grass is up and growing.

In the Middle, Lower, and Coastal South, warm-season grasses, such as Bermuda, St. Augustine, and Zoysia, will soon be going dormant. Apply a "winterizer" fertilizer, one with a low-nitrogen/high-potassium formula. This

Slow-release fertilizer applied after the first frost will help shrubs through the winter.
Photograph: Mary-Gray Hunter

should improve winter hardiness. Look for a product with about 1 part nitrogen to 3 parts potassium, such as 8-8-25, and apply it about four to six weeks before the first expected frost.

Roses are renewed by the cooler autumn weather, so they will appreciate a light application of a good rose

food. Cool-weather annuals and vegetables will be growing rapidly, too. Apply a liquid or slow-release fertilizer at the recommended rate.

Trees and shrubs could use a fall feeding also, but in South Florida and South Texas it is best to wait until after frost. The plants will be dormant and less likely to sprout new growth in response to the fertilizer. However, the roots will continue to be active as long as the soil is not frozen. Slow-release fertilizer will help them get through winter and boost them into vigorous growth next spring. In South Florida and South Texas, you should fertilize trees and shrubs this month because, even as their growth slows toward winter, they store food in their roots for spring. Plants that go into winter properly fed will stand cold better than hungry plants.

injured stem into the depression, cover it with soil, and anchor it in place with a forked stick, brick, or rock. Let it remain in place all winter. Then in spring, cut the rooted stem free from the parent plant.

☐ **Soil**—Winter is too cold, summer is too hot, and spring is too busy. So now is the best time to prepare new beds for flowers, vegetables, and herbs. Double-digging is laborious but worth the time and effort. It involves removing one shovel's depth of topsoil, then amending the next 6 to 8 inches of soil with organic matter, fertilizer, and lime or sulfur as recommended by your soil test results. Do the same for the top layer as you replace it. This makes a slightly raised bed of loose, fertile, well-drained soil that is 12 to 15 inches deep. Plants will be deeper rooted, more drought resistant, and more vigorous in such a well-prepared bed.

☐ **Winter squash**—Cure butternut and hubbard squash before storing them for the winter. When you harvest, leave the stems attached; then place the fruit in a warm location with good air circulation for about two weeks. This curing process will harden the rinds and increase the storage life of these squash selections.

SPECIAL TIPS FOR THE SOUTHEAST

☐ **Cover crops**—Enrich bare beds used for vegetables and flowers by sowing clover or rye, which will grow all winter. Next spring, turn the crop under with a fork or tiller two to three weeks before you plan to plant.

☐ **Seeds**—This is a good time to sow seeds of cool-season annuals. They will germinate early, grow into healthy plants, and produce flowers in spring. These include forget-me-nots (*Myosotis*), Shirley poppies, bachelor's button, larkspurs, and Johnny-jump-ups. Sow them in a prepared garden bed at the spacing recommended on the seed package. It's a good idea to sow them in bulb beds where the color, height, and flowering season will complement the bulbs or conceal the fading foliage.

☐ **Summer bulbs**—A blanket of mulch should protect summer bulbs through winter in the Lower South. But in the Middle and Upper South, these tender bulbs should be dug each fall and replanted in spring. Store them in a cool, dry place, such as a basement or heated garage. Temperatures should be no cooler than 50 to 60 degrees. **Cannas** should be dug each year in the Upper South and divided every three years throughout the South. Discard the old rhizomes, saving the younger ones that have growing points called eyes. **Dahlias** need to be dug and divided each year whether they are hardy or not. After the first frost, cut the stem back to about 6 inches, and uproot the tubers. Clean and label each clump; then store them in boxes of slightly damp sphagnum peat moss, perlite, or vermiculite. Divide clumps in spring before planting, leaving a growing point on each stem. **Elephant-ears** can be killed by a hard freeze in the Middle and Upper South. Dig after a light frost has browned the leaves.

☐ **Vegetables**—Knowing when to harvest can make the difference in the flavor of root crops. For tender beets, pull them when they are 1 to 3 inches in diameter. If the seed packet says that round, red radishes mature in 22 days, that's when you should harvest them. If left in the ground too long, they'll become quite woody. Carrots can be harvested anytime from very young to fully mature; trim the tops as soon as you pull them. Salsify needs to be left in the soil until after frost for best flavor; harvest only as needed.

SPECIAL TIPS FOR FLORIDA

☐ **Lawns**—Gardeners in North Florida can overseed lawns with annual ryegrass to enjoy a lush green carpet all winter. Mow your lawn about an inch tall, and rake it deeply to scratch up the thatch. Using a fertilizer spreader or a seeder, broadcast the grass seed over the lawn at the rate of about 5 pounds per 1,000 square feet. (Don't be tempted to scatter the seeds by the handful.) Then drag the back of a rake over the entire area to work the seeds into the turf. Feed with a starter fertilizer, and water daily until the grass is about 3 inches tall. Continue watering once or twice a week through winter.

☐ **Mulch**—October begins Florida's dry season, so you'll need to water more now. To conserve the moisture in flowerbeds, around shrubs, and in the vegetable garden, apply a layer of organic mulch 2 or 3 inches thick. The mulch will also help keep down weeds. Popular organic mulches include pine straw, pine bark, and shredded cypress. As an alternative to cypress, most of which is made from virgin stands of trees, try new mulches made from pesky melaleuca trees.

☐ **Strawberries**—Start strawberries now so the plants will grow large before they begin bearing fruit in late winter and early spring. The three most popular varieties for the state are Florida 90, Sequoia, and Florida Belle. Tioga is another variety sometimes available, but it is susceptible to leaf spot diseases. Strawberries need a sunny spot in the garden where the soil is well drained. However, you can also grow strawberries in hanging baskets, window boxes, or strawberry jars (big pots with pockets or holes in the sides for plants). Whether you plant strawberries in pots or in the ground, be sure to work in a couple of tablespoons of slow-release fertilizer per plant to encourage growth and plenty of fruit.

☐ **Vegetables**—Gardeners in North Florida can plant cool-weather vegetables now. Sow seeds of lettuce, radishes, carrots, and spinach for fresh salads this fall and winter. You can also grow broccoli, cabbage, kale, collards, Swiss chard, and turnip greens. Each may be started from seed. Broccoli, however, will take about a month longer if started from seed rather than from transplants. This is also a good time to plant root crops. Turnips and beets are always sweetest in the fall.

SPECIAL TIPS FOR TEXAS

☐ **Frost dates**—Knowing approximately when to expect the first frost of the year helps you plan when to sow, harvest, and protect your garden. Average frost dates across Texas include late October for the Panhandle, mid-November for Central, West, and East Texas, late November for South Texas, and early December for the coastal areas. Contact your county Extension agent for specific information about your area.

☐ **Onions**—Though growing onions from seeds is a bit more difficult than planting onion sets, seeds will offer you a wider choice of selections. After working in ¼ cup of 10-10-10 fertilizer per 10 feet of row, sow seeds thickly in ½-inch-deep furrows 1½ feet apart. Water well. When seedlings are about 4 inches tall, thin to a 2- to 4-inch spacing. Recommended selections for Texas include Red Granex, White Granex, and Evergreen White Bunching.

November

Greenish-yellow flowers appear in candelabra-like clusters in spring.

THE SOUTHERN GARDEN®

SASSAFRAS
Fascinating History, Beautiful Leaves

*Early settlers considered this tree a medicinal gold mine.
Today Southerners treasure the colors of its autumn foliage.*

by STEVE BENDER

Much has been written concerning the fall spectacle of sassafras, one of our finest native trees. But perhaps Donald Culross Peattie, the superb naturalist, put it best when he wrote:

"Against the Indian summer sky, a tree lifts up its hands and testifies to glory, the glory of a blue October day. Yellow or orange, or blood-orange, or sometimes softest salmon pink, or blotched with bright vermilion, the leaves of the Sassafras prove that not all autumnal splendor is confined to northern forests. Deep into the South, along the snake-rail fences, beside the soft wood roads, in old fields where the rusty brook sedge is giving way to the return of forest, the Sassafras carries its splendid banners to vie with the scarlet Black Gum and the yellow Sweet Gum and other trees of which the New Englander may hardly have heard."

Given the rich history of sassafras (*Sassafras albidum*), it's hard to believe even a few people, much less an entire region, could be unaware of it. According to Peattie, the tree first gained fame in 1574 when Nicholas Monardes, the "physician of Seville," published *Joyfull Newes Out of the Newe Founde Worlde*. Monardes wrote: "From the Florida, . . . thei bryng a woodd and roote of a tree that growth in those parts, of great vertues, and great excellencies, that thei heale there with greevous and variable deseases. . . . The name of this Tree . . . is . . . Sassafras."

The aromatic oil present in the leaves, bark, and roots led Europeans to believe sassafras could cure all sorts of things—malaria, ague, various fevers, colds, and lameness. Moreover, the wood was said to repel insects. Before long, European demand for sassafras was such that English expeditionary companies set off for Virginia for the sole purpose of acquiring it. In fact, as late as 1610 England required shipments of sassafras from Virginia as a condition for the colony retaining its charter.

Meanwhile, in the South sassafras oil gained fame as a healthful "spring tonic." It was also used to flavor root beer, candy, pharmaceuticals, and tea. Today some Cajun cooks still grind the leaves for filé. However, health authorities discount possible medicinal benefits and even discourage the making of sassafras tea, suspecting the oil—safrole—of causing cancer if ingested in large quantities. (You can purchase sassafras concentrate with the safrole filtered out.) But this doesn't detract in any way from sassafras's ornamental value.

FROM THE WILD
TO THE GARDEN

In the Gulf South sassafras can become a large tree, 70 to 80 feet high. In most places, however, it's much smaller, perhaps 25 to 30 feet. In shape, it resembles flowering dogwood (*Cornus florida*), possessing layered, horizontal branches tipped with plump flowerbuds.

(Above) *Blazing yellow and orange, this sassafras extends a flamboyant greeting at the entrance to a driveway.* **(Right)** *Leaves may have several lobes or none at all, with fall color ranging from bright yellow to orange and red.*

Trees can be either male or female. Males sport showier flowers, but females develop shiny, blue berries, which birds absolutely relish. Birds distribute seed wherever they perch, which is why you often see sassafras sprouting beneath large trees, electric lines, and along fencerows. Left to itself the tree suckers readily and forms thickets in fields and on roadsides.

Two characteristics distinguish sassafras from other trees. The first is the bark, which on young trees is bright green. The second is the varying shapes of its leaves. The leaves may be oval or lobed—and if lobed, may have one, two, or three lobes. Often all four shapes appear on the same tree. The lobes remind some people of fin-gers—hence the "hands" to which Peattie refers.

Few trees surpass this one's fall spectacle. The leaves assume colors of scarlet, yellow, and gold, but the most memorable is bright orange tinged with pink. Trees in full sun exhibit more of the red and orange shades.

In home landscapes sassafras is perfect for naturalized areas, where it spreads to fill the understory beneath large shade trees. You can also use it in mixed borders or as a specimen or lawn tree. If possible, plant it in front of tall evergreens. This displays the fall foliage to best advantage.

Sassafras isn't fussy. It grows in just about any well-drained soil and does well in either full sun or light shade.

Except for Japanese beetles and gypsy moths, pests generally leave it alone. Don't try to transplant it from the wild, as sparse root systems make successful digging of established trees nearly impossible. Instead, purchase container-grown trees from a nursery. Plant in either fall or spring.

People seldom keep sassafras in the medicine cabinet anymore. But for spicing up the autumn landscape, it may be just what the doctor ordered.

Sassafras is rarely available at local garden centers. For sources, send a stamped, self-addressed, business-size envelope to Sassafras Editor, *Southern Living*, Box C-119, Birmingham, Alabama 35282.

Chinese pennisetum (Pennisetum alopecuroides) *is known for its soft, flowing blossoms that spill in the wind.*

THE SOUTH EMBRACES
ORNAMENTAL GRASSES

Popular in pockets of the South and catching on fast, ornamental grasses are just what the name implies. Use them for accents, specimens, and as massed ground covers. And be prepared to answer the question "What is that?"

by LOIS B. TRIGG / photography MARY-GRAY HUNTER

In Maryland and the District of Columbia two men have been working quietly and diligently to kindle our taste for ornamental grasses. One is Landscape Architect Wolfgang Oehme, whose bold landscape design of the Federal Reserve building in 1977 provided one of the first public introductions to the gentle rustle and flowing forms of this underused group of plants. The second is Kurt Bluemel, a Baldwin, Maryland, nurseryman and landscape architect who began selling a few grasses and now ships thousands to gardeners each year. Having come

from grass-rich Central Europe in the late fifties and early sixties, Oehme and Bluemel were challenged by our landscapes' obvious lack of the many handsome grasses they knew back home. Each man set out to do something about it. And now, as one of Oehme's friends put it, "Pennsylvania Avenue looks a little like Hamburg."

While Oehme and Bluemel weren't

(**Left**) *Thick plumes of compact pampas grass* (Cortaderia selloana *Pumila*) *gleam brightly against the darker, wispier* Miscanthus sinensis.

the first to use ornamental grasses here, their work and vision awakened gardeners and designers to the virtues of this overlooked group. So much so, in fact, that we now look to our own land and its rich grasses for jewels such as little blue-stem (*Schizachyrium scoparium*) and Indian grass (*Sorghastrum avenaceum*). "The use of grasses is more than vogue," says Landscape Architect James Turner of Austin. "It's a growth in our appreciation of beauty in America, by that I mean our own mental growth as a culture."

WHAT ARE ORNAMENTAL GRASSES?

Perhaps the clearest way to define ornamental grasses is by saying what they are not. These are not grasses to be walked on. In fact, they are used more like shrubs. Ornamental grasses function as accents, hedges, specimens, and ground covers just like so many other shrubs—both short and tall. Some grasses grow only a few inches in height, and others tower 10 to 12 feet. Some spread; some form clumps. From a botanical standpoint the group includes not only grasses but also sedges and rushes.

Anyone looking for tough plants that require very little maintenance will be happy with ornamental grasses. Think about where you've seen grasses grow naturally—sand dunes, prairies, marshes, poor fields—areas where weaker plants can't make it. Most tolerate drought, and others will thrive in low, wet areas and poorly drained soil.

"Grasses provide a means of appreciating nature in its various stages rather than just green," says Jackie Gratz, a Baltimore gardener who admits the only gardening she once cared about was growing vegetables and herbs—until she discovered grasses. "When they come up in early spring, they're just a beautiful, soft, delicate green. In early summer before they bloom, the green is cool and peaceful. Then in late summer and fall, when one is beginning to feel that things are going to die soon, here comes the marvelous display of blooms. It's a kind of reawakening. You know that the grasses will be with you through winter, rustling in the wind. . . . And the grasses are beautiful in the snow."

USE GRASSES AS YOU WOULD OTHER PLANTS

If at first you are intimidated by the exotic look of grasses, put your fears away. "I think one of the biggest mistakes one could make is to say that grasses are different from any other plant," says Bluemel. "The regrettable thing is that they have never been incorporated into our landscapes, when actually one should take them as a matter-of-fact element of design. They have the same kind of uses as other plants, so instead of a forsythia, you might use a grass."

Can you use ornamental grasses in a traditional setting? "It depends on how much courage and imagination you have," says Designer Edith Eddleman of Raleigh. "I like to use them as an accent, maybe worked into low evergreens so the grass rises up behind and you can see the plumes dancing above.

"In my foundation planting I have some of the smaller grasses," she adds. "There are some charming ones. I have *Deschampsia flexuosa* Aurea that's only 8 inches tall and has lovely gold-green leaves planted with *Ajuga metallica* Crispa and a little lavender veronica that also has purple leaves. It's a lovely combination."

Sometimes you can incorporate grasses throughout a design. "We use them on a big scale to create a kind of meadow," says Jim van Sweden, Oehme's partner in Washington, D.C. "But when we run into people who want just a few grasses, then we use them as special elements as you would a special shrub. The grass reads as an exclamation point—like a sculpture coming out of a ground cover."

In placing grasses, van Sweden offers two important observations. "Grasses are very natural looking, and they need to breathe and move in the wind and not be plastered against a wall," he says. "And they don't look good planted in rows—there's nothing worse."

In Memphis, Landscape Architect Bob Green loves to place grasses next to pools. "We typically cut planting spaces into the pool deck, and the first plant to go in is a clump of fountain grass so that it overhangs the pool coping. We also mix it with ground covers, such as Bar Harbor and blue rug junipers, around the pool because these plants don't shed." The fountain grass Green uses is *Pennisetum setaceum*.

Grasses also are excellent when used as ground covers. They grow dense enough to keep out weeds the same way traditional ground covers do. "Basket grass (*Nolina texana*), bear grass (*N. erumpens*), and rescue grass (*Bromus unioloides*) are excellent for Texas," says James Turner. You can put an edge around them the same as for masses of English ivy, Asian jasmine, or liriope. Jim van Sweden likes many of the evergreen sedges for ground cover. "They look a lot like liriope," he says.

Another way to use grasses is in a flower border. Edith Eddleman likes their softening effect and the contrast in textures among grasses and the flowers. "Many perennials are sort of

*(Left) The pink, fuzzy blossoms of Oriental fountain grass (*Pennisetum orientale*) feel like a cat's tail. (Center) Miscanthus sinensis Purpurascens is a sea of red foliage. (Right) Maiden grass (Miscanthus sinensis Gracillimus) blooms red then turns silvery in winter.*

(**Above**) *Variegated Japanese silver grass* (Miscanthus sinensis *Variegatus*) *sports leaves marked with creamy variegation—a nice contrast with its reddish, late-summer blooms.*
(**Left**) *At the Baltimore home of Jaqueline Gratz, reed grass acts as an accent while it rises boldly from a ground cover of English ivy. In the background* Miscanthus sinensis *Yaku Jima does the same at the base of the front porch.*

SO WHAT'S THE CATCH?

Really, there is none. Once you master placement, planting and maintenance are easy.

Most grasses need full sun—a few, such as Japanese sedge (*Carex morrowii*), will tolerate shade. Most also like well-drained soil, but a few, such as variegated Japanese silver grass (*Miscanthus sinensis* Variegatus) and Japanese sedge, will grow in poorly drained spots or even at the edge of a pond.

Like any other plants, grasses will need watering the first year or so until they are established. If you buy grasses in pots, set them at the same depth as they were growing in the container. If you order by mail, your treasures might arrive in bare-root clumps. In this case, set the crown well above the ground as you would with strawberry plants.

Once a year most grasses need trimming back. This is done in late winter, before the grasses resume spring growth. Trim the dried leaves and flowerheads as far back as you can to the base of the plant. If you have just a few grasses, you can do this with a pair of loppers or pruning shears. But if you're working with a large area, you'll need a power tool. Eddleman finds that a string trimmer with a plastic blade installed works best.

Occasionally a grass needs dividing. Jaqueline Gratz recommends dividing clumps of miscanthus every second or third year; otherwise, they get too thick and fall over. She uses an ax to cut through the dense clump after lifting it out of the ground.

rounded or mounded, so it's nice to include a grass that is strongly vertical or even those with a weeping form," she says.

"In the typical English border, there is often a marvelous grass with great plumes coming out of delphiniums or whatever else," says van Sweden. "Calamagrostis is so vertical—it really speaks. It is very sculptural and yet still compact."

(**Above**) *A golden sweep of fountain grass leads into a side yard tinted with the beginnings of autumn.* (**Right**) *White flowering fountain grass* (Pennisetum caudatum) *echoes the tranquil feeling of an adjacent meadow.*

FAVORITE GRASSES, MORE INFORMATION

Ornamental grasses are a book-size subject, so these we've mentioned can serve only as a start. For a good overview of grasses and inspirational photos on their uses, we recommend *Ornamental Grass Gardening,* by Thomas A. Reinhardt, Martina Reinhardt, and Mark Moskowitz, HPBooks, Los Angeles.

We asked Kurt Bluemel and another respected grower, Andre Viette of Fishersville, Virginia, to recommend some of the best grasses for beginners in the South. A list of their choices follows.

ORNAMENTAL GRASSES TO TRY

Here is an assortment of ornamental grasses, offering a variety of texture, color, and size.

Calamagrostis arundinacea Karl Foerster / Karl Foerster feather reed grass
Calamagrostis acutiflora Stricta / feather reed grass
Calamagrostis brachytricha / reed grass
Carex morrowii Variegata / silver variegated Japanese sedge
Chasmanthium latifolium / northern sea oats
Cortaderia selloana Sunningdale Silver / Sunningdale Silver pampas grass (Lower South only)
Cortaderia selloana Pumila / compact pampas grass
Deschampsia caespitosa / tufted hair grass
Erianthus ravennae / ravenna grass
Helictotrichon sempervirens / blue oat grass
Imperata cylindrica Red Baron / Japanese blood grass
Miscanthus sinensis (most selections) / miscanthus

Molinia caerulea Arundinacea Karl Foerster / Karl Foerster tall purple moor grass
Panicum virgatum / switch grass
Pennisetum alopecuroides (most selections) / Chinese pennisetum
Pennisetum orientale / Oriental fountain grass
Pennisetum setaceum Rubrum / purple-leaved fountain grass

Remove the fleshy, red pulp before sowing dogwood seeds.

Dogwoods From Scratch

As you admire a spectacular flowering dogwood (*Cornus florida*) in either fall color or spring bloom, you can't help but want two or three for your garden. But you don't have to buy them from a nursery. If you're patient and willing to do a little work, you can grow your own dogwoods from seeds. Here's how.

Just as soon as dogwood berries turn bright red in early fall, harvest a handful. Timing is the key here, because a tree loaded with fruit one moment might be stripped of it by hungry birds or squirrels the next.

The next step is to peel the fleshy, red pulp from each berry, revealing a hard, yellowish seed. Place the seeds in a small glass jar or plastic, zip-top bag, and store them in the refrigerator for three months. At the end of this time, sow the seeds ½ inch deep in a seed flat filled with moist, seed-starting soil mix. Provide bottom heat of about 70 degrees and the seeds should germinate in several weeks. Give the seedlings bright light, and feed every two weeks with water-soluble 20-20-20 fertilizer diluted to half-strength.

When the seedlings are about 2 inches high, transplant them to individual 4-inch pots. As soon as their roots have filled the pots, transplant them into the garden, provided that the chance of a late-spring frost has passed. Your new dogwoods may take several years to begin blooming, but you'll have the satisfaction of having grown them yourself.

LETTERS

TO OUR GARDEN EDITORS

Sweet olive: Can I grow sweet olive outside, or should I plant it indoors in a container?
M. N. C.,
Cullman, Alabama.
Sweet olive (*Osmanthus fragrans*) is hardy outdoors in the Lower and Coastal South but may need some protection in North Alabama, where winter temperatures sometimes fall below 10 degrees. Plant it where it receives sun in summer and shade in winter. It prefers moist, well-drained, slightly acid soil. In a favorable location, this evergreen shrub can grow 10 to 12 feet high. Gardeners in the Middle and Upper South should grow sweet olive in a large container that can be brought indoors for the winter. A potted plant usually grows 6 to 7 feet high. Give it a sunny window, and feed monthly with water-soluble 20-20-20 fertilizer. In early spring, the shrub's tiny, white flowers will fill the house with their delicious perfume.

Oleander: Can you tell me if oleander will survive the winter in my area?
P. M. G.,
Richmond, Virginia.
An evergreen shrub grown for its extremely showy flowers, common oleander (*Nerium oleander*) isn't winter hardy in Richmond. Although nurserymen have introduced hardier selections in recent years, oleander remains primarily an outdoor plant for the Coastal South. However, you can easily grow it in a large container if you'll keep it outdoors from spring until fall and then move it indoors to a sunny window for the winter.

Texas mountain laurel: Would you please tell me how to germinate the seeds of Texas mountain laurel?
H. A. W.,
Seguin, Texas.
To get the seeds of this small evergreen tree to sprout, first use a nail file or clippers to make a small nick in the hard coating of each seed. Then soak

Don't Forget To Rake

Most of us welcome autumn's colorful falling leaves. But these same leaves can spell trouble for a lawn. During rainy weather, a thick surface layer of leaves can mat down and smother the grass. This results in large dead patches the following spring.

Fallen leaves are particularly nettlesome for cool-season grasses. These grasses emerge from summer dormancy and start growing again in fall. They need plenty of sunlight during autumn to build up food reserves, which help them weather winter cold.

Leaf litter can also turn the soil quite acidic. Most grasses grow poorly in highly acidic soils, preferring a near-neutral pH.

Obviously, the solution is to diligently remove the leaves as they fall. Raking is the traditional method, but some people prefer using leaf blowers

It's important to rake fallen leaves so they won't pack down and smother grass.

or lawnmowers to do the job. However, these latter methods can create both noise and exhaust, so if you're loath to disturb the peace and fresh air of a crisp autumn morning, pick up that trusty rake.

Whether yours has metal, rubber, or plastic tines, just be sure they are flexible so that you can rake either firmly or lightly. A light touch is especially important when raking leaves on a newly seeded lawn. In this case, you should consider using a leaf blower or rake with a gentle, sweeping motion through the grass blades and never actually scratch the soil's surface.

the seeds overnight in water. Next, sow them about ½ inch deep into moist potting soil. They should begin to germinate shortly.

Perennials: Could you recommend some perennials that would grow for me in hot, all-day sun? *K. M., Ocala, Florida.*
Good choices for northern Florida include African iris (*Dietes vegeta*), butterfly weed (*Asclepias tuberosa*), threadleaf coreopsis (*Coreopsis verticillata*), daisy bush (*Gamolepsis chrysanthemoides*), daylily (*Hemerocallis* sp.), fern-leaf yarrow (*Achillea filipendulina*), four-o'clock (*Mirabilis jalapa*), moss verbena (*Verbena tenuisecta*), and Victoria mealycup sage (*Salvia farinacea* Victoria).

Gladioli: Please advise how to store gladioli for the winter and how to divide them in spring. *R. B., Harahan, Louisiana.*
Gladioli are hardy in most areas of the Lower and Coastal South, so gardeners there can leave them in the ground. However, if you choose to dig them for the winter and divide them, wait until the foliage turns yellow. Then use a garden fork or shovel to lift the corms. Shake off all of the soil, and remove the leaves. Dust the corms with garden sulfur to prevent rot; then place them in a mesh bag, and store in a cool, dry place. When next spring arrives, separate the offsets from the corms, and plant them in the garden.

Dogwoods: I have pink dogwoods growing among native, white dogwoods. Will the seedlings from the pink dogwoods be true to color? *D. W., Hattiesburg, Mississippi.*
It's possible, but unlikely. The seedlings of flowering dogwood (*Cornus florida*) exhibit great variability, not only in growth rate, habit, and amount of blooms but also in flower color. This really isn't a disadvantage, for without such variability, we wouldn't have the many fine dogwood selections that beautify our gardens today.

Plants for red clay: We just bought a home, and our soil is red clay. Would you advise us as to which trees and shrubs will tolerate this soil? *A. W. R., Raleigh, North Carolina.*
Provided that your soil is reasonably well drained (water doesn't stand for hours following a heavy rain), there are a number of plants that will do quite well. Trees to try include oaks, ash, Chinese elm, ginkgo (be sure to get a male tree), red maple, crabapple, flowering pear, pines, and hawthorn. Among the better shrubs for clay are juniper, barberry, pyracantha (firethorn), Chinese holly, yaupon, nandina, quince, and forsythia.

Tulips: Last year my tulips sent up nice, healthy foliage. But when the flower stalks started to come up, the blossoms just split on the end and didn't bloom. What went wrong? *R. N. P., Eutawville, South Carolina.*
Although the problem could have been caused by overly dry soil, it's more likely that your tulip bulbs didn't receive enough winter chilling. To prevent this from happening again, take your bulbs soon after you purchase them, and place them in the crisper compartment of your refrigerator for 10 to 12 weeks. Then plant them outside in the garden. Make sure that the soil is loose, fertile, and well drained. Sprinkle a teaspoon of slow-release fertilizer in each hole as you plant them. You should get lots of flowers next spring.

Ferns: What can I do when I bring my ferns indoors to keep the leaves from falling? *R. E. J., Arlington, Texas.*
Tender ferns brought indoors for the winter often drop leaves due to dimmer light and drier air. One way to reduce this is to move the plants into full shade for several weeks prior to bringing them inside. This will help them adjust to less light. Once they're indoors, be sure to keep the soil moist. To increase humidity around them, place the plants close together (but not touching) and mist several times per day. You may also consider using a room humidifier or placing the ferns on gravel-lined saucers filled with water. Finally, keep the plants well away from drafts, cold windows, and heating vents.

Sumac: I wanted to collect some sumac leaves and berries to use in a fall arrangement, but a friend told me that they were poisonous. Is this true? *C. S., Stainville, Tennessee.*
Most sumacs are *not* poisonous and don't cause dermatitis. The only poisonous species, appropriately named poison sumac (*Rhus vernix*), is far less common than the others. The easiest way to identify it is by the fruit clusters that ripen in fall. Poison sumac has white fruits, while the safe species bear red fruits. Unfortunately, poison sumac has turned the gardening public against all of its brethren. Gardeners daring enough to try sumacs discover them to be excellent landscape plants. They're drought resistant and grow in just about any soil. They grow at a rapid rate and can take over an area easily if left unchecked. Their fall foliage is a spectacular blend of scarlet, orange, and gold; their scarlet fruits attract birds and other wildlife. The fruits of shining sumac (*R. copallina*) can be used to flavor tea.

Walking iris: A few years ago, I was given a plant called a walking iris. It sends out a long stem, like a spider plant, and a new plant forms on the end. Could you give me some guidelines regarding light, water, and fertilizer requirements? *D. M. T., Cobb Island, Maryland.*
Walking iris (*Neomarica gracilis*), an old-fashioned plant seldom seen today, requires bright light and moist, well-drained soil. It's hardy outdoors only in the Coastal South, so gardeners in your neck of the woods must grow it in a pot and bring it indoors for the winter. While the plant is inside, let the soil go slightly dry between waterings. Divide and repot in February if the plant gets too crowded.

TIP OF THE MONTH

I wanted to plant crocus bulbs around my front yard, but the soil was so hard and the grass so thick, it was impossible to dig 300 holes. Then my husband came up with the ingenious idea of using his electric drill and 1½-inch spade bit to drill holes in the lawn 6 inches apart. The drill not only made perfect holes but also pulverized the soil. I had the most beautiful crocuses in town. *Elaine Gentry, Ranson Canyon, Texas.*
Editor's note: We would like to have your ideas—the ones that have worked for you. We're especially interested in vegetables, houseplants, shrubs, trees, and garden care. For each tip that is published, we will pay $10 and send you one of our garden books.

Submit as many ideas as you wish, but each must be on a separate sheet or card, along with your name, address, and telephone number. We may need to edit the tips, and none will be acknowledged or returned. Send to Gardening Tips, *Southern Living*, Box 523, Birmingham, Alabama 35201.

CHECKLIST
For November

☐ **Amaryllis**—This spectacular bulb makes an ideal gift. If you are lucky enough to receive one, select a pot large enough to leave about an inch of soil around the sides of the bulb. When handling the bulb, be especially careful not to break the roots. Plant your amaryllis in potting soil, leaving about an inch of the neck exposed above the level of the soil. Water well, and place it near a bright window. If the light is too dim, the stalk will grow tall and may break off. You can prevent this by staking plants if heavy blooms appear on the same side of the stem. After the flowers fade, treat amaryllis as one of your houseplants. Fertilize monthly with soluble 20-20-20 or similar analysis. Remember, the foliage has to grow to replenish the food reserves in the bulb. You can move it outdoors in summer. Then let it dry out and go dormant during autumn. You'll see the fat bud emerging when it's ready to grow again.

☐ **Clover**—Enrich soil in vacant areas of the vegetable garden by planting clover. The roots are hosts to bacteria that trap nitrogen from the air. So when the crop is tilled into the soil, you get more than just organic matter. Seed can be obtained from farm supply stores as well as mail-order companies. Sow about 1 pound per 1,000 square feet by broadcasting seed over the bed and scratching it in with a rake. Water daily until seedlings appear, then weekly thereafter. Two to three weeks before spring planting, turn the clover under with a fork or tiller.

☐ **Compost**—Keep compost moist during dry weather, or the pile won't decay. Water using a small sprinkler set atop the bin, and let it run for about an hour. As you add fall leaves and other debris to the pile, work in 2 cups of fertilizer for every foot of fresh material. Debris will make compost more rapidly if you turn the pile every couple of weeks—but if you're a lazy gardener, don't worry. The material will eventually decay, although you may have to dig into the center of the pile for the best compost (that on the outside dries out and will decay more slowly).

☐ **Garden cleanup**—Dead stalks and other debris left in the garden provide choice locations for insects and diseases to overwinter. Remove and destroy any infested material, and add the rest to your compost heap. Fallen leaves may be composted as well. Do not allow leaves to pile up on the lawn, as serious damage to grass can occur. It's also time to remove old mulch from camellias and azaleas and replace it with fresh to help protect the plants from petal blight, a disease that causes the flowers to turn brown prematurely.

☐ **Houseplants**—Fall and winter bring reduced light and cooler temperatures. This means your houseplants won't need as much water. Jade plant, sansevieria, and cactus will probably be happy with just one watering per month. Plants with large leaves, such as spathe flower and Chinese evergreen, lose more moisture but may need water only every 10 days or so. Always check the moisture by poking your finger about an inch into the soil; water when the soil feels dry.

☐ **Lawns**—If your lawn is scheduled for spraying by a lawn maintenance service, it's wise to water the day before treatment. A drought-stressed lawn is more likely to burn. Be sure to follow the applicator's directions for watering after treatment so the chemical is not rinsed away.

☐ **Propagation**—Deciduous plants, such as crepe myrtle, forsythia, wisteria, spirea, and flowering quince, can be propagated from cuttings this time of year. Take a cutting by making a slanted cut about 6 inches from the end of a stem, just below a node. Fill a pot with equal parts moistened sphagnum peat moss and builder's sand. Dip the cutting into a rooting hormone, and stick it 1 to 2 inches into the pot. Store the container in a cool, dark place, and mist the cuttings every day or two. This method will also work with many evergreens, including juniper and yew.

ANNUALS SURVIVE WINTER, BLOOM IN SPRING

No matter where you garden, there are cool-season annuals you can sow now for a bounty of blossoms in late winter or early spring.

Larkspur's tall spikes of pink, white, blue, or purple make it a spring favorite. Because seedlings can survive subzero cold, this annual can be sown now throughout the South. Larkspur reseeds prolifically, as does Johnny-jump-up, a cousin of the pansy. Plant seeds this fall in full sun to partial shade, and enjoy them for years. (Be prepared to stake larkspur because it will grow about 3 feet tall.)

Forget-me-nots (*Myosotis*) are also

Sweet peas, poppies, bachelor's-button, and nasturtiums can be seeded now to provide flowers next spring.
Photograph: Mary-Gray Hunter

sown in fall. These tiny blue flowers are great for overplanting bulb beds to provide a carpet of blue underneath tulips or narcissus. They'll grow in full sun or partial shade.

Sweet peas can be planted this month if you live in the Middle or Lower South; wait until February or March in the Upper South. Sweet peas are aptly named because their delicate perfume makes them a joy to cut and bring indoors in spring. Plant vining types at the base of a trellis, or choose self-supporting selections. Even if seedlings appear to be killed back this winter, they'll sprout from their roots in early spring.

Bachelor's-button, Shirley poppies, and nasturtiums can also be grown from seed. Follow a similar planting schedule as described for sweet peas, and you'll have bouquets of flowers in 9 to 12 weeks.

For best results, sow seeds in a well-tilled bed with good drainage and rich soil. Because these are cool-season annuals, you can expect their performance to lag in late spring when warm weather arrives. Then simply replace them with warm-season annuals for the summer.

☐ **Roses**—A new brochure is available from All-America Rose Selections. "The Wonderful World of Roses" includes information on selecting, planting, and care. It also lists all the AARS display gardens throughout the U.S. To obtain a copy, send a stamped, self-addressed, business-size envelope and $1 to Dept. RR, All-America Rose Selections, Inc., 221 North LaSalle Street, Chicago, Illinois 60601.

☐ **Scale**—Keep scale from building up on camellias, euonymus, tea olive, citrus, and other evergreens by spraying with dormant oil. The oil coats the pests so they suffocate. It's a good idea to spray again in spring to get a second chance at scales that survived the first spray. Oil sprays, such as Volck, are relatively safe; however, they can burn foliage if you spray when temperatures are below 40 degrees or above 85. That's why fall and spring are the best times to spray.

☐ **Shrubs and trees**—Fall is a great time to plant trees and shrubs, but be sure to select the right ones for a particular spot. One of the most important considerations is the ultimate size a plant will attain. Also consider the amount of sunlight or shade an area receives, and select a species adaptable to those conditions. Next, determine how much water will be available. Shrubs planted beneath overhangs will receive little rain, and competition from nearby trees lessens available water as well. Plants in low, soggy areas must be able to tolerate having their feet wet. Place tender plants in locations protected from cold winter winds.

☐ **Trunk wrap**—Young trees usually have thin bark that is easily split by winter sun on a cold morning or nibbled by hungry wildlife. You can protect newly planted trees by wrapping their trunks with paper or plastic products made for this purpose. These can be bought at garden centers or hardware stores. After a year or two, the trunk will be tougher, and you can remove the wrap.

SPECIAL TIPS FOR THE SOUTHEAST

☐ **Bulbs**—In the Middle and Lower South, begin planting spring blubs now. In the Upper South, get them in the ground as soon as possible. When you buy bulbs, check the box for recommended depths and spacings. To ensure even flowering, dig out an entire bed to the recommended depth, and set them on the soil in a staggered grid pattern. Mix a slow-release fertilizer into the backfill soil along with a generous portion of organic matter. Carefully refill the bed so you do not disturb the bulbs. Water well to settle the soil, and add more soil to level the bed. Apply a mulch of pine needles or finely ground bark to keep out weeds; the bulbs will have no problem pushing up through it.

☐ **Cold frames**—Lettuce and other cool-weather greens can be sown in cold frames now for winter salads. Although these seedlings will need water less often than if planted in an open bed, you will have to provide moisture because rain cannot reach them. Vent the cold frame on warm days by propping open the lid several inches. Or buy an automatic cold frame opener, which opens the lid when temperatures rise and closes it again as they cool.

☐ **Equipment**—Sprinklers and water timers can be destroyed if they contain water when freezing temperatures arrive. Drain, and store them so they will be in good shape when you need them next season. Even your garden hose can be split by water expanding as it freezes. Drain it after use to prevent damage.

SPECIAL TIPS FOR FLORIDA

☐ **Citrus**—Check citrus trees for spider mites. They can be especially troublesome during dry weather in fall and winter. These pinpoint-size, spiderlike pests attack the foliage, stems, and fruit, causing defoliation and weakening the plant. Signs of these mites include yellowing foliage and a light webbing on the underside of leaves. To control mites, apply insecticidal soap according to label directions. Be certain to spray the entire tree, thoroughly covering the underside of leaves.

☐ **Watering**—Although the weather is cooler now, trees, shrubs, and flowers still need supplemental water during periods without rain. This is especially true of anything recently planted. Regular watering helps keep citrus from splitting when a rain finally comes after a dry spell. Thorough watering will also help lessen the damage a hard freeze can cause to citrus and many other plants. To help conserve the water once it has been applied, spread a 2- to 3-inch layer of mulch under shrubs and in flowerbeds.

SPECIAL TIPS FOR TEXAS

☐ **Herbs**—Gardeners living north of a line from Austin to El Paso will need to protect rosemary, bay, and lemon verbena from winter cold. Plants already growing in containers can simply be brought inside. However, you would be wise to spray them with insecticidal soap two weeks before you move them, and again just prior to moving. Plants in the garden can be transplanted into pots. Get as much of the roots as possible when you dig. Rinse soil from the roots, and replant in potting soil. Then give them a sunny window in a cool room. If you live in an area where these plants are marginally hardy, try mulching the roots. When particularly cold weather is predicted, cover the entire plant.

☐ **Lawns**—Gardeners south of a line from Dallas to Abilene can feed lawns through winter using a fertilizer higher in potassium than nitrogen, for example, 8-8-25. The extra potassium helps the lawn resist cold, while the lower supply of nitrogen provides just enough energy to keep the grass healthy without encouraging new growth that can be killed by a freeze. Also, be sure to keep the lawn watered—even if it is dormant. Lawns that are drought stressed are more likely to be hurt by a sudden, severe cold spell.

☐ **Ranunculus tubers**—In the Southern half of the state, plant this month for a showy array of yellow, orange, red, pink, or white flowers in March or April. (Gardeners farther north should wait until late winter to plant.) Soak tubers overnight before planting in a sunny spot with well-drained soil. Plant them about 2 inches deep with their "claws" pointed down, and space them 6 to 8 inches apart. Tubers can be lifted after blooming and replanted next year, but they are best treated as annuals because their performance in successive years is unpredictable.

☐ **Seeds**—Leftover seeds from this year's garden must be stored properly to ensure their viability next spring. Place them in a wide-mouth canning jar or other airtight container, and keep it in the refrigerator or freezer. If seeds are more than 3 years old or have been exposed to moisture or heat during the summer, they should be discarded.

December

The soft pinstripes and velvety sheen of Calathea ornata *distinguish it as one of the most elegant.*

THE SOUTHERN GARDEN®

CALATHEAS: BEYOND GREEN

If you enjoy the color fresh flowers add to your home but wish for the lasting quality of a foliage plant, then calatheas may be for you.

by LOIS TRIGG / photography VAN CHAPLIN

Native to the jungles of South America, these tropical treasures are equally contented in the confines of heated and air-conditioned homes. Besides needing only minimal care, calatheas boast some of the richest colors to be found in foliage plants. With leaves in a tapestry of silver, pink, purple, or green, they enliven any decor.

"Some people think potted flowers are old hat," says Designer Sue Davidson of the Organized Jungle in Orlando, "so we like to use calatheas because they're different. They are especially dramatic with interiors in neutrals or white."

Besides rating a 10 on looks, calatheas also earn high marks in the survival category. "We like to call calatheas 'second chance plants' " says Susan Griffith, whose nursery in Plymouth, Florida, grows dozens of types for wholesale. "If one dries out completely, you can cut it all the way back, and the new growth that appears will be tougher and even better conditioned to the indoors."

Of course, Griffith doesn't recommend treating your plant this way. "Benign neglect" is what she recommends. "The main thing most people

do wrong is fertilize and water too much," she says. "They need fertilizer only about once every three months, and you should let them run slightly dry between waterings." A plant will tell you when it needs water because the typically stiff leaves begin to relax.

As for light, the amount a calathea should receive depends on how long you want to keep it. "If there's just enough light to cast a shadow, the

All-green Calathea gandersii Ruffles *wears a shiny iridescence that makes the leaves look patterned.*

plant will look good for at least a year," says Griffith. In filtered, bright light they will last indefinitely. However, calatheas don't like full sun; the leaves will burn in direct sunlight.

You can clean the leaves with a damp cloth or put the whole plant in the shower. Griffith cautions against oil-based plant shines because calatheas are sensitive and will burn.

FIVE GREAT CALATHEAS

Of the many types and sizes of calatheas available, here are a few good selections for the tabletop.

Calathea picturata Argentea wears an iridescent, silvery green that makes it one of the most popular of all calatheas. It grows a little more openly than most types, with a form reminiscent of a spathiphyllum. You can expect one of these in a 6-inch pot to get 12 to 18 inches tall.

Calathea ornata is marked by colorful pinstripes on dark-green, velvety leaves. The color of the stripes indicates age. Youngest plants have red stripes; middle-aged ones, pink; and older ones, white. Mature plants will eventually lose their striping altogether, but this takes a couple of years. A plant growing in a 6-inch pot

Calathea picturata *Argentea grows like a spathiphyllum, but its leaves are variegated and therefore much brighter.*

will get 12 to 20 inches tall.

Calathea roseopicta has large, spoon-shaped leaves whose purple undersides are as attractive as the pattern on the top of the leaves. It grows 12 to 16 inches tall in a 6-inch pot. Royal Picta is a similar but larger hybrid selection whose leaves are slightly scalloped. It grows up to 20 inches tall in a 6-inch pot.

Calathea gandersii Ruffles is one of the few calatheas that have solid-green leaves. Yet because the leaf is ruffled and its surface iridescent, light striking at different angles gives the leaf a patterned look. You can expect Ruffles to get 12 to 16 inches tall in a 6-inch pot.

A FINAL NOTE

Calatheas are related to prayer plants and share the same curious habit of folding up for the night. This begins in late afternoon and is more prominent with some species than with others. So when you notice this, don't think something is wrong with your plant—it's just curling up for the night.

Roseopicta *and the larger hybrid Royal Picta are much appreciated for the purple on the underside of their leaves.*

WHITE FLOWERS FOR THE HOLIDAYS

Lilies and spider mums spotlight these decorations in an imaginative way. Tiny tubes of water keep flowers fresh for several days.

photography MARY-GRAY HUNTER

The allure of fresh blooms in wintertime. The excitement of decorating for the holidays. Put these together, and the results are fascinating—flowers in arrangements, on packages, even on your tree.

The key to working fresh flowers into arrangements is using tiny tubes called florist vials or water picks. Each pick holds enough water to keep a blossom fresh for about two days.

The decorations shown here were designed by Norman K. Johnson of Birmingham. He chose spider mums to decorate a Christmas tree tucked into the base of a stairwell. The starburst-like blossoms seem to light the tree. Only 4 feet tall, the tree rests atop a skirted table for extra height and prominence. Glimmering with strings of white lights, branches support a dozen 4-foot lengths of gold-bead garland that hang vertically from the top of the tree. A much longer garland of silver stars winds around the tree horizontally. Bunches of baby's-breath brighten the deep spaces between the dark-green branches.

Behind the tree, two garlands dress a curving banister. The first garland, dotted with sprays of baby's-breath, attaches underneath the handrail. The second is draped like a swag and fastens to the first. A spider mum tied with metallic ribbon highlights each point where the garlands are fastened together. At the bottom of the stairs, the newel is draped with a bough of balsam fir, baby's-breath, a spider

(Above) Huge spider mums, resting on the tips of branches, seem to light this tree. (Right) In place of a traditional bow, a large spider mum punctuates this newel.

mum, and a skirt of the same ribbon.

In the dining room, a double-sided wreath of balsam fir graces the table. Studded with lilies and tiny bunches of statice tucked into the greenery, the wreath forms an elegant, simple centerpiece that can be made quickly. Before working with lilies, always remember that it's best to pinch off the anthers (structures that hold pollen) with a pair of tweezers. The pollen will stain hands, clothing, tablecloths, walls—nearly everything it touches.

Also in the dining room, a foliage arrangement on the buffet ties in with the tabletop centerpiece. Large branches of leucothoe, magnolia, and

This balsam fir wreath becomes an elegant centerpiece when studded with lilies and statice.

white pine make up this design. Except for a sprig of asparagus fern, all of the materials were gathered from the garden. The branches stay fresh in a 3-quart bowl stuffed with blocks of florist foam; this large base holds a two- to three-day supply of water. Chicken wire taped over the top of the bowl helps hold the branches securely in the foam. Magnolia branches are placed in the back of the arrangement since their large leaves can still be seen even when slightly covered by other foliage. Stems of leucothoe and white pine gently arch in front of the magnolia. Anchored in the center of the arrangement, elegant lilies turn this handsome design into an outstanding one. The lilies in their vials are taped to 18-inch-long florist picks and then inserted into the foam base.

For a final decorative touch, offer a gift topped with a nosegay. The one shown (below, left) is made from a carnation, leatherleaf fern, and statice. The fern and carnation are inserted into the florist pick; the statice is fastened to the outside with florist tape. Nosegays can be made a day early and kept fresh in the refrigerator. After it has adorned a present, this little bouquet can double as a corsage.

(**Left**) *A package decoration made from a white carnation, leatherleaf fern, and statice can double later on as a corsage.*
(**Right**) *Handsome in its own right, this rich foliage arrangement becomes outstanding when pale-colored lilies are added.*

Position the plant and backfill the hole so the plant sits at the same level as it was previously growing. Lay a yardstick across the hole as a guide for leveling.

Planting Trees and Shrubs

Fall and winter are the seasons when smart Southern gardeners are busy planting trees and shrubs. Plants set out now have a chance to become established before summer's heat and possible drought set in.

If you're planning to plant soon, here's some information you will find interesting. It may change the way you prepare the soil from now on.

Dr. Carl Whitcomb, a horticultural researcher in Stillwater, Oklahoma, has spent years comparing the progress of plants set in planting holes amended with organic matter against those planted in native soil. His findings challenge the tradition of adding sphagnum peat moss, pine bark, and other amendments to the backfill because the plants set in unimproved planting holes did as well or better than those pampered with soil amendments. Whitcomb's work has prompted other researchers to explore the same concept, and many came up with similar results. The exceptions are blueberries and azaleas, which always do better in soil made more acid by adding sphagnum peat moss or sulfur.

So do you plant with amendments or without? If you have used amendments in the past and have been satisfied with the plants' growth, it's fine to continue amending. It probably won't hurt un-less you add so much organic matter that as it decays and loses volume, the plant sinks. Then the crown becomes buried, increasing the chances of rot.

However, if you have very poor soil, or perhaps even subsoil, such as on graded lots, it's good to work amendments or rich topsoil into the entire area—not just the planting hole—with a tiller or tractor. Whitcomb's work shows that amendments do make a difference when worked into the entire area, for example, a 20- x 8-foot strip that will be planted with shrubs.

Guidelines for Planting

In most of the South, late winter and early spring are the best times to plant evergreens and bare-root plants, such as roses and fruit trees. Gardeners in Florida and South Texas can plant now. Dig a hole at least twice as wide as the root ball. Roughen the sides of the hole with your shovel so they're not entirely smooth.

For bare-root plants, pile soil in the center to make a mound over which you spread the roots of the plant. Holding the plant in place, refill the hole making sure the crown of the plant is slightly above ground level. If it's buried, the plant will suffer. Tamp the soil with your foot to eliminate air pockets, and water thoroughly.

To plant balled-and-burlapped plants, leave the burlap around the root ball intact. A broken root ball often results in a dead plant, so handle carefully. Once it is set, you can cut wire or cord that wraps the ball so it won't girdle the trunk or roots, but leave the burlap in place. Pull off any burlap that is up around the trunk so it won't be above ground where it will act as a wick to pull away water.

Plant container-grown plants in a similar manner, only this time there's no need for the mound of soil. When setting the plant, be sure it is at the same level as it was growing in the container. Slip container-grown plants from their pots carefully. If they're not too big, you can turn them upside down and spread an open hand over the top of the container to catch the root ball as it slips out.

If the roots are matted and tangled, spread them by cutting crosswise through the bottom one-third to one-half of the ball and gently part the sections. Don't worry about the cut roots; they will branch like a cut stem.

Handle plants growing in plantable pots one of two ways. If the roots grow into the sides of the cardboard-like material, then plant the whole thing—pot and all. The pot will decompose. Just peel away the rim, or be sure the top is completely buried. Like exposed burlap, an exposed portion of the pot will wick moisture from around the roots.

On the other hand, if the plant is just being held in the pot to prevent drying of the roots (as is often done with bare-root roses) and the roots are easily separated from the pot, then remove the plant. That way there is no waiting for the pot to decompose. Plant as you would a bare-root plant.

Fertilization

You might think it's not necessary to fertilize now because plants don't seem to be growing. But actually, the roots are, and they will appreciate a fertilizer, such as 5-10-10, that is low in nitrogen and high in phosphorus and potassium. Scatter it over the ground after the plants are set. Then in early spring and after frost in fall, apply a fertilizer that contains slow-release nitrogen to feed the plants slowly and steadily throughout the year.

This Tree Won't Drop A Needle

How would you like a Christmas tree fashioned from natural materials and guaranteed not to drop a needle? Well, here it is—a handsome pine cone tree. You can make it yourself in just a few hours. And the supplies you'll need are inexpensive.

Karren King of our staff designed the tree pictured at right. Because she planned to display the tree atop a sideboard, she made the frame approximately 3 feet tall. She began by rolling a sheet of chicken wire into a cone-shaped frame and fastening it together with florist wire. Placing the frame on a cardboard base during the construction phase makes the tree easy to pick up and move when you're finished.

The next step is to twist florist wire around the base of each pine cone, and then attach it to the frame. "Start at the bottom," she explains, "and arrange the cones as close together as possible. It's easier to turn the frame as you work. Then just keep going until you reach the top." Although almost any type of pine cone will do, Karren

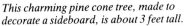

This charming pine cone tree, made to decorate a sideboard, is about 3 feet tall.

recommends choosing ones of consistent size to keep the tree from looking jumbled or uneven. For this tree she selected cones from Virginia pine (*Pinus virginiana*) because they're small and easy to work with.

After you've covered the frame with cones, decorate the tree with twinkle lights, ribbons, bows, strings of beads, or bundles of baby's-breath. Add presents around the tree, matching or coordinating the wrapping paper and ribbon to the colors of the tree.

When the holidays have passed, you'll find this decoration is as easy to put away as it is to put up. Just remove the lights and beads; then store the tree in a large plastic bag to keep it from getting dusty.

(Left) *Begin by rolling a sheet of chicken wire into a cone-shaped frame; then attach the cones.* **(Right)** *Wire the cones as tightly to the frame as possible.*

Face-lift for a Fifties House

Rosalinda and Donald Ratajczak's house has always been easy to spot. "We used to tell people to drive down the street until they saw the ugliest carport in Atlanta, and that was our house," Rosalinda says with a laugh. Now, however, their home stands out for a different reason: It's one of the prettiest in the neighborhood.

The Ratajczaks loved the convenient Midtown location and comfortable interior of their 1950's ranch-style home, but the exterior definitely needed a face-lift. Overgrown landscaping, a flat-roofed carport with a

dog-eared fascia, and an ill-defined pathway to the front door showed every one of the house's "thirty-something" years. As Landscape Architect Ron Hadaway tactfully puts it, "The place had not aged gracefully."

Solving their parking problem was a top priority, but the first two architects consulted couldn't come up with any viable solutions. "One suggested we tunnel under the house!" Rosalinda says. Then they called Hadaway. "In about 20 minutes he had conceptually solved our problems."

"First I suggested we tear off the carport and build it back in a different shape with a higher roofline," says Hadaway, ASLA, with HDH Partners in Marietta, Georgia. The previous carport had been attached directly to the front of the house; the new one is connected by a series of 2 x 12 timbers that forms a trellis between the house and garage. "When you come out of the garage, the trellis is overhead," Rosalinda explains, "but standing at the kitchen window, you look out over it." The trellis allows lots of light into the new structure.

A set of steps beneath the trellis offers quick access from the garage to

(**Top**) *A white railing of sturdy posts and slender pickets leads guests from the driveway to the front door.*
(**Above**) *Before, a flat-roofed garage, overgrown plants, and an unattractive color scheme made this house look dated.*

the front door. But guests use another walkway that ascends the grade change more slowly and passes through a brick-paved forecourt. This space is enclosed by a white railing, which draws the eye to the front door. Raised planters separate the forecourt from the garage, and a bench rests in a nook on the opposite side. "We sit out there, especially in the winter, to enjoy the sun," Rosalinda says.

The only other improvements done to the house itself were a new roof to match that of the garage, and a coat of paint in a contemporary-looking shade of gray. To complement the transformation, Hadaway redesigned the planting, which includes a simple sweep of holly and liriope around the foundation of the forecourt.

"It's amazing how much updating your landscape can accomplish," Rosalinda says. "It makes you feel better about your whole house."

The brick-paved forecourt features a raised planter next to the garage and a recessed seating nook on the other side.

LETTERS

TO OUR GARDEN EDITORS

Wood ashes: I have lots of wood ashes I would like to use in my garden. Would you please tell me which trees, shrubs, and flowers would benefit most from them?
S. C. P., Boyce, Louisiana.
Wood ashes especially benefit those plants that enjoy soil having a pH of between 6.5 and 7. This includes most vegetables, annuals, perennials, and roses, as well as many trees and shrubs. However, you shouldn't place ashes around acid-loving plants, such as azaleas, hollies, and blueberries, because the ashes are alkaline. Also, gardeners living in areas with alkaline soil should temper their use of ashes, as adding them may raise the soil pH higher than their plants like.

African violet: My African violet looks healthy, but some of the bottom leaves have started dying. What can I do to stop this?
R. G., Somerset, Kentucky.
The problem you describe is a condition known as petiole (or stem) rot. This happens when the petiole of a bottom leaf touches the rim of a porous pot that has absorbed mineral salts from houseplant fertilizer. The salts burn the stem, and it rots through. Rot can also occur when the lower petioles contact the sharp rims of plastic pots. One way to prevent petiole rot is to wrap the rims with aluminum foil. Or you can coat them with paraffin.

Christmas cactus: I have a Christmas cactus that has never bloomed. I put it outside last summer and gave it morning sun and afternoon shade. This fall I put it in a dark closet each day for six weeks and withheld water as I was instructed to do. What's wrong?
T. W. B., Fredericksburg, Virginia.
Perhaps flowerbuds are forming, but they're dropping before they open due to environmental conditions. This is a very common problem. Bud drop can be caused by too warm temperatures, too dry air, cold drafts, and soil that stays too wet. In addition, although you should water in fall just enough to keep the stems from shriveling, once flowerbuds form, increase watering so that the soil stays moist but not soggy.

Pyracantha: I cut some pyracantha branches and placed them in water to use in holiday decorations. But within a few days the berries shriveled, and I was forced to throw them out. Is there a way to treat the cut branches to keep this from happening?
T. L. C., Hilton Head, South Carolina.
Unfortunately, pyracantha (firethorn) doesn't last very long in water. You might try spraying the berries with clear lacquer and see if this helps preserve them. Or you could substitute the red berries of nandina; these berries last practically forever and need no special treatment.

Anthurium: I was recently given a "sweetheart plant." It has bright-red, heart-shaped flowers and shiny green leaves. Can you give me more information about this plant, including how to care for it?
D. P., Plano, Texas.
"Sweetheart plant" is another name for flaming anthurium (*Anthurium andraeanum*). This tropical plant may grow 2 to 3 feet tall, but dwarf selections grow 1 foot or less. The "flowers" aren't really flowers at all, but specialized leaves called bracts. The bracts may be red, white, orange, or pink. Flaming anthurium blooms best when given plenty of bright light, but it should be shaded from hot afternoon sun. Don't let the air temperature drop

Flaming anthurium comes in many colors and sizes. Given proper conditions, it will bloom for weeks.
Photograph: Mary-Gray Hunter

below 60 degrees. Fertilize every two weeks from spring until fall with water soluble 20-20-20 diluted to half-strength. To maintain adequate humidity, mist daily or place the plant atop a gravel-lined saucer filled with water. The soil must provide excellent drainage. A soil mix consisting of equal parts of potting soil, perlite, and coarse sand should suffice. Let the soil become slightly dry between thorough waterings.

Termites: I was told by a neighbor not to use any kind of bark mulch around the plants near the foundation of my house, as it may attract termites. Is this sound advice?
E. M. C., Naples, Florida.
Shredded bark mulch really shouldn't cause a problem, as long as it is placed against concrete, brick, or pressure-treated wood. However, just to be safe, you might want to substitute pine straw for mulching plants next to the house and save the bark for plants farther out in the garden.

TIP OF THE MONTH

When cutting a fresh pineapple, slice off the top, leaving about an inch of fruit attached to the leaves. Set the top aside for two days; then plant it about a half-inch deep in a 6-inch pot filled with potting soil. In about a week, the pineapple will root. After a year, move it to a 12-inch pot. In about three years, the plant should be about 3 feet tall and ready for a 20-inch pot. Pineapple plants tolerate a lot of forgetfulness, provided they have well-drained soil. They thrive on little water and should be fed with houseplant fertilizer every four months. Before you know it, you have an exotic plant for the price of a piece of fruit.
Mary Ann Edenfield, Savannah, Georgia.
Editor's note: We'd like to have your ideas—the ones that have worked for you. We're especially interested in vegetables, houseplants, shrubs, trees, and garden care. For each tip that is published, we will pay $10 and send you one of our garden books.

Submit as many ideas as you wish, but each must be on a separate sheet or card, along with your name, address, and telephone number. We may need to edit the tips. Those unpublished will not be acknowledged or returned. Send to Gardening Tips, *Southern Living,* Box 523, Birmingham, Alabama 35201.

CHECKLIST FOR DECEMBER

☐ **All-America Selections**—Six new flowers and four new vegetables earned AAS recognition for 1990. Each year AAS judges new flowers, bedding plants, and vegetables grown in trial gardens throughout the U.S., and only the most outstanding earn designation as All-America Selections. Flower winners for 1990 include **Summer Pastels** achillea, a 2-foot yarrow that includes yellow, pink, and apricot colors; **Pink Castle** celosia, a bright-pink celosia with plumes that hold up in drought, heat, or rain; **Jolly Joker** pansy, a combination of purple petals with an orange face; and **Scarlet Splendor** zinnia, a dwarf type with red flowers.

In the bedding plant category, two multiflora petunias prove that these small-flowered types outdo the large-flowered types in the garden. **Polo Salmon** is a heat-tolerant, long-lasting salmon-pink petunia. **Polo Burgundy Star** is a bicolored, burgundy and white one that boasts the same tough qualities.

Finally, a pepper, a bean, and two squash selections also took AAS honors. **Super Cayenne** pepper grows up to 2 feet tall and works as an ornamental as well as a source of fiery pods. **Derby** green bean is a bush-type bean with pods that stay tender to lengths of 7 inches. **Cream of the Crop** acorn squash sports an unusual creamy color and yields 2- to 3- pound fruit. **Sun Drops** bush-type squash grows in an unusual oval shape. It's a tasty variety comparable to yellow crookneck types.

☐ **Bird feeders**—It's a delight to watch the many birds attracted to a feeder during winter. Hang your feeder in an open area where cats cannot hide. Likewise, keep the feeder away from shrub beds and other areas where sunflower and other seeds knocked to the ground could become weeds next spring. A post or tree limb over an open lawn is an ideal spot. Remember, once you have begun feeding the birds, they depend on you for much of their food. So don't stop, particularly during cold periods.

☐ **Christmas trees**—It may seem a little early, but buy your tree as soon as the tree lots open. Not only will you have a better selection, but the tree you choose will be fresher if it spends the next couple of weeks in a pail of water than on a sunny lot nailed to a tree stand. When you get it home, saw 2 inches off the trunk to open clogged water channels, and place it in a stand that holds water or in a bucket. Check the water daily, as a tree can use much more than you would expect. If your family buys a living tree, be aware that it can stay decorated for only a week to 10 days. These trees are dormant, and when brought into a warm house, they respond as if it were spring, sending out new shoots. Then when planted outdoors, they can be killed by the first freeze. Choose a tree that will grow well in your area. For example, a deodar cedar is beautiful in the Lower South but not dependable in the Upper South. The opposite is true for a blue spruce or Fraser fir.

☐ **Garden detective**—When plants die, don't just cut them down or dig them up—look at their roots. Examine them for problems that might have killed the plant. For example, if a dead plant has roots growing in circles, as if they were in the pot, you may need to amend the soil in the garden. You'll probably find that the soil is so hard roots could not penetrate it. If the roots have rotted, you can assume the culprit is either poor drainage, soil fungus, or both. Modify the bed to improve drainage or build a raised bed. Loosen the soil and add organic matter so the water runs through it more quickly.

☐ **Houseplants**—Rotate houseplants from dim locations to sunny ones to keep them in good condition through winter. Remember to place them away from vents where dry, heated air will damage the leaves. Check containers weekly to be sure the soil is moist.

☐ **Mistletoe**—This traditional holiday greenery is actually a damaging parasite that obtains all of its water and nutrients from its host plant. Breaking off the mistletoe will make the tree look better, but the mistletoe will grow back unless you cut a chip

GIFTS FOR GARDENERS

From the most practical to the most indulgent, gifts for the gardener are plentiful. In this season for decorations, garden ornaments seem especially appropriate. Those that hang on a wall or fence are similar to pictures in your home. A wall plaque of St. Fiacre, the patron saint of gardeners, is a traditional favorite. You also may find architectural remnants or outdoor paintings to fill a bare spot with interest.

Freestanding ornaments, such as an urn, a statue, or even a sundial, commonly serve as a focal point. The gardener on your list may have put off purchasing one in favor of plants. So take a cue from his or her garden plan.

A thatched-roof birdhouse, a plaque of St. Fiacre, an armillary sphere sundial, and iron plant hooks are gift ideas.
Photograph: Mary-Gray Hunter

Because this is a good time to set out trees and shrubs in most of the South, a plant is an excellent choice, particularly if you know what the gardener has been wanting. Even if the plant is leafless, you can give it appeal by tying a red ribbon around its trunk.

Many gardeners enjoy having birds in the garden. The obvious gift is a birdhouse or a feeder, but a bird identification guide or even binoculars would be appreciated.

Similarly, wind chimes have no direct bearing on the garden itself, but they make the outdoor experience more pleasant. Choices range from interesting visual designs to the most melodic chimes.

A practical gift of garden equipment cannot miss. Decorative iron plant hangers or a fine pair of gloves or clippers will bring a smile to any gardener's face. But don't forget the bookshelf. At this time of year when chores are fewer and the weather is not always cooperative, perhaps the greatest gift of all is a book to inspire visions of the season to come.

from the tree where it is attached. If the limb is small, consider removing the entire branch. Then treat the wounded area with pruning sealer or orange shellac.

☐ **Nematodes**—For those who are tired of fighting the knotty roots and stunted growth brought on by soil nematodes, there's hope. A new nematocide called ClandoSan promises to be much easier to use and safer than fumigation. While ClandoSan is still too new for definite assessment, initial research and experience show that it controls nematodes well, especially in vegetable gardens. ClandoSan also may be used in flowerbeds and on the lawn. A granular product that you can work into the soil or spread like fertilizer, ClandoSan is made from the ground shells of crab, shrimp, and other shellfish. It is on the market now, but if you are unable to find it at a local nursery or garden center, ask someone there to help you locate the nearest source.

☐ **Poinsettias**—To select a poinsettia that will last all season, look at the true flowers—the small yellow beads in the center of the red bracts. The true flowers should be fresh, that is, still closed or newly opened. Keep your plant in bright, indirect light and away from heating vents and drafty doors. Water when the surface of the soil dries out. Do not let the soil dry to the point of wilting or the leaves will drop.

☐ **Potpourri**—Make a Christmas potpourri for next year by collecting dried needles from your wreath or tree when this holiday season is over. Combine them with bay leaves, cinnamon sticks, whole cloves, star anise, and juniper berries. Store the mixture in an airtight container in a cool location.

SPECIAL TIPS FOR THE SOUTHEAST

☐ **Evergreens**—When you cut greenery from your garden, remember that you are pruning your plants. While most pruning is best left until January and February, you can safely trim branches of boxwood, American holly, pine, cryptomeria, Eastern red cedar, Southern magnolia, leucothoe, and others. You can also cut branches from your azaleas, but remember that you'll be removing spring flowers. Condition your greenery to make it last longer. Submerge entire branches in a tub of water for 3 to 4 hours; then place only the stem ends in water while the foliage dries. Before arranging, recut the stem ends at an angle with a sharp knife or shears, and add floral preservative to the water. Spraying broad-leaved evergreens with acrylic floor wax will give them a shine and slow the loss of moisture from foliage.

☐ **Tree maintenance**—Check deciduous trees now for unusual knots, galls, bark discoloration, or holes that might indicate a problem. If you see anything suspect, consult a professional arborist or your county Extension agent. This is also a good time to thin the canopy of a tree so more light passes through to the lawn or shrubs.

☐ **Trees and shrubs**—When you go to the nursery to select a plant that is already leafless, you may be at a loss to determine whether it is alive or not. First look for a plant with good form. If the nursery does not have a greenhouse, the pot or root ball should be insulated by a covering of soil, hay, sawdust, or similar material. Lift the pot, and look for signs of white roots at the bottom of the pot; black roots are a bad sign. Examine the twigs as well. If the buds are firm and the twigs do not break when gently bent, it is probably a healthy plant. Finally, ask about guarantees. Most nurseries will ensure that the plant will sprout leaves in spring.

SPECIAL TIPS FOR FLORIDA

☐ **Annuals**—You can still set out transplants of baby's-breath, cornflowers, calendulas, pansies, petunias, pinks, snapdragons, and sweet alyssum. They will bloom through late winter and early spring. To give them a good start, be sure to prepare the soil by adding plenty of organic matter, such as compost or sphagnum peat moss. Also work in a slow-release fertilizer at the rate recommended on the label to feed the plants through the growing season. You may need to apply again in February or March. Be sure to keep the plants well watered.

☐ **Citrus**—This is peak time for the citrus harvest and a good time to choose which variety you like. Lemons, kumquats, tangerines, and calamondins ripen now, along with Hamlin, navel, and pineapple oranges. Grapefruit that are ready for a taste test include Duncan and Marsh. Buy different selections at the market; then check their availability at a local nursery. Plant container-grown citrus trees now; just be sure to keep them well watered during the dry winter season.

☐ **Daffodils**—Gardeners in the coolest areas of North Florida can grow certain daffodils dependably from year to year. A recent trial by the Extension service in Leon County found that the daffodil selections Ice Follies, Fortune, and Gigantic Star will naturalize and bloom as dependably as the old standbys, Tete-a-Tete and Paper White.

SPECIAL TIPS FOR TEXAS

☐ **Camellias**—East Texans are now enjoying camellias at their peak of bloom. Because you can see the color of the flowers and know what you're getting, this is an excellent time to buy new plants. If you have acid soil, plant camellias directly in the garden; otherwise, grow them in containers. Plant camellias in a hole or pot at least twice the size of the root ball. Into the backfill or potting soil, work a generous amount of organic matter, such as sphagnum peat moss, compost, or leaf mold, and ½ cup of azalea-camellia fertilizer.

☐ **Hollyhocks**—Seeds of hollyhock may be sown now in South Texas and along the Gulf Coast. Choose a sunny, well-drained site; barely cover the seeds with soil, as they need light to germinate. Recommended selections include Chater's Regular Mixture, which grows 6 feet tall and produces 5-inch-wide double flowers; Clause's All Double Chater's Mixed, which bears double flowers on long sturdy stems; and Hollyhock Powderpuff, a 4-foot-tall dwarf selection with large, double flowers.

☐ **Kohlrabi**—Gardeners living in areas of Texas where freezes are rare should consider growing kohlrabi this winter. This unusual-looking member of the cabbage family is easy to grow. Start by working in ½ pound of a complete fertilizer (10-20-10) for every 8 feet of row. Form 20-inch-wide rows with two furrows ½ inch deep and a foot apart. Sow at the rate of 6 to 8 seeds per foot of row. Keep soil moist. Seedlings should emerge within two weeks. Once seedlings reach a height of 1½ inches, thin to a 6-inch spacing, and mulch lightly. If kept well watered, kohlrabi won't need to be fertilized again. You can expect a harvest in about 50 to 60 days. The "bulbs" are mature when they reach the size of a tennis ball.

Index

(Italicized numbers indicate illustrations.)